CW00669588

Hans Gál
MUSIC BEHIND BARBED WIRE
A Diary of Summer 1940

Hans Gál
MUSIC BEHIND BARBED WIRE
A Diary of Summer 1940

With a Foreword
by Sir Alan Peacock

Translated
by Anthony Fox and Eva Fox-Gál

TOCCATA
PRESS

First published in 2014 by Toccata Press
© Anthony Fox and Eva Fox-Gál, 2014

British Library Cataloguing in Publication Data
A catalogue record for this book is available from the British Library.

ISBN 978 0 907689 75 1

Toccata Press gratefully acknowledges contributions towards the costs
of this book from The Hans Gál Society
and The International Centre for Suppressed Music.

Set in 11 on 12 point Minion Pro
by KerryPress Ltd, Luton
Printed and bound in Great Britain
by CPI Group (UK) Ltd, Croydon, CR0 4YY

Contents

List of Illustrations

Foreword
SIR ALAN PEACOCK

To Sir John Anderson, famous Scots statesman and Home Secretary at the outbreak of the Second World War, it seemed to be sound sense that confinement of German aliens should be restricted to known Nazi sympathisers. But when Holland suffered the Blitzkrieg the following spring, allegedly helped by a German 'fifth column', the British government assuaged fears of a repetition, were the UK invaded, by extending the net to non-naturalised Germans and Austrians, including known refugees from Nazism. Thus in May 1940, Dr Hans Gál, one of the most distinguished musicians and composers ever to live and work in Scotland, already almost 50 years old and forced to flee, not long before, from Germany and then his native Austria, was whisked off first to Huyton, outside Liverpool, and then to the Isle of Man to live behind barbed wire – a fate shared by some other eminent and talented Jewish scholars, artists and scientists, some of whom subsequently repaid their incarceration by outstanding contributions to the improvement of life in post-War Britain. The core of this book is Gál's absorbing diary of their reactions to what proved to be a traumatic experience.

Conditions in the camp were tough, probably tougher than those encountered by German prisoners-of-war. A particular problem was hygiene. Gál was one of the few who was awarded a hot bath – but only as medical treatment for a most unpleasant and painful skin disease.

Adjustment to hard physical conditions is probably much less difficult than to the emotional effect of being cut off from communication with families and friends, denied newspapers and other reading matter, and not knowing when and how one would be released. But the imprisoned intelligentsia were a resourceful lot and soon proved to their rather unintelligent, awkward but not totally unfriendly guardians that winning the co-operation of the internees would make their job easier. The imprisoned formed a most effective organisation for obtaining concessions, such as restoring contact – though still supervised – with the outside world and the self-provision of educational and cultural activities, thus maintaining morale. But nothing would move the obstinate authorities to recognise that refugees from Nazism would bitterly resent being lumped together behind barbed wire with its fanatical proponents. For many, this insensitivity born of ignorance left a sour taste in the mouth well after their release.

Gál's graphic account of the burden of incarceration details his own contribution to alleviating its effects: seeking out the musical talent available, organising concerts where it could be displayed, and writing music – both as a form of personal therapy and for the manifest enjoyment of his fellow prisoners. The result was the delectable *Huyton Suite*, a trio for flute and two violins (the only instruments he had to hand), and the incidental music for *What a Life!*, a very clever revue put together by fellow-Austrian Georg Höllering, a pioneer in German film-making. As the title suggests, the revue offers ironic commentary on camp life, but, although reminiscent of the famous Bertolt Brecht-Kurt Weill satirical cabaret, it exercises its appeal in a different way, with a tone of resignation in both the fine music and lyrics.

The text of his diary would be difficult to savour without details concerning the cast in Gál's personal drama. His daughter, Eva Fox-Gál, herself a German scholar and excellent musician, offers an account of the fortunes of the Gál family and pen pictures of a cast of remarkable persons in the drama, which includes such diverse figures as Otto Erich Deutsch, the Schubert scholar, Franz Reizenstein, well known fellow-composer and pianist, Ekke von Kuenssberg, to become one of the best-known physicians in Edinburgh, and Klaus Fuchs, the atomic physicist who later gained notoriety as a Soviet spy. Her introduction is complemented by an essay by Richard Dove which reminds us that the clumsy internment policy excited strong opposition from public figures who risked accusations of being unpatriotic but who induced government to realise that they were alienating internees whose release would be not only just but expedient.

Economics has long shouldered the sobriquet of 'the dismal science', but economists themselves are not necessarily a dismal lot, and although I have made my career in economics, music has been an important part of my life for as long as I can remember. My first contact with Hans Gál goes back to October 1960, when my dentist, Mr Nathan, a keen amateur musician who lived round the corner from the Gáls, took me to a meeting of the Edinburgh Society of Musicians to hear Hans give the first performance of his new 24 Preludes, Op. 83, and so the youngest professor at the University of Edinburgh, as I then was, was introduced to probably the oldest member of the University staff. (Amazingly, twenty years later, he was to follow up the 24 Preludes with a set of 24 Fugues, Op. 108, written in his early nineties.) That concert was a wonderful musical experience and accordingly, when I saw an announcement in *The Scotsman* that Dr Gál would take a limited number of private students of composition, I submitted some feeble manuscript offerings as evidence of minimal competence.

Perhaps intrigued at the prospect of having a professor as a student and, of all things, an economist, he agreed to teach me. In the eighteen months that followed, I was kept hard at it, at least reaching the stage where I had learned enough to know what I didn't know about composition. Eventually, my appointment to the new University of York brought my apprenticeship to an end but in the years which followed, the new vistas of music opened up by Hans' teaching provided a welcome antidote to the fantasy world of academe. I am proud to be a vice-president of The Hans Gál Society and hope I can help promote the appreciation of the work of a man who was my esteemed teacher and became my personal friend.

But I suspect that, even without that personal connection, I would still be deeply impressed and profoundly moved by Gál's account of his misfortunes. There is a musicality about his writing which calls for the use of the right timbre at the right time. And it serves a double purpose: those not familiar with his music should be lured to the growing number of opportunities now available to hear it; and those familiar with it will surely gain in their understanding of its value to them and to the importance of supporting the growing efforts to re-establish Hans Gál's work in the contemporary repertoire of serious music.

QUARTET

‹ ‹ ‹ B DUR › › ›

FÜR
KLAVIER · VIOLINE
BRATSCHE & VIOLONCELL

VON

HANS GÁL

OP. 13

Variationen
über eine Wiener
Heurigenmelodie

für
Violine, Violoncell
und Klavier

von

Hans Gál

Op. 9

Prelude

Hans Gál photographed in Vienna in 1925, two years after the success of his second opera, Die heilige Ente, *had launched his career.*

Hans Gál:
A Biographical Introduction
EVA FOX-GÁL

Born in Vienna in 1890, of Jewish descent, Hans Gál was destined to a life of turbulence and dislocation. In the 1890s, under the Bürgermeister Karl Lueger,[1] Vienna was already fertile ground for the anti-Semitism that was to pave the way for the agenda Hitler expounded in *Mein Kampf*; it is indicative of the ideological climate that Hans was refused a place at the nearest neighbourhood primary school because it had filled its Jewish quota.

Although from a modest background – his father was a homeopathic doctor with four children to provide for, in a flat that also housed the practice – Gál's musical interests and abilities were recognised early and were encouraged, especially by his Aunt Jenny,[2] who had been an opera singer under Richard Strauss in his early Weimar years. By the end of his school days Gál was already a proficient pianist, having been a pupil of one of the foremost teachers in Vienna, Richard Robert, who also taught Rudolf Serkin, Clara Haskil and Georg Szell. In 1908 Gál obtained an appointment to teach harmony and piano at the Vienna New Conservatoire. This position, along with private teaching and a Rothschild scholarship, enabled him to pursue his compositional studies in two years of intensive private study with Eusebius Mandyczewski,[3] who had belonged to Brahms' inner circle of friends and in whom Gál found his ideal mentor and 'spiritual father'. At the behest of his real father to get a 'genuine' qualification, he

---

[1] Lueger (1844–1910), a zealous Catholic, was Bürgermeister, or mayor, of Vienna from 1897 to 1910, the politics of his Christian Social Party openly espousing anti-Semitism, and at several points in the first edition of *Mein Kampf* (Eher Verlag, Munich, 1926), Hitler pays him effusive tribute. But Lueger's anti-Semitism was more 'flexible' than Hitler's: when it was pointed out that there were many Jews in his circle, he famously retorted: 'Wer ein Jude ist, bestimme *ich*' – '*I* decide who is a Jew'.

[2] Jenny Fleischer-Alt, born in Bratislava in 1863, the sister of Hans' mother, Ilka, enjoyed a successful operatic career, singing in her early twenties at the court theatre in Wiesbaden and the court opera in Weimar. Marriage in 1890 obliged her to give up her career.

[3] Mandyczewski (1857–1929), born in Ukraine (then part of the Austro-Hungarian Empire), studied in Vienna under Hanslick, Fuchs and Nottebohm, was a composer and conductor as well as a seminal musicologist, editing the Schubert Gesamtausgabe in 1887–97. For over four decades (1887–1929) he was the librarian and archivist of the Gesellschaft der Musikfreunde in Vienna.

*Two early influences: Eusebius Mandyczewski, Gál's mentor and 'spiritual father',
and the soprano Jenny Fleischer-Alt, Gál's 'Tante Jenny',*

also studied music history at Vienna University under the renowned Guido
Adler, graduating in 1913 with a doctoral dissertation ('On the stylistic
characteristics of the young Beethoven, and their relationship to the style
of his maturity') which was accorded the rare distinction of publication in
Adler's own series, *Studien zur Musikwissenschaft.* Through teaching, as
well as freelance editing and performing, Gál was able to maintain a degree
of financial independence and to devote every spare moment to what really
mattered to him: composition. In these early 'apprentice' years, as he called
them, he composed vast amounts, including operas, symphonies, chamber
and choral music, piano works, and about a hundred songs.

The declaration of war in 1914 was inevitably a shattering blow to Gál's
career as a composer, which had been crowned with considerable early
success, culminating in the Austrian State Prize for Composition in 1915.
Thanks to his poor eyesight, at least, he was posted far from the firing-line,
first to Belgrade, then to a remote outpost in the Carpathians, where he
was an officer in charge of the construction of a railway, and finally served
in Italy. When it became clear to him that the war was lost and the front

collapsing on all sides, he escaped back through Italy with his men. An officially stamped receipt from the municipal authorities in Bolzano for the due return of his full complement of three horses, five oxen and three wagons, dated 6 November 1918, documents his unofficial exit from the field of war.

The enforced hiatus in Gál's career did have one welcome by-product, for which, in retrospect, he remained enduringly grateful: it delayed the possibility of publication until after the War. This pause allowed him the necessary detachment from the entire body of his earlier compositions, with the result that he discarded the vast bulk of them, including the symphony for which he had won the State Prize, and published only those works which he felt fully able to endorse – and to which, indeed, he was to remain committed to the end of his life. But he did compose a number of other works during the war years, including the cantata *Das Bäumlein, das andere Blätter hat gewollt* ('The little tree that wanted other leaves'; later published as Op. 2), his *Serbian Dances*, Op. 3, and a string quartet, subsequently published as the First Quartet, Op. 16 (its two predecessors having been discarded); moreover, he arrived back in Vienna with a completed opera in his bag: *Der Arzt der Sobeide* ('Sobeide's Doctor'), Op. 4, which was given a successful premiere in Breslau in 1919. Given the unprecedented death-toll of the First World War, Gál had been exceedingly fortunate. But the Vienna to which he returned was not, and never again would be, the cultural hub of a great historic superpower. The War had irretrievably torn apart the Austro-Hungarian Empire, which had long been like a seething crater just waiting to erupt, and left Austria, hitherto its ruling nucleus and centre, in political and economic ruins.

The period immediately after the First World War was extremely hard, and the Great Inflation of the early 1920s wrought further material and moral devastation. It was nevertheless a time when Gál was able to build up a rapidly rising career, particularly in Germany. His second opera, *Die heilige Ente* ('The Sacred Duck'), Op. 15, following its successful premiere under Georg Szell in Düsseldorf in 1923, was immediately adopted by six other theatres, and continued to be performed until 1933. It was followed by a third opera, *Das Lied der Nacht* ('The Song of the Night'), Op. 23, first performed in Breslau in 1926, and a large body of compositions in all genres. His *Overture to a Puppet Play*, Op. 20, was a huge international success, receiving over one hundred performances, conducted by, among other distinguished conductors, Fritz Busch, Furtwängler, Keilberth, Szell and Weingartner. For five years, from 1924, he had a contract with Simrock (the publishers of Brahms and Dvořák), for 'first refusal' of any new work.

In March 1929 Gál's opera Die heilige Ente *became the first contemporary opera to be broadcast by RAVAG, Austrian Radio, announced with a photomontage from the Prague and Weimar productions in* Radio-Wien.

For his Symphony in D, Op. 30, he was awarded a prize in the Columbia Schubert competition of 1928.[4]

In 1929, following his successes as a composer, Gál was appointed Director of the Municipal Conservatoire in Mainz. The following years in the Rhineland were amongst the happiest of his life. The family occupied a beautiful apartment overlooking the Rhine. He threw himself wholeheartedly into the life of the college, teaching harmony, counterpoint and composition, as well as conducting the orchestra and opera classes and a madrigal choir, and even taking on a few piano pupils. He was, alongside Alban Berg and Ernst Toch, on the selection committee of the *Allgemeiner Deutscher Musikverein*, the German Society of Musicians (founded by Franz Liszt and abolished by Adolf Hitler), which organised annual festivals of new music. Several major compositions also stem from this period, including a Violin Concerto, Op. 39, and a fourth opera, *Die beiden Klaas* ('The Two Klauses'), Op. 42.[5]

Hitler's accession to power in 1933 was undoubtedly the most fateful turning-point of Gál's life. At a stroke he was suspended from office, and performance and publication of his works were banned in Germany. The Violin Concerto had received its first performance only a month before, but *Die beiden Klaas*, which was about to be staged in Dresden under Fritz Busch, was cancelled (a fate it was to suffer again in 1938, when it was due to be performed in Vienna). Initially, like thousands of others, Gál did not believe that the Germans could take Hitler seriously, and he spent the next few months in a village in the Black Forest to see how the situation would develop. But by August it had become clear that there was no future for himself or his family in Germany, and they reluctantly had to clear their flat in Mainz. He was always profoundly moved when recalling how their landlord in Mainz had refused to take any rent for those months, as his personal protest against the Nazis.

At this point he could have gone to America, where there were possible openings for him, but he was temperamentally unwilling to expatriate himself, especially to a culture that felt so alien. Like so many fellow-Austrians who, in order to build a career, had had to leave the narrow straits of

[4] In 1927 the Gesellschaft der Musikfreunde in Austria and the Columbia Graphophone Company in Britain and the USA announced a competition to mark the centenary of Schubert's death the following year. Initially calling for a completion of Schubert's Symphony No. 8 in B minor, the so-called 'Unfinished', the terms of the competition provoked such a storm of protest that they were changed to allow original symphonic compositions in which melody was a primary consideration. For an outline history of the competition, *cf.* Arvid O. Vollsnes, *Ludvig Irgens-Jensen: The Life and Music of a Norwegian Composer*, Toccata Press, London, 2014, pp. 113–16.

[5] Posthumously premiered as *Rich Claus, Poor Claus* in May 1990 in York (England), by York Opera, conducted by Leslie Bresnen.

post-war Austria for the relative affluence and cultural buoyancy of Germany during the Weimar Republic, he now decided to return to Vienna, where he at least had family roots. But, in common with so many others, including Alban Berg and Zemlinsky, he found Austria an illusory homeland. The political situation was exceedingly unstable, with a progressive dismantling of democratic structures, as the Hitler regime cast its long shadow over the border. Most of these composers were unable to re-establish themselves during the years between 1933 and 1938. Gál had to earn his livelihood from private teaching and a little conducting, and performances of his music were drastically reduced. Having experienced the events of 1933, the Gáls were resolved not to be taken by surprise again. His wife Hanna[6] now trained as a speech therapist, so as to be equipped for all eventualities with a professional qualification of her own, and insisted that they both take English lessons, to which Hans reluctantly submitted. With Chancellor Schuschnigg's surrender of Austrian independence and its formal annexation to the Third Reich, and the apparent failure of the Allies to recognise the full implications of Hitler's expansionist policies for Austria and Czechoslovakia, Gál knew that Austria (and indeed Europe) was lost and that they had to leave without delay. On 8 March 1938, even before Hitler's forces had crossed into Austria, Hanna left on her own, to check whether the borders were still open, embarking on a nightmare journey through Switzerland and France and eventually to England, with passengers being arbitrarily hauled out of their carriages by young Gestapo guards, who, as it transpired, were themselves fresh out of prison. Hans followed a week later by the same route, but, to his utter despair, was detained by the Home Office on arrival in England and refused entry. Fortunately Hanna was able to mobilise the good services of a fellow refugee, the art historian Ernst Gombrich (later Sir Ernest Gombrich),[7] who had already established himself in England and was able to give the guarantees necessary for Gál's release. Their two sons (Franz[8] and Peter[9]), aged thirteen and fifteen, followed four months later, and two of Gál's sisters (Gretl[10] and Erna[11]) also fled to Britain. The eldest sister (Edith[12]) stayed behind to look after her elderly mother and Aunt Jenny in Weimar. Faced with imminent deportation, Edith and Jenny took their own lives in April 1942, swallowing poison. His mother had died of natural causes the previous month.

---

[6] *Cf.* Appendix One: Personalia, pp. 184–85, below.

[7] *Cf.* Appendix One: Personalia, pp. 190–91, below.

[8] *Cf.* Appendix One: Personalia, pp. 183–84, below.

[9] *Cf.* Appendix One: Personalia, p. 185, below.

[10] *Cf.* Appendix One: Personalia, p. 185, below.

[11] *Cf.* Appendix One: Personalia, p. 183, below.

[12] *Cf.* Appendix One: Personalia, p. 183, below.

*Gál, now director of the Städtische Musikhochschule in Mainz,
at home in his study.*

Like all the other refugees in 1938, the Gáls were initially not allowed to do any work, paid or unpaid. They stayed in a variety of boarding houses and otherwise depended on hospitality. Gál, provided with a cordial letter of introduction from Fritz Busch, had the good fortune to meet Sir Donald Tovey,[13] who immediately recognised in him a kindred spirit and hoped to obtain a post for him in the Reid School of Music at the University of Edinburgh, where he was Professor. In the interim he found a temporary job for him, cataloguing the Reid Library collection, which was still stacked in boxes. Gál always maintained that the six months he spent working with this rare collection of books and manuscripts, among which he even found a hitherto unpublished Haydn symphony, laid the foundation for all the books he was later to write, in that he had never, before or after, been able to spend so much time reading. Sadly, Tovey suffered a stroke, from which he never really recovered, and the plan to find Gál a permanent post at the University never went through. The cataloguing job came to an end and Hans had to leave Edinburgh. Hanna, meanwhile, had obtained a work permit and had started working as a speech therapist in a London clinic, and the Gáls had also been offered the use of a family house for a year, which meant that the family could finally live together again.

The next blow came with the declaration of war on 3 September 1939. England had been intended only as a transitional stop, prior to obtaining visas for America, which they now had; but the onset of war put a final end to any further plans of emigration. The nightly bombing raids and screaming sirens particularly affected their younger son, and they decided to leave London. Gál had found Edinburgh most congenial as a city and had made good friends during his short time there. Hanna managed to obtain a position as housekeeper for Sir Herbert Grierson,[14] emeritus Professor of English at the University, who lived on his own in a large town-house and was able to offer the Gáls a whole floor, including a drawing room with a grand piano. It was a highly cultured environment in which the Gáls quickly felt at home. Hans was able to compose again, and founded a madrigal ensemble and a refugee orchestra – there were a large number of refugees in Edinburgh, connected both to the University and to the major teaching hospital, the Royal Infirmary.

But just as life was resuming some sort of normality, Gál and his elder son Franz were arrested on Whit Sunday 1940 and whisked off to internment. It is perhaps strange, in view of so many previous and major traumas, that Gál should have found this one so terrible. But for him the four-and-a-half

---

[13] *Cf.* Appendix One: Personalia, p. 195, below.
[14] *Cf.* Appendix One: Personalia, p. 191, below.

Sir Donald Tovey, whose initiative brought Hans Gál to Edinburgh

months of internment probably represented the worst period of his life. Many others looked back on it through almost rose-coloured spectacles, in spite of separation from home and family and considerable physical deprivation, remembering the stimulating company and boarding-school-like escapades. Gál found the sheer powerlessness of his situation, the mindless bureaucracy, the incomprehension of the officers guarding the camp, for whom there was apparently no difference between Nazi prisoners of war and these refugees who had fled from Nazi persecution, the intrinsic absurdity of the whole operation, intolerable. These feelings come out in the opening pages of the diary, where he gives expression to his shock and outrage. Yet life as an internee also had high points: the composition and performance of his trio for flute and two violins, the only instruments available in the camp at this point, and the camp revue, for which he wrote the music from his hospital bed. His exhilaration in the face of the daily challenge of collaborating in the creation and performance of a camp music-drama expresses the ultimately life-affirming stance of one who was blest with the gift of extraordinary creativity and for whom music was his salvation.

This diary is the only piece of directly autobiographical writing Hans Gál ever produced – his way of coping with this particularly stressful episode of his life. It was based on short-hand notes in his diary, which he then typed out as his first task following his release. He made four copies only: one for himself, and one for each of the comrades with whom he shared a room: Willi Gross,[15] Hugo Schneider[16] and Max Sugar,[17] all close friends and fellow refugees from Edinburgh, who emerge from the pages of the diary like characters in a novel. Gross and Sugar, particularly, were highly influential figures in the camp organisation, and Gál was at the hub of musical events, so that one gets a vivid impression of camp life from the centre.

The diary was never intended for publication, and the copies given to his three fellow internees were emphatically 'for private use only!' Furthermore, Gál was exceedingly unforthcoming in interviews on the subject of the internment. One can only speculate about his reasons. Perhaps it was because he felt that it could too easily be misrepresented as disloyalty to the country which had, after all, provided him with a home and, in 1945, a permanent university post and finally, in 1946, British citizenship; perhaps, too, it was out of his realisation that the 'internment' experience could not, and must not, be compared with the unspeakable horrors of life under the Nazi terror, let alone in a Nazi concentration camp; or perhaps because of an innate reluctance to bare his soul, particularly in an area of deep personal pain. He was extremely reticent about self-expression, with a constitutional dislike of any form of self-importance or pathos. Indeed, the closest one can get to any sort of self-characterisation is in his writings on other composers, notably his works on composers with whom he felt a strong affinity, such as Brahms or Schubert. His remarks on Schubert, for instance, where he speaks of the composer as living in a kind of 'incognito', behind a 'protective mask', are particularly illuminating:

> He needed it as a shield against trivial curiosity, as a protection for the artist's most essential, most secret possession, the tabernacle of his creative soul, which, shunning the light, is sensitive to touch like a mimosa.[18]

My father sent me the typescript, with the following, characteristically understated, note, saying:

[15] *Cf.* Appendix One: Personalia, p. 191, below.
[16] *Cf.* Appendix One: Personalia, pp. 194–95, below.
[17] *Cf.* Appendix One: Personalia, p. 195, below.
[18] *Franz Schubert and the Essence of Melody*, Victor Gollancz, London, 1974, p. 12.

Here's the business: I've just had another look at it and seen that there are all sorts of things that could interest you. I had pretty much forgotten it – and tomorrow once again there's an interviewer coming who wants to get information about the 'internment' of 1940. I'll be very sparing in my comments.[19]

This was the first time I had ever set eyes on the diary and, because I found it so emotionally overwhelming, I put it aside for when I would have more time to read it properly. In the event, alas, I did not actually come to read it until after his death, so I missed the opportunity to discuss it with him. I immediately felt that it was a text of such quality, intrinsic interest and documentary importance that it merited publication, but I was uncertain as to whether such a step was appropriate or not, given the expressly private spirit in which it had been written, and the inevitably personal impact it had on me, which could cloud my judgement as to its wider interest. I initially showed it to people who had either been interned with Gál or had had parallel experiences in another camp, and then began to show it to people for whom the material was completely unfamiliar. The consensus was that it was of such general interest, and so exceptionally readable, that it ought to be published, particularly now that more than half a century had elapsed since the events that it records. Willi Gross' widow was instrumental in encouraging its publication, and any remaining hesitations were swept aside by the encouragement of the publishers of the original, German-language edition, Peter Lang.[20]

There are always issues of tact where individuals are named and described, sometimes with irritation or frustration, sometimes with a wicked eye for caricature. But although Gál is outspoken and impulsive in his views, and judgements sometimes appear harsh at first, they are usually tempered with humanity when seen in their fuller framework and should not be taken out of context. Personal vanity is lambasted, particularly where individual artists wanted to make their mark in camp concerts at the expense of the whole, but, again, Gál was usually ready to revise his opinion where the talent proved commensurate.

The text offered here is just as I was given it in its typed form. The diary shorthand would be equivalent to the manuscript sketch of a piece of music, the typed version like the fully realised score. In this instance, the only original that survives is the typed version. It sometimes shows a dual time-frame: the time of experiencing events, and the time of writing, which

[19] Letter dated 2 March 1982.
[20] *Musik hinter Stacheldraht. Tagebuchblätter aus dem Sommer 1940*, Exil Dokumente, Vol. 3, Peter Lang, Bern, 2003.

may include retrospective comment; thus the actual raw material of lived experience is inseparable from the way in which it is shaped into narrative. The text represents Gál's existential need to give expression and form to his experiences and to articulate them with precision and clarity; it is not directed at public reception. But even the most personal diary becomes, in a sense, public by virtue of transmuting emotions, perceptions, sensations, into the trans-personal medium of language.

Gál's prose style has much in common with his music, and is characterised by wit, conciseness, lucidity and understatement, rather than pathos. One might expect a work written in extreme circumstances, as was the *Huyton Suite*, to be more of a 'cry from the heart', an expressionistic scream, expressing pain with dissonance. Instead it is a serenade, a work of supreme clarity, lightness of texture and artful playfulness, drawing its substance from deeper layers of the psyche than the raw experience of the moment. But there are glimpses of something darker, as in the profoundly expressive, soulful melody on which the slow-movement variations are based; and even amid the exuberance of the final movement there are contrasting, deeply poignant passages hinting at a world that feels far removed and irretrievably lost. The genesis of the *Huyton Suite* is vividly documented in the diary and gives considerable insight into Gál's creative process. It would be wrong to conclude that he was simply an escapist, in denial of the reality around him. As is abundantly clear from the pages of the diary, he was fully involved and personally engaged. He was acutely aware of the irony and absurdity of his situation, and fully conscious of the incongruity between art and external reality. What the composition affirms in him is the creative power to bridge this gulf and transcend the abyss:

> In sober moments it is clear to me that I am mad. Here I am, writing music, completely superfluous, ridiculous, fantastic music for a flute and two violins, while the world is on the point of coming to an end. Was ever a war more lost than this one now? Each possibility seems as hopeless as the other. I must, as so often in my life, think of the 'Man in the land of Syr' in the parable by Rückert. I hang above the abyss eating berries. How wonderful that there are such berries! Never in my life have I been as grateful for my talent as I am today.[21]

---

[21] Entry for 12 June 1940; *cf.* p. 76, below.

Acknowledgements

I would like at the outset to record my grateful thanks to Martin Anderson for committing his Toccata Press to this first published translation of Hans Gál's internment diary. Martin's personal knowledge of Gál and his music, as well as his encyclopaedic knowledge of *émigré* musicians in general, make him the ideal publisher for this English edition of the diary, which has been enriched by his own unique brand of dedication to detail, erudition and humanity. The editorial footnotes are his.

It is a particular sadness that Sir Alan Peacock, who passed away on 2 August 2014, just as this book was passing through its final stages of preparation, did not have the satisfaction of seeing it in print. It would have meant much to him. I am immensely grateful to him for his Foreword and for his dedication to my father.

Conversations with several fellow-internees from Central Camp, among them Dr Walter Kellerman, Dr Rudolf Sprintz, Dr Eric Conrad, Professor Werner von Simson and Gitta Deutsch (the daughter of Otto Erich Deutsch), who has recorded her own very gripping wartime and internment experiences in her *Böcklinstrassenelegie*,[1] supported me in my decision to proceed with the publication of the German original (Peter Lang, Bern, 2003). I am all the more grateful to have had the opportunity to speak to each of them, because all have now passed away.

In collecting information for the biographical notes, I was reliant on many kinds of personal help and owe a large part of the life-stories to the recollections of family members of the individuals concerned; these include Dr Julian Gross, Professor Hans Schneider, Andrew Höllering and Dr Liselotte Kastner-Adler. Dr Kastner-Adler helped me most generously with her research, especially into refugee doctors, and I am deeply grateful to her for all the information she gathered about medical practitioners who figure in the text.

I thank Marion Camrass, who, through her valuable recollections, extended in a lively manner my image of my aunt, 'Tante Gretl'. I also thank Dr Janet Wasserman and Esther Brumberg, curator of the Collection of the Museum of Jewish Heritage – A Living Memorial to the Holocaust, for biographical information on Paul Humpoletz, Dr Primavera Gruber

---

[1] *Böcklinstrassenelegie: Erinnerungen*, Picus Verlag, Vienna, 1993.

and her database of the Orpheus Trust, Berlin, for valuable notes on Dr Rosenzweig, and the late Professor Hamish Ritchie and the Glasgow University Archive Services for information about Dr Guder. For the original compilation of the biographies, I owe a deep debt of gratitude above all to Regine Prelle-White, whose assistance in collecting and organising material was indispensible.

For the English publication, additional biographical notes have been added about the musicians Alfred Blumen, Hermann Baron, Hans Karg-Bebenburg and Nicolo Draber. For the information about Blumen and Draber I am indebted to Suzanne Snizek, who has meticulously researched the musicians mentioned by Gál;[2] Primavera Gruber supplied Blumen's date of birth.

Special thanks are owed to my daughter Tanya for sifting through our family documents, which made a lot of previously unknown material available to me, and for all manner of practical assistance in managing to excavate the relevant versions of various documents and save me from despair over the vagaries of my filing.

Another invaluable addition to this edition are contemporary pictures that have been supplied from the papers of the late Major Cecil Francis, Commandant of Central Camp, Isle of Man, handed down via the family of Hazel Spicer, great-niece of Major Francis; she has most generously made them freely available for this publication, for which we are most grateful. The pictures and documents sent to Major Francis (presumably as leaving presents) from internees in Central Camp in November 1940, two months after Gál's release, testify to much warmer relations between the internees and the military command. Paul Weatherall of the Manx Museum provided help in trying to identify one of the internees involved, and Anthony Grenville of the Association of Jewish Refugees provided information on other points.

For the CD I thank above all my son Simon, who masterminded every aspect of the recording, and extracted the material for the revue *What a Life!* from the original manuscript, found in a bundle of Gál's 'laid aside' works. Michael Freyhan played a major part in the decipherment and preparation of performance material, and we thank him not only for typesetting the score and parts but also for directing the revue from the piano, as well as performing the Suite. I am grateful to all the performers, especially the singers Norbert Meyn and Thomas Guthrie, for their enthusiastic

---

[2] *Cf.* her 'Hans Gál and the Musical Culture of British Internment Camps of WWII', in Erik Levi (ed.), *The Impact of Nazism on Twentieth Century Music*, Böhlau Verlag, Vienna, 2014; and '"The trio is growing like an asparagus": Hans Gál and the Huyton Suite trio', in Fabien Théofilakis (ed.), *Captivité de guerre au XXe siècle: des archives, des histoires, des mémoires*, Armand Colin, Paris, 2012.

participation in the whole enterprise. A particular thank-you to Thomas Guthrie and Michael Freyhan for the addition of the 'Ballad of Poor Jacob', which was not included with the original German publication; this is its first performance and recording in English. I would also like to record our grateful thanks to Professor Hermann Korte for permission to print the text of the 'Ballad of Poor Jacob' (copyright The Norbert Elias Foundation).

I owe a huge debt of gratitude to my husband, Dr Anthony Fox, who has been involved at every stage of seeing this book into print, first in German and now in English, and who has played a major part in the materialisation of this translation, including the first English translations of Otto Erich Deutsch's 'Ballade vom deutschen Refugee' and Norbert Elias' 'Ballade des armen Jakob'.

The biggest debt of gratitude, of course, is to the author himself, my father: I thank him for the spirit, the humour and the love which live in his music and in the pages of his diary.

Eva Fox Gál
York
September 2014

'Most Regrettable and Deplorable Things Have Happened': Britain's Internment of Enemy Aliens in 1940

RICHARD DOVE

On 22 August 1940, as the threat of German invasion hung over Britain, the House of Commons devoted its adjournment debate to the contentious topic of the internment of 'enemy aliens'. Opening the debate, the Labour MP Rhys Davis strongly criticised government policy, declaring that 'the treatment meted out to our alien population in the last few months is not the result of cruel intentions, but of panic and sheer stupidity'. Major Victor Cazalet, a Conservative member, went even further: 'Frankly, I shall not feel happy, either as an Englishman or as a supporter of this government, until this bespattered page of our history has been cleaned up and rewritten'.[1]

Such forthright language confirms the strong feelings the issue had inspired in Britain since the introduction of mass internment three months earlier. Responding to the debate, the Home Secretary, Sir John Anderson, was almost apologetic, conceding that 'most regrettable and deplorable things have happened in the execution of internment policy'.[2] How had such 'things' come about? The issue has continued to attract interest among British historians, particularly since the partial release of official records began in 1972, the first substantial account being Peter and Leni Gillman's *Collar the Lot!*[3] Nonetheless, as the Gillmans record, the culture of secrecy cultivated by successive British governments continues to cast its shadow over this episode. Many Home Office records for the crucial period of internment policy have never been released; even today, almost three-quarters of a century after the event, some crucial documents are still withheld, and others have been destroyed.[4]

---

[1] Hansard, Vol. 364, 1939–40, 6–22 August 1940, debate 22 August 1940.

[2] *Ibid.*

[3] *Collar the Lot! How Britain Interned & Expelled its Wartime Refugees*, Quartet Books, London, 1980. *Cf.* also Louise London, *Whitehall and the Jews, 1933–1948: British Immigration Policy, Jewish Refugees and the Holocaust*, Cambridge University Press, Cambridge, 2001.

[4] The most comprehensive recent consideration of internment and its effects is Alison Garnham's *Hans Keller and Internment: The Development of an Emigré Musician, 1938–48* (Plumbago Press, London,

When war broke out in September 1939, there were over 70,000 German and Austrian refugees living in Britain, many of whom regarded the outbreak of hostilities with mixed feelings. Although most of them welcomed an outcome they had long considered inevitable, their response was understandably qualified by their apprehension as to the anomaly of their own situation. Under the terms of the Aliens Act (1919) the declaration of war had transformed all Germans and Austrians overnight into 'enemy aliens', subject to curfew and travel restrictions. The very phrase 'enemy aliens', with its suggestion of hostility, must have seemed threatening to men and women who had already endured insult and persecution before arriving in Britain.

In fact, the general internment of 'enemy aliens' was one of a number of contingency measures which the British government had considered, and rejected, in 1939. The decision was not a rousing affirmation of liberalism, but a practical conclusion drawn from the experience of mass internment during the First World War, when Britain had interned some 30,000 German nationals, most of them in the outbreak of 'spymania' which had followed the sinking of the liner *Lusitania* in May 1915. A post-war review of this policy had suggested its essential futility; this time it was decided that such wholesale measures were unnecessary. On 4 September 1939, the day after war was declared, Sir John Anderson, recently appointed Home Secretary,[5] rose to make a short statement to the Commons. On the one hand, Sir John reported, the government had taken decisive action, moving rapidly to detain some 300 German nationals in Britain, including journalists, businessmen, and a sprinkling of merchant seamen, whose ships had happened to be in British ports. On the other hand, there was to be no immediate resort to mass internment. Instead, there was to be a policy of review, under which all German and Austrian refugees were to appear before specially constituted tribunals, charged with categorising them according to the degree of security risk they were perceived to represent. Refugees from Czechoslovakia were exempted from these measures, perhaps in a belated attempt to atone for the betrayal of the Munich Agreement. Indeed,

---

2011). Garnham's narrative interweaves official discourse and policy pronouncements with letters from the 21-year-old Hans Keller (1919–85) to his family. Keller was interned first at Kempton Park racecourse, then at Huyton and finally in Mooragh Camp, Ramsey, on the Isle of Man. His letters suggest that it was easier for younger internees to adapt to their constrained circumstances than for older men of Gál's generation and above, as Gál himself surmises (*cf.* p. 105, below).

[5] His name was to become synonymous with the Anderson air-raid shelter which once graced a million suburban gardens.

a handful of Germans and Austrians who had come to Britain under the auspices of the Czech Refugee Trust Fund, were also exempted.[6]

Each of the 120 local tribunals was in effect a 'one-man' court, chaired by a King's Counsel or county-court judge, assisted by a police secretary, whose function was to act as an additional check against spies masquerading as refugees. The task of the tribunals was to place each refugee into one of three categories, according to the degree of risk they were deemed to represent. Category 'A' was intended for those aliens who were considered a threat to national security and were therefore to be interned. Category 'B' indicated those who were exempt from internment, but subject to certain restrictions, most notably a ban on travelling more than five miles without prior police permission and on owning a car, a camera or a large-scale map. Category 'C' was reserved for those whose anti-Nazi credentials were recognised, and who were therefore exempted from internment and from restrictions. The tribunals were required to make a further distinction, one which cut across these categories – between 'refugees from Nazi oppression' and 'non-refugees'.

The mere enunciation of these administrative measures conveys none of the uncertainty they induced, nor of their emotional impact on men and women who had been forced to flee their own countries and who now found themselves penniless, unable to work and dependent on the charity of others, in a foreign land whose language few of them spoke and whose customs even fewer understood. There was certainly general resentment amongst refugees at being classified as 'enemy aliens'; there was also particular apprehension about the workings of the tribunals. They were to be held in secret, and aliens were not permitted legal representation, though they were allowed to bring a friend.

The tribunals began work in the first week of October 1939. They worked fast, and by the end of November they had considered over 35,000 cases. In all they examined 71,600 refugees, placing 600 in category 'A', 6,800 in category 'B' and 64,200 in category 'C'. Of those examined 55,460 were classified as 'refugees from Nazi oppression'. But the decisions reached by the tribunals were often inconsistent, even arbitrary, depending very much on the whim of the tribunal chairmen, some of whom were clearly ignorant of the anti-Jewish measures in Nazi Germany and Austria. They were perhaps most inconsistent over their application of the compromise category 'B', but also over the very definition of who was a refugee. It was widely recognised that most Austrians and Germans had been the victims

---

[6] *Cf.* Charmian Brinson and Richard Dove, *Politics by Other Means. The Free German League of Culture in London 1939–1945*, Vallentine Mitchell, London, 2010.

of persecution. By contrast, those who had left Germany or Austria in the early days of Nazi rule had not generally suffered persecution or torture, and tribunal chairmen were therefore required to assess whether they could have had 'reasonable grounds for anticipating oppressive treatment'. Many of those placed in Category 'B' wished to appeal against their classification and, indeed, the Home Office agreed to review all 'B' category cases once the tribunals had completed their work, although this review had barely started before it was overtaken by events.

From late January 1940 there was a growing press campaign against the refugees, conducted largely in *The Daily Mail* and *Sunday Dispatch*,[7] instigated above all by the very journalists[8] who had been most vociferous in supporting pro-appeasement policies in the 1930s. They accused the tribunals of being dangerously lenient, asserting (without providing the slightest evidence) that enemy agents were masquerading as refugees. This campaign continued for three months, though it seems to have had little effect on public opinion. Nor did the authorities react at this point. In fact, Sir John Anderson made a statement to the Commons, pointing out that the majority of refugees were bitter enemies of the Nazis, and concluding that the government saw no reason for a policy of general internment. This attitude was reversed in May 1940.

The military situation had drastically deteriorated with the German occupation of Denmark and Norway. In the wake of the fall of Norway,[9] and the humiliating failure of the British Expeditionary Force,[10] rumours began to surface in the British press that the Germans' lightning invasion had been prepared by a 'fifth column' of Nazi agents inside Norway itself.[11] Such stories, however unfounded, nurtured latent fears that there was a similar fifth column at work in Britain – with the finger of suspicion

---

[7] Like *The Daily Mail*, the *Sunday Dispatch* – then the best-selling British Sunday newspaper – was owned by the Harmsworth family; in 1961 it merged with *The Sunday Express*. In the 1930s Harold Harmsworth, the First Viscount Rothermere, had unashamedly used his raft of national papers to promote appeasement with Nazi Germany and he corresponded with Hitler and his inner circle until shortly before the outbreak of the Second World War.

[8] Chief among them were G. Ward Price (*cf. The Daily Mail*, 24 May 1940, p. 4) and Beverley Nichols (*cf. Sunday Chronicle*, 26 May 1940, p. 2).

[9] Germany invaded Norway on 8–9 April 1940 and swiftly established control over most of the country; the last pockets of resistance surrendered on 10 June.

[10] At the outset of war in September 1939, the British Expeditionary Force, founded in 1938, was deployed to the Franco-Belgian border, with an initial strength of 158,000 men; during the period known as the 'Phoney War' its size was doubled, to 316,000 men. It failed to withstand the German Blitzkrieg launched on 10 May 1940 and fell back to the Channel coast, leading to the evacuation from Dunkirk in the last days of May and first of June.

[11] *Sunday Dispatch*, 14 April 1940.

inevitably pointing at German-speaking refugees.[12] Such fears reached panic proportions after the fall of the Netherlands.[13] Sir Neville Bland, the British minister to the Dutch government, arrived back in London to report that Holland had been subverted by a fifth column of Nazi agents. Bland was quite clear that the danger was to be found partly 'below stairs':

> Every German or Austrian servant, however superficially charming and devoted, is a real and grave menace [...]. I have not the least doubt that, when the signal is given, as it will scarcely fail to be when Hitler so decides, there will be satellites of the monster all over the country who will at once embark on widespread sabotage and attacks on civilians and the military indiscriminately. We cannot afford to take this risk. ALL Germans and Austrians, at least, ought to be interned at once.[14]

In May–June 1940 the British government introduced its policy of indiscriminate internment, the course of which ran parallel to the course of the military campaign. Selective internment of enemy aliens was introduced following the German invasion of the Netherlands and Belgium; the order for mass internment was issued in the wake of military defeat in France and the growing fear of invasion. On 12 May, the third day of the battle for Holland and Belgium, the government announced the establishment of a 'protected zone', comprising some thirty coastal counties, within which all male Austrians and Germans between the ages of sixteen and 60 were arrested for 'temporary internment'. The 'protected zones' encompassed a wide area, running from Devon to Inverness. In Devon it extended to Dartington Hall, causing the internment of the ballet-master and choreographer Kurt Jooss, and other accomplished dancers and musicians working at the Dartington Arts Centre. In the east it included Cambridge, resulting in the arrest of numerous refugee academics and students. In Scotland, the 'protected zone' encompassed Edinburgh, where a number of émigrés had settled, among whom was Hans Gál: his diary of internment duly begins on 13 May 1940.

Two days later, as the Netherlands surrendered, the government ordered the internment of all male 'enemy aliens' in category 'B'. The arrests were carried out in some secrecy, usually early in the morning, adding considerably to the uncertainty and anxiety of the victims. They were allowed to pack only a small suitcase, containing the barest essentials, since their internment was intended to be temporary.

---

[12] *The Daily Telegraph*, 16 April 1940.

[13] The bulk of the Dutch armed forces surrendered on 14 May 1940; troops stationed in Zealand held out for another three days.

[14] Quoted in Gillman, *op. cit.*, p. 102.

By mid-June an estimated 7,000 men and 4,000 women had been interned. On 20 June the government reversed its previous position, abandoning any talk of temporary internment. By 25 June the order was given to intern all 'C' category men – precisely those already acknowledged as 'refugees from Nazi oppression', a designation stamped, moreover, in their police registration book. (There were a few, though important, exceptions, including men of 70 or over, those in essential war work and those working for refugee organisations.)

During these initial weeks, the implementation of internment bore all the marks of hasty improvisation. Refugees were arrested by local police and taken to local 'aliens collecting stations' (in Gál's case the Donaldson deaf-and-dumb school, which had been hastily vacated at the beginning of the war) and later transferred to makeshift 'transit camps' which were under military control.[15] Even before the war, the government had designated various sites for use as internment camps, should they be required. They included the Isle of Man, where enemy aliens had been interned in the First World War, and Huyton, near Liverpool. But such preparations proved completely inadequate. The number of internees exceeded by far the capacity of the camps – something which was obvious at Huyton: sleeping arrangements were inadequate, hygiene was primitive and food was often sparse (Gál noted that the dining-hut at Huyton quickly became known as Starvation Hall[16]). Among the sites for these makeshift camps was Kempton Park race-course, where men were billeted in the Tote building and even in the stables. There were several tent camps, such as Prees Heath in Shropshire, where the entire camp was under canvas and difficult conditions were made worse by appalling weather which finally forced the dispersal of the camp.[17] Among the worst of these makeshift camps was Warth Mills, a disused cotton mill near Bury, which housed some two thousand prisoners in terrible conditions; there were only eighteen water taps for all the prisoners; the 'lavatories' consisted of sixty buckets in the factory yard. Among the internees there was the lawyer and journalist Rudolf Olden, who was later drowned when the liner *City of Benares* was sunk by a German U-Boot.[18] At

---

[15] *Cf.* pp. 55–79, below, and Robert Neumann, internment diary (untitled), manuscript, 123pp., Österreichische Nationalbibliothek, Vienna, ser. n. 21.608.

[16] *Cf.* p. 58, below.

[17] *Cf.* Richard Friedenthal, *Die Welt in der Nussschale*, Piper, Munich, 1956, which is a fictional account of the author's internment, notably in Prees Heath.

[18] François Lafitte, *The Internment of Aliens*, Penguin, Harmondsworth 1940, pp. 101–2; rev. edn. Libris, London 1988. A prominent human-rights campaigner in pre-Nazi Germany, Olden was the author of *Hitler der Eroberer: Entlarvung einer Legende* ('Hitler the Conqueror: Debunking of a Myth'), published by Querido in Amsterdam in 1936 and, in English translation as *Hitler the Pawn*, by Gollancz in London, also in 1936.

Huyton, which became the largest of the transit camps, the government had requisitioned the newly completed Woolfall Heath Housing Estate[19] and turned it into an internment camp by the crude expedient of throwing barbed wire around its perimeter. Although the houses had been completed, they contained neither beds nor other items of furniture: the internees slept on straw palliasses. Initially, conditions there were reasonable, as Gál's account makes clear,[20] but they rapidly deteriorated as more and more prisoners began to arrive. Robert Neumann, one of these later arrivals, described Huyton in his diary as 'hell on earth'.[21]

Most internees were profoundly shocked both by their internment and by the abrupt change in British attitudes it signified. The early months of war had generally produced a strong sense of solidarity with their British hosts, inspired by the feeling that everyone was in the same boat, a feeling which had now vanished.

Though overcrowding and primitive living conditions were unpleasant and dispiriting, most internees had more immediate and more tangible concerns. They suffered from feelings of frustration and anxiety, the trauma of arrest and detention being compounded by concern for the well-being of family or friends. Most were initially held virtually incommunicado, unable to communicate with their loved ones, except for simple messages, requesting clothing or other necessities. These restrictions were later relaxed: internees were allowed to write two letters a week, though each had to be limited to a maximum of 24 lines. Even then communication was highly erratic, all letters being subject to censorship and hence to considerable delay.

Throughout the early weeks of internment, prisoners were cut off from all other contact with the outside world as well; denied access to newspapers or radio, they were kept in ignorance of the progress of the war. In the absence of factual information, each camp became a hotbed of rumour and counter-rumour. As news of the fall of France filtered through, and the fear of invasion grew, many internees felt increasingly anxious about their situation, seeing themselves as 'sitting ducks', destined to be handed over to the Germans in the event of a successful invasion. One of the bitterest complaints by refugees was that Jews and anti-Fascists were interned together with 'Auslandsdeutsche' (Germans living abroad), most of whom had been arrested on the outbreak of war as known or suspected Nazis.

---

[19] In 1932 Liverpool City Council had purchased a large amount of land from the Knowsley estate of the Earl of Derby; Woolfall Heath was one of four housing estates intended to absorb population overspill from metropolitan Liverpool.

[20] *Cf.* pp. 55 *et seq*, below.

[21] *Loc. cit.*, p. 20.

Some ninety per cent of refugees were Jews and the decision to intern these two groups cheek by jowl caused much distress, confirming the insensitivity of the authorities and their complete lack of preparation. Both the soldiers responsible for guarding the camps and the officers commanding them seemed woefully ignorant of the history of the refugees whom it was now their duty to guard.

Although internment itself initially found general support amongst the British public, there were also some critical voices, including such luminaries as the Archbishop of Canterbury, the Bishop of Chichester, the MPs Eleanor Rathbone and Josiah Wedgwood, J. J. Mallon, the warden of Toynbee Hall, and the classicist Professor Gilbert Murray. He had played host to Rudolf Olden in Oxford and criticised 'public hysteria' about aliens, condemning those 'who can see no difference between one German and another'.[22] H. G. Wells, in a letter to *The Times*, attacked the 'slovenliness and stupidity' of official policy.[23] But public opinion in general was not yet ready to change.

The Isle of Man

By the end of May, the British government had begun the process of transferring internees to more permanent camps, mainly on the Isle of Man. Many of these camps consisted of hotels and boarding houses in the resorts on the island, which were requisitioned by the government and surrounded by barbed wire. In this way, the authorities created a number of camps, mostly in Douglas, the capital, on the east coast, the largest four being Central (often known as Central Promenade) Camp, to which Hans Gál was transferred from Huyton, Hutchinson, Onchan and Palace; there were also Granville (not used), Metropole, Regent (also unused) and Sefton. Outside Douglas, there was Peveril Camp in Peel, on the west coast, which eventually played host to members of the British Union of Fascists; Mooragh Camp in the north-eastern coastal resort of Ramsey; and Rushen Camp, for women and children, was formed by enclosing Port Erin and Port St Mary (this time without barbed wire), on the southern peninsula of the island.

Material conditions of internment gradually grew better after internees were transferred to the Isle of Man, as administration slowly caught up with requirements. Meals improved and internees were eventually able to buy provisions from local shop-keepers. Above all, the internees were allowed a considerable degree of autonomy, enabling them to organise various

---

[22] 'Judex' (i.e., Herbert Delauny Hughes), *Anderson's Prisoners*, Gollancz, London, 1940, p. 112.
[23] *The Times*, 2 July 1940.

educational and cultural activities which the authorities encouraged as a means of relieving boredom and maintaining morale.

At first sight, the range and variety of cultural events which took place in internment camps is astonishing, but in fact, a high proportion of internees were scholars or arts professionals – actors, musicians, artists, writers, film-makers. Hutchinson Camp, for example, contained a number of artists, including Fred Uhlman, Siegfried Charoux, Helmut Weissenborn and Kurt Schwitters. It also held the writer Richard Friedenthal, who would fictionalise his experience in the novel *Die Welt in der Nussschale* ('The World in a Nutshell'),[24] the journalist Heinrich Fraenkel and the cabaret-artist Peter Herz. There was also a theatre group, comprised mainly of professional actors, which performed seven full-length plays in the course of 1941 alone (many of them were not released until early 1942) and various distinguished musicians, including Maryan Rawicz (of the piano duo Rawicz and Landauer), the composer Egon Wellesz and the concert pianist Richard Glas, who gave concerts and recitals. Most camps established an educational programme of lessons and lectures.

Central Promenade Camp, where Gál was held, could boast no such array of talent, but Gál also records examples of the concerts which were held there, emphasising the extraordinary concentration of musical talent which the British had chosen to intern. Some careers were advanced or even launched by internment. Ernest Bornemann, who was deported to Canada, was released to work for the English documentary-film-maker John Grierson. The musical partnership of Rawicz and Landauer, who enjoyed extraordinary popularity in post-war Britain, began with recitals given in internment on the Isle of Man; it was also there that three members of the future Amadeus Quartet first met and played together. Peter Herz who established the 'Stacheldraht Cabaret' in Hutchinson Camp on the Isle of Man, to amuse and entertain his fellow-internees, went on to found the Blue Danube Club in London, where he performed with much success until 1954. In spite of the efforts of scholars like Michael Seyfert,[25] most of these cultural events have inevitably gone unrecorded, the ephemeral nature of artistic performance being compounded by the material circumstances of internment. Part of the value of Hans Gál's diary undoubtedly lies in its record of his own creative endeavours in internment: the composition and performance of the *Huyton Suite*, and later of music for the revue *What a Life!*

---

[24] *Op. cit.*
[25] Michael Seyfert, *Im Niemandsland. Deutsche Exilliteratur in britischer Internierung. Ein unbekanntes Kapitel der Kulturgeschichte des zweiten Weltkriegs*, Das Arsenal, Berlin, 1984.

Gál's *Huyton Suite* was written in adverse circumstances: the almost complete absence of privacy for composition was matched by the lack of simple necessities such as sheet music and, even more seriously, musical instruments. Adapting to the circumstances, Gál wrote the music for flute and two violins, corresponding to the instruments and musicians available to him. When the work was finally performed on the Isle of Man, the audience, most of whom had passed through Huyton, sat spellbound, their emotional involvement complete.[26] The writer Robert Neumann organised a course in creative writing in the nearby Mooragh Camp, inviting participants to explore the theme 'Huyton Camp', a subject which, he reported,[27] gave participants considerable food for thought.

Gál's diary also gives the best description yet of the production of the 'bilingual camp revue' *What a Life!*, which has become one of the notable cultural events of internment. It was devised by the film director G. M. Höllering, who had produced the Brecht-Dudow film *Kuhle Wampe*[28] and who would later become the owner of the Academy Cinema in London. Gál's text contains a striking portrait of Höllering,[29] at whose insistence he wrote the music for the revue. It also involuntarily confirms how rapidly such creative activities took control, gaining, in the daily tedium of internment, an almost compulsive importance. The last third of Gál's diary is devoted to his work on the revue, and to his efforts to secure release from internment: two conflicting projects which finally converged when he agreed to stay one day longer in the camp in order to take part in the first performance.

Deportation

Even as the government took measures to consolidate most internees on the Isle of Man, it also launched a policy of large-scale deportation, an idea enthusiastically adopted by the new Prime Minister, Winston Churchill, who declared himself 'strongly in favour of removing all internees out of the United Kingdom'.[30] Planning for the operation had begun at the end of May. On 3 June, in a note to the Cabinet Secretary, Sir Edward Bridges, Churchill demanded to know whether 'anything [has] been done about shipping 20,000 internees to Newfoundland or St. Helena?'[31] Neither of

---

[26] *Cf.* p. 124, below.
[27] Neumann, *loc. cit.*, p. 60.
[28] *Kuhle Wampe, oder: Wem gehört die Welt* (a left-wing film dealing with unemployment: 'kuhle Wampe' means 'empty belly' in Berlin slang) was conceived and written by Brecht and directed by him and Slatan Dudow. Banned on its release in 1932, a cut version was re-instated after protests.
[29] *Cf.* pp. 107 and 131, below.
[30] Quoted in Gillman, *op. cit.*, p. 133.
[31] Quoted in *ibid.*, p. 163.

these destinations was ever envisaged, but Churchill's question catches the urgency of the affair. The first ship carrying deportees left for Canada on 21 June, an operation conducted in considerable secrecy: none of the internees was actually aware of their ultimate destination.

The deportation of 'enemy aliens' contains some of the most disreputable aspects of this entire episode. When the troopship *Dunera* transported 2,400 'enemy aliens' to Australia, they were robbed and mistreated by soldiers on board, an occurrence which caused much public disquiet when the story emerged through the press in Australia.[32] Many internees, particularly younger men, were subjected to considerable moral pressure to persuade them to join one of the shipments for deportation. And although the first shipments consisted almost entirely of younger, unmarried men, pressure was swiftly exerted on older men to encourage them also to 'volunteer' for deportation. Gál records the assurances given to married men that their interned wives would be allowed to accompany them in the same convoy – only to discover that it was not true. In an entry dated 20 July, he writes:

> It is so despicable that at first we didn't want to believe it. Our comrades who went voluntarily with the third overseas transport on 10 July, trusting that their wives would join this transport, were deceived.
>
> A letter from one of the wives in Port Erin, the women's camp on the island, led to this discovery. Even today, the wives still have no idea that their husbands were sent away. No-one has told them anything, they know nothing. Meanwhile it has also become known that the destination of this, the third transport, was not Canada but Australia.[33]

In fact, this shipment never took place. In an entry dated 5 August Gál noted: 'The Australia transport has been stopped for unknown reasons.'[34]

The reason – as yet unknown to Gál and his fellow-internees – was that the government had halted any further deportations. Public opinion had begun to move strongly against internment after the loss of the *Arandora Star*. This luxury cruise liner, commandeered for war duties, set sail from Liverpool on 1 July, bound for Canada. It was carrying some 1,200 internees, including some 700 Italians and 500 Germans and Austrians. At 6am on 2 July the vessel was torpedoed by a German submarine off the coast of Ireland, sinking with the loss of more than 700 lives. Over two-thirds of the Italians on board were drowned and nearly one-third of the Germans and

[32] *Cf.* Cyril Pearl, *The Dunera Scandal*, Angus and Robertson, London, Sydney and Melbourne, 1983.
[33] *Cf.* p. 117, below.
[34] *Cf.* p. 128, below.

Austrians.[35] Public concern at the incident, and the policy of deportation which it brought to light, finally led the government to change course. In mid-July Churchill – in a striking *volte face* – felt able to tell the House of Commons that he had always thought that 'the Fifth Column danger [was] somewhat exaggerated in this island'.[36] By that time over 27,000 'enemy aliens' had been arrested and interned, some 7,500 of whom had been deported.

Within weeks of announcing measures to intern all 'C' category men, the government was confronted with the problem of releasing them. On 23 July Sir John Anderson told the Commons that certain classes of internee were eligible to apply for release. The first 50 walked free from camps on the Isle of Man on 5 August.[37] On 31 July the government issued a White Paper listing eighteen categories for release from internment, including 'the invalid or infirm', those holding key positions in vital war-industries, 'scientists, research workers and persons of academic distinction for whom work of national importance in their special fields is available', as well as doctors and dentists. For younger men, the quickest method of securing release was to volunteer for the British Army's non-combatant Pioneer Corps (auxiliary units performing light engineering tasks), an inducement which proved highly effective. By January 1941, some 4,600 internees had already enlisted.

Although the White Paper was cautiously welcomed by the various refugee organisations, it also drew criticism for its naked self-interest. In the parliamentary debate of 22 August, Rhys Davies declared that 'these men should be let out of the internment camps because they are innocent and not because they are useful'.[38]

By early October 1940 over 4,000 men and women had been freed, by the end of that year a total of 10,000. The releases continued during 1941 at the rate of a thousand a month and by October 95 per cent of all internees in categories 'B' and 'C' had been released. (Gál himself emerged on 27 September.[39]) The reversal of fortunes was virtually total. 'Enemy aliens' who in 1940 had been rigorously excluded as a potential threat were transformed into 'friendly enemy aliens', who were rapidly integrated into the British war-effort. Many younger internees joined the Pioneer Corps and, later, regular units of the British Army; many others – both men and women – started work in armaments factories and other branches of

---

[35] *Cf.* also p. 100 and note 20 on p. 112, below.
[36] Quoted in Gillman, *op. cit.*, p. 231.
[37] *Cf.* Gillman, *op. cit.*, p. 232.
[38] Hansard, *loc. cit.*
[39] *Cf.* pp. 168–72, below.

British war-production. The deportees posed a particular problem for the government. In view of the difficulties and dangers of shipping, some chose to stay in Canada or Australia after their release, but many elected to return to Britain, arriving back by various roundabout routes, thus completing a remarkable odyssey, the original purpose of which had long been forgotten.

Historians have taken only intermittent interest in the wartime internment of refugees.[40] Those who have considered it have judged it harshly. Peter and Leni Gillman called it 'a disreputable story',[41] Francois Lafitte 'monstrously unjust'[42] and Eric Koch (himself a victim) 'a wartime blunder'.[43] A more recent critic, Tony Kushner, has described it as 'part of a tradition of anti-alienism, where restrictive measures, whatever their intolerant impulses, have been and continue to be defended'.[44] Sir John Anderson himself conceded at the time that internment was 'a matter which touches the good name of this country',[45] a phrase which might serve as a suitable epitaph for the whole sorry story of internment.

---

[40] A useful review of the literature on internment can be found in Sean Lewis' review of London's *Whitehall and the Jews*, online at http://www.history.ac.uk/ihr/Focus/War/reviews/revkellysean.html.

[41] *Op. cit.*, p. 6.

[42] Lafitte, *op. cit.*, p. viii.

[43] Eric Koch, *Deemed Suspect. A Wartime Blunder*, Methuen, Toronto, 1980.

[44] 'Clubland, Cricket Tests and Alien Internment, 1939–40', in David Cesarani and Tony Kushner (eds.), *The Internment of Aliens in Twentieth Century Britain*, Routledge, London, 1993, p. 96.

[45] Hansard, *loc. cit.*

...son Hospital, Edinburgh
...ai 1940

...er sitzen wir nun seit 24 Stunden, bewacht von grimmig drein-
...enden Soldaten mit Gewehr und Bajonett; sie müssen uns für ganz
...liche Gesellen halten. Gestern waren wir gegen hundert......,-
...ungen Leute unter achtzehn, darunter meinen Sohn, hat... man gleich
...iert untergebracht-, und heute sind noch etwa vierzig dazuge-
..., Nachzügler aus Edinburgh und Leute aus Glasgow, Aberdeen,
...ndrews. Von allen hört man die gleiche Geschichte: weggeholt
...inem Zivilpolizisten, mit gerade genügend Frist um das Notwendigste
...n paar Tage in ein Köfferchen zu packen, und fort zur Polizei-
...on. Von dort in verschlossenem Gefängnisauto- das Vehikel, das
...i uns zulande den "grünen Heinrich" nannte- zum Donaldson
...al, einem düsteren, kasernartigen, häßlichen Gebäude, wo wir
...einem kahlen, geräumigen Saal beisammen sitzen. Die Fenster
...zu hoch, um einen Ausblick zu gewähren. Draußen in der Ecke
...tiegenhauses steht eine große Statue der Hygiea (das Gebäude war
...ein Spital), aber ///// nach den sanitären Einrichtungen zu
...t Hygieia hier längst ihre Herrschaft aufgegeben. Die

Music
behind Barbed Wire

131

...ihrem Gatten und es geht ihm merklich besser. Bei ...einem Zustand wie
dem seinigen bedeutet der innere Auftrieb unendlich viel für die
Möglichkeit einer Genesung. Das war es ja, was wir uns vor allem
von einer Befreiung aus dem Stacheldrahtviereck für ihn erhofft
...atten; vielleicht war es noch immer nicht zu spät.
Ich bin in diesen Wochen gemeinsamer Sorgen um unseren Freund
...t Höllering ... vertraut geworden. Er ist ein prächtiger
..., die denkbar glücklichste Mischung ... eines Künstlertemperaments
Phantasie und Unternehmungslust und eines ordnungliebenden,
...kterfesten Menschen. Er hat ... eine neue Filmidee, die wir
...ander durchbesprochen haben und bei der sich allenfalls eine
...enarbeit... ergeben könnte. Aber das ist Zukunftsmusik.
...unausgesetzt tätig mit Entwürfen, Verbesserungen, Material-
...ein Mensch aktivster, positivster Art. Ich beneide ihn um
...eitsfähigkeit. Ich fühle mich wie ein Wrack mit meinem
...esicht, das wie ein Fremdkörper auf mir steckt. Ich werde
...n für das Konzert im Theater wie eine Gipsr...
...el sein.

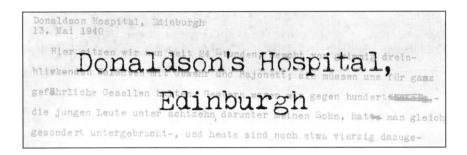

13 May 1940

We have now been stuck here[1] for 24 hours, guarded by grim-looking soldiers with rifles and bayonets; they must think we are very dangerous fellows. Yesterday we were getting on for a hundred – the young people under eighteen, including my son, were given separate accommodation – and today around forty more have arrived, late-comers from Edinburgh and people from Glasgow, Aberdeen and St. Andrews. One hears the same story from all of them: taken away by a civilian policeman with just enough time to pack the necessary things for a few days into a suitcase and then off to the police station. From there in a closed prison van – the vehicle that at home we used to call the 'Green Henry' – to Donaldson Hospital, a gloomy, barrack-like, ugly building, where we are now all together in a large, bare room. The windows are too high to see out of. Outside, in the corner of the staircase, there is a large statue of Hygieia (the building was once a hospital), but to judge from the sanitary arrangements Hygieia has long since given up her dominion. The question that is exercising us at the moment is: will we get straw sacks or at least straw bundles to lie on? For pampered people, which is what we are, after all, the first night was torture; we had to camp out on the hard floor with two hairy, dirty blankets, packed so closely together that we poked our neighbour in the face whenever we turned over.

Both my hip-bones are sore, I didn't get a moment's sleep. But the worst of all was the rain-water butt, at least that is what it is in my memory of

---

[1] Donaldson's Hospital, situated in the west end of Edinburgh (between Princess Street and Murrayfield stadium), was opened in 1850 to cater for destitute and vulnerable children; the building, in effect a Victorian palace, was designed by William Playfair and built with funds (£220,000) left for the purpose by the printer and newspaper-publisher James Donaldson (1751–1830). It soon evolved into a school for the deaf, although it also admitted hearing children. The school, now Donaldson's College, occupied the premises until 2008, when it moved to Linlithgow, to the west of Edinburgh. The conscription of the building for use as an internment camp was the only interruption to its continuous use as a school for those 158 years.

that night. I am lying sleepless with aching bones. My neighbour on the right, anxious little Dr. Adler,[2] is writhing about just like me; the one on the left, my friend Dr. Gross,[3] the zoologist, is sleeping like a child. Lucky man! All the time we can hear groaning, scraping, snoring sounds; of the hundred people some are always on the move. Suddenly a noise like rain on a tin roof. A pattering and drumming. Strange, I think, it was such a clear evening! The rain suddenly stops but after a short time it begins again. It keeps raining, with interruptions, until, at the first light of dawn – perhaps around three o'clock – I see the connection: the presumed tin roof is a dustbin standing at the entrance to the room. The guards locked us up in the evening and won't open up again until the morning. It was therefore wise to cater for emergencies. There is really no reason for such a thing to annoy one. But it makes you starkly conscious of the fact of being a prisoner, this most senseless of all pieces of senselessness. Yesterday, anyone who wanted to excuse himself was accompanied by a sentry with fixed bayonet; not for the world would they have let anyone walk the twenty yards across the corridor alone. Every entrance to the building is guarded; a double barbed-wire fence has been placed around us, with sentries patrolling in between. What an atrocious waste of manpower and energy for such a farce! This is an inexhaustible subject in our conversations: stunned horror at the transformation that has taken place for us since yesterday in the friendly, human face of this country. Almost all of us who come from Edinburgh know one another. There is not a single one among all of these for whom I would not stake my life that he is as harmless as I am, like me driven out of his homeland and hounded, that he, like me, has found helpfulness and decent, splendid people who have become his friends and would be willing to testify for him. Every one of us is worried, with every fibre of our being, about the outcome of this war, which is *our* war, the war against *our* oppressors, against those who have ruined our livelihood, plundered our property and left us unprotected and homeless! And now we are imprisoned because we have been mistaken for the enemy – our enemy! And we are put into a building – this is like a grim mockery – in which a few hundred German civilian prisoners from captured ships are interned. These people have already settled in quite comfortably, manage the kitchen and dish out the food to us, while we have to line up in turn with our tin bowls. The flaxen-haired Hamburg type predominates; there are good-natured-looking, pleasant lads among them, but also some real Nazi faces, who greet us with sneering grins and evident satisfaction. Comments fly

---

[2] *Cf.* Appendix One: Personalia, p. 187, below.
[3] *Cf.* Appendix One: Personalia, p. 191, below.

1

Donaldson Hospital, Edinburgh
13. Mai 1940

Hier sitzen wir nun seit 24 Stunden, bewacht von grimmig drein-
blickenden Soldaten mit Gewehr und Bajonett; sie müssen uns für ganz
gefährliche Gesellen halten. Gestern waren wir gegen hundert ~~stark~~, -
die jungen Leute unter achtzehn, darunter meinen Sohn, hat man gleich
gesondert untergebracht-, und heute sind noch etwa vierzig dazuge-
kommen, Nachzügler aus Edinburgh und Leute aus Glasgow, Aberdeen,
St. Andrews. Von allen hört man die gleiche Geschichte: weggeholt
von einem Zivilpolizisten, mit gerade genügend Frist um das Notwendigste
für ein paar Tage in ein Köfferchen zu packen, und fort zur Polizei-
station. Von dort in verschlossenem Gefängnisauto- das Vehikel, das
man bei uns zulande den "grünen Heinrich" nannte- zum Donaldson
Hospital, einem düsteren, kasernartigen, häßlichen Gebäude, wo wir
nun in einem kahlen, ~~geräumigen Saal~~ Raum beisammen sitzen. Die Fenster
~~sitzen~~ sind zu hoch angebracht, um einen Ausblick zu gewähren. Draußen in der Ecke
des Stiegenhauses steht eine große Statue der Hygiea (das Gebäude war
einmal ein Spital), aber ~~nach~~ nach den sanitären Einrichtungen zu
schließen, hat Hygieia hier längst ihre Herrschaft aufgegeben. Die
Frage, die uns momentan bewegt, ist: werden wir heute Strohsäcke
bekommen oder wenigstens Strohbündel, um darauf zu liegen? Für
verwöhnte Leute, die wir nun einmal sind, war die erste Nacht eine
Tortur; mit je zwei haarigen, schmutzigen Decken hatte man sich ~~sich~~ auf
dem harten Fußboden sein Lager zu bereiten, eng genug zusammengedrängt,
um, wenn man sich umwandte, seinem Nachbarn mit dem Ellbogen ins
Gesicht zu fahren. Meine beiden Hüftknochen sind wund, ich habe nicht
einen Augenblick schlafen können. Das Schrecklichste von allem aber

The first page of the typescript of Gál's internment diary

around. Although newspapers are forbidden in the house, these people are surprisingly well-informed about the events of the war and, understandably, remarkably optimistic about the victory of the German cause. And these are our fellow prisoners, our fellow sufferers!

Meanwhile our people have been presented in groups to the officer in charge, a grey-haired captain who makes a pleasant impression. He took down personal details and gave each of us a number which from now on, it seems, will replace our names. I took the opportunity to ask urgently for something reasonable to sleep on. And in the course of the afternoon we were indeed taken to a store where we were given straw sacks which we were allowed to fill with sparingly measured-out straw. We are overjoyed by this favour. Towards evening we were led up into an upper storey – before this we were allowed to walk around for half an hour in the yard, always alongside the wall – and we were quartered in individual rooms, fourteen men in each. I was unlucky and got an especially small room which likewise – this seems to be what the rule requires – had to accommodate fourteen men. The room is gloomy, three-quarters of the only window deprived of its normal function by the blackout, the air could be cut with a knife. But all this is marvellous compared with the mass accommodation of yesterday and we feel almost comfortable. As we were divided up randomly, we could hardly choose our company. But among my room-mates are some of my friends, and little Dr. Adler, the anxious family man, has remained my sleeping-neighbour.

Franz,[4] my older boy, who was brought here with me yesterday, comes running in. This evening he will be taken away, along with the whole group of young men under eighteen, to a special camp in the south of England. I tried unsuccessfully to protest; boys are not allowed to stay here with the adults, that is a rule that admits no exception. The boy, who is otherwise a rough diamond, is gentle and almost tender at our parting. I share with him the small amount of money that I've been allowed to keep (bank-notes were taken away, together with all knives, scissors and other suspicious articles, e.g., books), then he is chased away by a non-commissioned officer, as he was naturally not allowed on our floor, with the adults. I am somewhat consoled by knowing that he is in the company of the Wittingeham boys. They are splendid, fresh, cheerful and resolute young people, among whom he will probably be better looked after than among us adults. Wittingeham is a farm camp with exemplary facilities, where young people are prepared for emigration to Palestine. I once gave a concert there with my friends from Edinburgh, and we were delighted by the whole atmosphere of the house

---

[4] *Cf.* Appendix One: Personalia, pp. 183–84, below.

and the enthusiasm of the teachers as well as the pupils.[5] They are boys who were brought here to safety from the November pogroms in Germany and were looked after and educated in the best manner in Wittingeham. Now they have been taken away from their work and locked up. According to the current regulations, emigration to Palestine is only possible under the age of eighteen, the time will shortly run out for many of the boys. But no-one is bothered about that now.

At eight o'clock it's 'Roll Call'; an officer goes from room to room and checks the number of prisoners. Each of us has to stand by his straw-sack. As the lieutenant, a surly-looking man, comes into our room, he points with his stick and says 'too full'. 'How intelligent', I think to myself, 'so he's noticed that we are suffering from overcrowding.' But no, he has merely pointed to a straw-sack that is stuffed full, against the regulations. We must have order! For these people we are prisoners for whose custody they are responsible. Nothing else concerns them. But why has no-one instructed them? Why are orders given to imprison people who are acknowledged to be for the most part loyal and reliable – merely as a safety precaution, and above all, so it is announced, for their own protection – and no instructions are given to the executive authorities as to how these friendly, loyal elements are to be treated? Was it really just a senseless, thoughtless panic measure? The war has entered a critical stage, Norway and Holland have fallen, Belgium and France are in the middle of a severe struggle. There has been treason everywhere. In one section of the press there has long been deliberate agitation against the refugees. Are there not other interests and other agendas behind this measure, which was carried out without any visible preparation and literally overnight, to arrest all 'enemy aliens' in the protected area on Whit Sunday? We have enemies in this country, that is beyond doubt. These enemies were Hitler's most loyal friends until the outbreak of war. Are secret forces of this kind now at work, are we, the *apparent* fifth column, ultimately the victims of the *real* one? And what will

---

[5] Whittingeham House, near Stenton in East Lothian, east of Edinburgh, was built around 1817 for James Balfour, father of the politician Arthur Balfour (1848–1930) who as British Foreign Secretary in 1917 wrote the Balfour Declaration, which stated that 'His Majesty's government view with favour the establishment in Palestine of a national home for the Jewish people, and will use their best endeavours to facilitate the achievement of this object'. With this background, Viscount Traprain, Balfour's nephew, opened Whittingeham Farm School on the estate to give shelter to some of the 10,000 refugee Jewish children arriving in Britain as part of the *Kindertransport* effort. When Whittingeham Farm School opened in 1939 it admitted 51 children, a number that expanded to 160 before it was closed in 1941, in part because many of the children were now older than seventeen but also because of financial difficulties. Whittingeham Farm School had an explicitly Zionist goal, teaching its pupils the agricultural skills that were intended to be useful in settlements in Palestine.

happen if such forces intervene here in the machinery of state and in the war?

These are the tormenting thoughts that keep me awake until deep into the night. All my fellow-sufferers are already asleep. Only little Dr. Adler is writhing about. He is in the same state as I am. And it is really so difficult to find even a half-tolerable position with aching hips on a narrow, skimpy sack of straw....

14 May

I have slept for a couple of hours. But how my bones ache! And how unspeakably disgusting everything is that reaches my five senses. This awful, stale barrack-smell made up of human sweat, lavatory odours, Lysol[6] and bad food in the whole house, in every corridor and staircase! How I hate this house! A large rectangle, laid out around a square courtyard, in the ugly sixties style. On the inside, along the windows overlooking the courtyard, there is an endless corridor, every side looks the same, you never know where you are or which of the many staircases which lead downwards from here on the first floor is the right one, the one to the dining room, the only one we are allowed to use. One part of this corridor leads past the place where the German civilian prisoners live. We avoid this area as best we can, but we can't stop the Germans coming to us to beg for cigarettes, to start conversations and let us know that we shall soon all be liberated by Hitler. The food is meagre. Bad tea and watery, sticky porridge for breakfast, cabbage and potato soup, tasting like dishwater, for lunch. The piece of bread and cheese for tea is far more tolerable and for many it is the only nourishment that they take. It is prisoners' rations and we are held like convicts, with all the harshness and lack of consideration that go with it. It is all punishment: the sleeping accommodation, the food, the hour-long walk in the courtyard, round and round, always along the wall, the impossibility of even telling one's family where one is. What are we being punished for? What crime have we committed? And *who is punishing us*? Are they our friends, the same Britons who accepted us so kindly, acknowledged our work, offered our children hospitality, gave us the feeling of being in a new homeland? I came to this country two years ago with the intention of emigrating to America, and I had made all the arrangements. But we got attached here, we could not separate ourselves from this wonderful land that was like a cultivated garden, from many dear, noble, well-disposed people, from the few possibilities for work and livelihood that we had found here. And we were tired of wandering. A year ago we renounced our American visas and

---

[6] A disinfectant.

decided to stay here. And now comes that friend, with a changed, cold and unapproachable face, says 'sorry' and treats you, the trusting, grateful guest, like the worst enemy and criminal! A newspaper has been smuggled in, God knows how. There is general satisfaction that the 'rounding up of aliens' has been carried out so successfully, according to plan and without a hitch. Voices among the public demand that more people should be interned, people from the unprotected area, women, children, everyone. Safety first! In a footnote it is remarked that correspondence opposing the internment cannot be considered. This is how public opinion is created in the land of democracy! I have the feeling that our position is hopeless.

15 May

Yesterday there was a little row that seems to have had a cleansing effect. In the afternoon there came an order to go down to the main room to receive a visit. The chief rabbi of Edinburgh, Dr. Daiches,[7] was announced. Almost all of us know him personally, he is a friendly man who completely understands our position and he is politically astute. He himself has adopted a German child who is interned alongside us. Perhaps he can help! We are assembled like the congregation in the synagogue, all full of eager anticipation. Dr. Daiches enters, accompanied by the commandant. He walks to the podium with quick little steps, smiling at us all like good friends and – his customary diplomatic shrewdness must for the moment have left him in the lurch, or he felt himself to be too much the preacher in the pulpit, or it was simply embarrassment in the face of the awkward and completely unusual situation – he blurts out the clumsiest address imaginable: 'I am so glad to see all my dear friends so happy together!' The effect was overwhelming. A hurricane broke loose which must have hit the hapless optimist as unexpectedly as the baffled officer, who didn't understand the situation at all. Cries of 'We are *not* happy!', 'What a scandal!', 'We are treated like beasts!', a hundred gesticulating arms, contorted faces, I would never have thought that a hundred people could have created such an infernal din. When a modicum of peace returned after a few minutes, I spoke up and tried to give some sort of a picture of our situation to the flabbergasted clergyman who had fallen out of the clouds. I did so with bitterness and spared the commandant who was present nothing of things that one prefers not to hear. Most of my comrades were afterwards of the opinion that I had done

[7] Dr Salis Daiches was chief rabbi to the Jewish community of Edinburgh from his appointment in 1918 until his death in 1945. In May 1931, at a ceremony laying the foundation-stone of the first purpose-build synagogue in Edinburgh, Dr Daiches pointed out that Scotland was the only European country which had never shed Jewish blood or erected ghetto walls – a consideration which may have made Gál's new circumstances all the more disquieting.

more harm than good and heaped reproaches on me that I could not regard as unjustified. I am not well-suited to being a spokesman on issues where my emotions are aroused. I then speak rashly and get carried away, saying things that I would not have said after careful thought. There are those among us who are more suited to such things and I shall not do it again, as anyone who speaks on behalf of all must keep within bounds. But on this occasion, as it later turned out, it was in no way detrimental. Afterwards Dr. Daiches had an interview with the commandant and seems to have told him all sorts of things about us that his superiors had unfortunately failed to notify him about. The behaviour of the guards and the officers towards us has changed considerably, we shall get newspapers every day, we shall be outside as much as possible, on the lawn in front of the house instead of in the horrible courtyard – and Dr. Daiches has taken messages for our wives, who in future will be allowed to visit us once a week. That looks far more humane! He has also promised that all steps will be taken by the community and the committee to clarify our position with the government and to accelerate as much as possible the promised 'reconsideration' of each individual case. But there are constraints, an enemy attack is feared daily, one must have patience, etc. The most important thing is: the authorities seem to have understood that we don't belong together in the same house as the Nazis, and everything will be done to restrict contact with them to a minimum.

16 May

What prisoners usually feel to be the worst thing has not yet set in: boredom. I have never found myself in better, more stimulating company. Lecturers, post-graduates und students from the universities of Edinburgh, St. Andrews and Aberdeen, doctors, lawyers, people of the highest intellectual level, are all here together. After a few days, working-groups, discussion clubs and student societies were formed, a complete, improvised little university. There are scientists, mathematicians, historians, theologians and philosophers. There is time to discuss interesting matters which would otherwise feel remote to us or which we would not get round to through lack of time. One thing is at the moment completely remote and alien: music. It has hidden itself away.

Beneath the intellectual layer the sediment of philistinism has settled, divided into bridge, skat and tarot games. Among the non-intellectuals there are, incidentally, some splendid types, people I instantly love, just as there are those I instantly dislike (this is not restricted to the non-intellectuals). The card-players are permanently in session, they begin after breakfast and are only reluctantly interrupted when we are called for a meal.

Of the non-intellectuals I already knew Julius Schwarz, a Munich grocer, from Edinburgh, with his smiling face, his touching helpfulness and his irrepressible optimism. A new acquaintance is Karl Heinrich, a veteran of the Spanish Civil War, a Viennese worker who was in the International Brigade and found himself stranded in Edinburgh after all kinds of wild adventures. He is a communist, and loves making political speeches, but if you are patient he can tell you the most interesting things about the Spanish campaign. He is a fellow of the clearest native wit; incidentally, he has an injured leg and an ailing lung, but would passionately love to be back in the war, if only they would let him. But he makes the grimmest predictions and asserts that France must be defeated, because the fascists there have systematically suppressed all dissidents. He was interned in France and has no kindly feelings for that country. His analysis of the reports from the general staff is sensible and shows that he has experience and can think.

My special friends are all from Vienna: Dr. Fabius Gross, a zoologist, research assistant at the University of Edinburgh; Dr. Hugo Schneider,[8] a dentist, in the process of setting up his practice in Edinburgh (I would probably have gone to him next week to have my teeth seen to); and Dr. Max Sugar,[9] a laryngologist. Gross is the youngest of them. He was the leader of my Refugee Orchestra in Edinburgh,[10] an enthusiastic amateur musician and a man of the most absolute honesty, objectivity and integrity – the epitome of what a researcher should be. In spite of his mere 33 years he is, with his wisdom, self-control and good English, the ideal person to represent us with the authorities here. He does it skilfully, discreetly and successfully. Schneider is the typical intellectual Viennese Jew, with a sharp understanding, incorruptible sobriety and a way of finding everything amusing, which can get on your nerves, but at the same time full of touching goodness and kindness. Sugar was a prisoner of war in Russia for five years. There's nothing new for him in what we are now experiencing. He is practical and helpful and the most reliable soul imaginable. Sugar, Schneider and Gross are in the room next to mine. I shall try to get a place with them as soon as I can.

Today there is bad news. The French front seems to have been broken through at Sedan,[11] this could lead to a catastrophe. I have never been a

---

[8] *Cf.* Appendix One: Personalia, pp. 194–95, below.

[9] *Cf.* Appendix One: Personalia, p. 195, below.

[10] Gál had set up a Refugee Orchestra and a madrigal ensemble during his first winter in Edinburgh, 1939–40; *cf,* also p. 175, below.

[11] The Battle of Sedan (sometimes referred to as the Second Battle of Sedan, an earlier battle having taken place in the Franco-Prussian War in 1870) was fought from 15 to 17 May 1940. A German tank force, having raced through the supposedly impenetrable forests of the Ardennes, captured Sedan, on

pessimist. The thought that this war could in fact be lost never crossed my mind until the Norwegian defeat.[12] Ever since, this thought has acquired a hellish reality. Everything is crumbling away! Every front collapses when the enemy just taps it. Where will this lead?

Well, we pass the time as best we can. Yesterday people came who are hungry for music. There are about a dozen of the best people from my Edinburgh Refugee Orchestra here. We could quite easily form a small string orchestra, if we had the instruments. The plan has already been made. Gross has obtained permission from the authorities to collect instruments, music-stands and music in Edinburgh tomorrow with a lorry. Then we can begin right away.

As things have turned out since the day before yesterday, life is more or less tolerable. The worst assignment of the day is the morning ablutions. We have three bathrooms, each with two wash-basins and a lavatory; that's tight for over a hundred people. A strict rota has been introduced. When I come to my wash-basin, everything is already flooded, soap and the remains of beards are floating around. On the most important object in the room sits Herr Weiss, a waiter from Grunewald in Berlin. He greets every new arrival with a jovial witticism, makes speeches, gives wise advice, and sits, and sits and sits. When he then begins his useful activity, he accompanies it with clever sayings, such as 'Where there's a will there's a way!', 'First things first, you know!' I've never wanted to strangle anyone so much. I finish as quickly as possible and escape. He's still sitting there and talking, and now he has a new audience. He will out-sit and out-talk more of them. His work seems to be difficult and time-consuming, but then he doesn't have anything else to do.

17 May

Nothing has come of our music plans. Marching orders! We are to leave tomorrow, supposedly for the Liverpool area. That hit us like a bolt from the blue. So we must be prepared for this situation to last a long time! We are moving away from our loved ones, beyond contact and reach. This is worse than we had feared! We have had permission to let our wives know, and each of us is allowed to receive a visit for a quarter of an hour. There's a commotion like in a disturbed ants' nest. The officer on duty is in despair over all the pointless questions that he can't answer, and all the unfulfillable wishes, the helplessness and hopelessness. One wants to send a telegram as long as your arm to the government, another wants to speak to his lawyer

---

the east bank of the Meuse on 12 May, allowing them to attack the French forces on the west bank and establish bridge-heads to cross the river in strength.

[12] *Cf.* note 9 on p. 31, above.

immediately, a third wants to make arrangements for his factory that will have to close, a fourth wants to give notice on his flat, a fifth to auction his furniture. The military are full of patience and kindness, calming everyone down as much as possible, promising that it will be better for us there. I know some people who will be jolly glad to be rid of us tomorrow.

The joy of being rid of us so soon seems to have put the commandant in a good mood. They are not going to be too strict about the visits, and anyone who comes will be let in. Orders to fetch people have been flying round all day, and the whole company is on the move.

My sister Gretl[13] came in the morning. She has always been the practical and energetic one in our family, and she has brought a large box full of welcome things, fruit, cake, chocolate. Half of it was intended for Franz, the poor boy, who is now locked up somewhere south of London. At lunchtime I was again summoned to the commandant's office; it was a pleasant surprise to see my friend Leslie Grant sitting there. He is an officer in the reserves; he lost one of his thumbs at Gallipoli in the last war, and is now once more in the army as a captain, entrusted with the organisation of the Scottish Protected Area. If anyone can help it is him; he also knows Franz, likes him and has promised to do whatever is in his power. In the afternoon Hansi[14] was here. I hardly recognised her, she looked so pale, tearful and run down. She was very unhappy about the removal of the boy. I could at least give her his address, which I had obtained in the meantime. She told me how our dear old gentleman – our host Sir Herbert [Grierson][15] – could hardly be consoled when he came home and heard that I had been arrested. He telephoned the police, the military command, the city council, but everywhere he was politely turned away, and simply couldn't understand that what had happened wasn't just a stupid mistake that could immediately be put right. The dear, good man! He invited us to live in his house at the start of the war; he is retired – he was professor of English literature at the university, and eventually the dean – his married daughters are scattered all over the world; perhaps he wanted to bring some life into his big, gloomy house, and my wife kept house for him very skilfully and successfully. We have become close friends, I love the Scottish clarity and uprightness of his way of thinking, his genuinely humanistic, deeply ingrained education, his stupendous knowledge and memory, his rugged goodness that is so reluctant to manifest itself. Some time ago, one of his daughters came to the house with her two children, they live in Leeds. Now she has accompanied

---

[13] *Cf.* Appendix One: Personalia, p. 185, below.
[14] Gál's wife: *cf.* Appendix One: Personalia, pp. 184–85, below.
[15] *Cf.* Appendix One: Personalia, p. 191, below.

Hansi, and I am pleased about that. How terrible it would be for Hansi to be alone at present! I know her to be among fine, understanding people who love her and with whom she feels completely at home. In spite of the war I had a busy, productive winter, establishing an orchestra and an excellent madrigal group, gave lots of concerts, laid all sorts of foundations for further useful work. There are many people in Edinburgh who are receptive to music and a still rather rudimentary musical life. Now that has all been interrupted, probably buried. Once more I am driven from my work. Will I ever be able to continue it?

We talk little. She strokes my hand and would most like to cry. So would I.

The soldier looks at the clock.

Never again will I let anyone visit me as a prisoner! Never again!!!

XXX Huyton bei Liverpool, 19. Mai

Ein sauberer, weißgetünchter Raum, nieder und sehr hell. Ich

liege auf einem Strohsack,

im Donaldson Hospital- und der Fußboden darunter ist ebenso hart.

Ich habe sehr wenig geschlafen, denn wir sind erst nach Mitternacht

zur Ruhe gekommen und die Sonne, die nun, um sechs Uhr morgens,

Huyton, near Liverpool

19 May

A clean, whitewashed room, low and very bright. I am lying on a straw sack – it is just as narrow and skimpy as the one in the Donaldson Hospital – and the floor under it is just as hard. I slept very little, as we didn't get to bed until after midnight and the sun's glare, which is now, at six in the morning, already falling on my bed, has woken me. My three room-mates are still asleep: Schneider, Sugar and Gross, my friends. We couldn't see much last night as it was already dark when we moved into our new quarters, and there is strictest blackout.

Looking out of the window I see a quite agreeable picture: a village street, nicely paved; small, two-storey houses with three front windows and little front gardens, still uncultivated. It looks like a workers' estate. To the left the road is cut off by a barbed-wire fence behind which there is a barrack building. To the right another road crosses, so that the whole estate looks like a T of which the vertical stroke is our road, Belton Road. In every house there is a kitchen and a bathroom, but not a single piece of furniture, no table, chair or bench. All of that will have to be improvised.

The small, neat, white houses look cheerful in the bright sunshine. A cold shower in a clean white bath is bliss after a week in the Donaldson Hospital. Gradually, everything begins to stir and at half past six there is a trumpet call, the reveille. The chap blows it like a pig, he has to try three times to squeeze out the final phrase. But in the next street, at the second attempt, he manages it. It is an attractive, characterful phrase. Perhaps I'll be able to make use of it?

Yesterday's journey was not at all bad. In buses to a remote little station outside Edinburgh, from there by express direct to Huyton, a few miles beyond Liverpool. We had glorious weather, comfortable compartments, plenty of room and friendly guards who probably also didn't exactly enjoy constantly baring their teeth with rifles, bayonets and ammunition brandished at such harmless freight. All these precautionary measures!

Es gibt viel musikempfängliche Maschen in Edinburgh und ein noch
sehr rüdimentäres Musikleben. Das ist nun alles abgebrochen, wahr-
scheinlich begraben. Man ist wieder einmal von seiner Arbeit ver-
trieben worden. Wird man sie je wieder fortsetzen können?

Wir reden wenig. Sie streichelt meine Hand und möchte am liebsten
weinen. Ich auch.

Der Soldat sieht auf die Uhr.

Nie wieder lasse ich mich als Gefangener besuchen! Nie wieder!!!

19./ Huyton bei Liverpool, 19. Mai

Ein sauberer, weißgetünchter Raum, nieder und sehr hell. Ich
liege auf einem Strohsack- er ist ebenso schmal und mager wie der
im Donaldson Hospital- und der Fußboden darunter ist ebenso hart.
Ich habe sehr wenig geschlafen, denn wir sind erst nach Mitternacht
zur Ruhe gekommen und die Sonne, die nun, um sechs Uhr morgens,
bereits grell auf mein Lager fällt, hat mich geweckt. Meine drei
Zimmerkameraden schlafen noch: Schneider, Sugar, Gross, die Freunde.
Wir haben gestern Abend nicht viel sehen können, es war bereits
finster, als wir in unser neues Quartier einzogen und es ist strengster
Blackout.
Ein Blick aus dem Fenster zeigt mir ein durchaus freundliches Bild:
eine Dorfstraße, sauber gepflastert; kleine zweistöckige Häuschen
mit Dreifensterfront und kleinen Vorgärtchen, die noch brach liegen.
Es sieht aus wie eine Arbeitersiedlung. Links ist der Blick durch
einen Stacheldrahtzaun begrenzt, dahinter steht ein Kaserngebäude.
Rechts geht eine Quergasse vorbei, so daß die ganze Siedlung wie
ein T aussieht, dessen vertikaler Stiel unsere Straße, Belton Road,

From Edinburgh to Huyton: the diary documents Gál's transfer on 19 May 1940

All this cordoning-off! I would have had Al Capone escorted like this. But then I would hardly have left the other side of the train unguarded when we boarded it; we could easily have simply got out again and made off, if anyone had taken it into his head to do such a crazy thing.

Incidentally, these non-commissioned officers and soldiers are nice, friendly chaps. The officers would probably also be like that if they didn't have to be professionally officious and if they themselves didn't apparently feel that they were the instruments of an enormous waste of energy. That sometimes makes them embarrassed, edgy and unfriendly.

In Huyton we were received by a whole company, transferred to buses and delivered to our destination. We were led into a hut with long tables and benches and were given tea, bread and cheese, and a burly captain made a speech of welcome in which he appealed for our good behaviour. We shall be able to arrange our lives as we wish. Anyone who wants to can take part in 'digging for peace'. He paused slightly before the last word: the slogan 'digging for victory' evidently seemed to him to be tactless when addressing German prisoners. How difficult it must be to understand what a refugee is!! He doesn't look nasty, but his face is completely expressionless, with eyes like a pig's and bloated, blue cheeks, suggesting much whisky.

After this we were distributed into our quarters. We are the first occupants of this camp, which has apparently just been evacuated for receiving internees. We immediately formed ourselves into groups, in order to stay together. Ten to twelve men were assigned to each house, filled straw sacks were there, and we made ourselves as comfortable as we could manage in the dark, as there is no light, although electricity is installed.

Today we had a late breakfast – as the kitchens are not yet working properly – in the same mess-hut in which we were received yesterday. There is a whole row of such huts behind the back of our road, and there are, as it now appears, all sorts of connecting roads all around that are still empty and blocked off. There will evidently be further arrivals. The breakfast was meagre, we would be glad now to get the despised porridge from the Donaldson Hospital, but we were assured that it would get better when everything was running smoothly. In the meantime we have nothing. The quickest thing to be organised was the kitchen detachment; there are all sorts of experts among us, and no-one will starve on kitchen duty.

I make a tour of the camp. On the far side of the mess-hut is a piece of heath and behind it a little wood, but this is separated from our area by barbed wire; the soldiers parade there in the afternoons. Quite a way beyond that is the semi-circle of houses of the village, which directly adjoins our camp at the other end – the left end of the T – and is separated from us only by the barbed-wire fence that limits our world. Inquisitive children stand there, no doubt puzzling over the strange people inside the cage. I must confess that we don't look nice. Most are unshaven, without ties, in a get-up in which one would, under normal circumstances, never have ventured out on to the street. The first mangy prison beards are beginning to sprout, unfortunately also on the cheeks of my room-mates. Schneider and Sugar have solemnly sworn not to shave in internment. I am curious to see how long they will keep it up.

22 May

We have settled in as best we could under the primitive conditions. Two new groups have already arrived, from Liverpool and Southampton; two streets have been added, and it is swarming with people when one walks along Belton Rd., the main road, in the evening. It is a crush like Piccadilly Circus, a grotesque mixture of fantastically undressed, bearded, dishevelled figures. This men's village will remain a nightmare in my memory. There is general agitation and bitterness, for the most sensitive point has been reached, that point at which the educated and uneducated, Germans and Austrians, bosses and workers are of one mind: there is nothing to eat. The catering arrangements are in a desperate mess, every newly arrived contingent – are they completely unexpected? – has turned the provision of food upside down. We are constantly being put on half rations, and the half rations are reduced still further by fraudulent private acts of self-help. There are artists who eat their way through three different mess-halls in succession, and yesterday it was established that five hundred more rations were distributed than there are supposed to be inmates in the camp. None of the miscreants will have suffered a stomach-enlargement by this means, I am sure of that, but such things are at the expense of the general good, and measures have been taken to prevent such abuse in future. We can't complain about the quality of the food, as our comrades cook it. But, between ourselves, it is pig-swill. I still have some of the things brought to me in Edinburgh by my wife and my sister; my room-mates also have some extra supplies, so there is still no real famine. But there is an atmosphere of hunger revolt in the camp, and the mess-hall has acquired the nickname 'Starvation Hall'. We have been granted permission to write home twice a week, no more than 24 lines, on small pieces of prisoners' notepaper, treated against invisible ink, which have been handed out. The ink blots on it, it is horrible to work on, but we were glad to be able to establish written contact at last.

Belton Road is occupied almost entirely by our Scottish group. I have many friends among them. In our house, in the room opposite, lives

Dr. Blumenthal,[1] a doctor from Berlin, a fine man with native wit, level-headed and unshakably good-humoured. He shares his room with our Edinburgh friend Julius Schwarz, the general grocer from Munich with the smiling full-moon face. He can sleep endlessly, and Blumenthal has his work cut out to get 'his Julius' off his straw sack in the morning. In the next house live two splendid young people, Dr. Kellermann[2] and Dr. Fuchs,[3] both of them assistants of Prof. Born,[4] the physicist, at the University of Edinburgh. Both of them are just 25. Kellermann, a good amateur violinist, was a member of my orchestra. I love him for his boyish freshness and his brilliantly sharp, straightforward manner. Fuchs, whom I met more rarely in Edinburgh, demands more and more respect the more closely I get to know him. He has the material for a great scholar, with all the necessary depth and speed of thought, absoluteness and integrity. Both have quickly achieved a sort of leading position in their house, in spite of their youth. One can trust their intelligence and sense of justice. A curious fellow in this house is the Hungarian communist Keresztesz, metal-worker, mechanic and electrician. He fled from Hungary after the Béla Kun episode[5] and has since then led a homeless existence, wandering though the world. Since no-one can remember his complicated name, everybody calls him by his first name, Béla. He is taciturn and often surly, but he is a good, helpful comrade and has an unusually clear intellect that has by no means got stuck in slogans. Then there is the little Dr. Auber,[6] who looks like a poor door-to-door salesman who hasn't sold anything yet today. God knows how he came to be a scholar, for in Vienna he really was a door-to-door salesman selling cotton goods, after he was made redundant as a bank official. He had a scholarship at the University of Edinburgh and his field is bird-feathers, in which he is said to be an authority. He must suffer inner torments of which no-one has any conception. Whatever one talks about, be it camp questions, politics or the War, his anguished face pops up, listening, with an expression of desperate anxiety, waiting to hear his final death-sentence. At present he is enthusiastically preoccupied with getting his beard to grow. His hand is for ever stroking the sparse stubble on his chin. Opposite us

[1] *Cf.* Appendix One: Personalia, p. 188, below.
[2] *Cf.* Appendix One: Personalia, p. 193, below.
[3] *Cf.* Appendix One: Personalia, p. 190, below.
[4] *Cf.* Appendix One: Personalia, p. 188, below.
[5] Béla Kun (1886–1938) was an Hungarian revolutionary who for 133 days in 1919 led the Hungarian Soviet Republic, the second Communist government in Europe after Russia's. A Romanian invasion brought down the Republic and Kun went into exile, first in Vienna and then in the Soviet Union. He disappeared during Stalin's 'Great Terror'. By coincidence, the maiden name of Kun's wife Iren, a music-teacher, was Gál.
[6] *Cf.* Appendix One: Personalia, p. 187, below.

lives Dr. Lewin,[7] a doctor in the Neurology Department at the Edinburgh Royal Infirmary, a spirited, wise fellow. He is already in his fifties, but always on the go, always passionate, and the best soul in the world. With him there lives a queer fish, the psychoanalyst Dr. Bien, a good-looking man well into his forties, a bachelor, very much a ladies' man, so naively opportunistic and so naturally lacking in character that I could never hold anything against him. A kosher dining group has been established and he immediately joined, assuming (probably rightly) that he would eat more and better there. He is also the happy owner of one of the beds that arrived the day before yesterday. There are only 170 – for a complement of over 2000 – and a regulation has now been introduced to the effect that only the sick and those over fifty are allowed a bed. Bien naturally did not hesitate to declare himself to be over fifty, and he will remain as old as that as long as is necessary.

There is also one living in our house who is devout on grounds of appetite, Herr Ziegler, a fat philistine from Munich. He appears good-natured and jovial, but his good nature completely disappeared when the meagre rations came, and since then he has not been a pleasant table-companion, with his greed and lack of consideration. Today he was absent from our table. I met him later and asked him why he had deserted our company. 'I have joined the kosher meals', he said, and added, with a demeanour of worthy dignity, 'It accords with my persuasion.'

We have set up a sort of self-government. Every house has elected a 'House Father' – ours is Gross – the House Fathers of each street have elected a Street Father, and the Street Fathers a 'Camp Speaker' and his deputy. The Camp Speaker is Professor Weissenberg,[8] a chemist, formerly at the Kaiser Wilhelm Institute in Berlin, and his deputy is friend Gross.

There was immediate unrest on account of an unpleasant rival who forced himself uninvited into the functions of a representative. He is called Störmann, no-one knows any more about him. He has ingratiated himself with the whisky-cheeked Captain Tanner and enjoys his confidence, as he speaks perfect English and was already interned here during the last war, and so has experience of matters in which the fat gentleman feels rather at a loss.

First of all Störmann has monopolised a key position: the post. Every letter that comes or goes must pass through his hands. He is arrogant and unpleasant in personal relations and is already behaving like a camp-leader, giving orders and avoiding as far as possible all contact with the 'misera

---

[7] *Cf.* Appendix One: Personalia, p. 193, below.
[8] *Cf.* Appendix One: Personalia, p. 196, below.

plebs'. I told Gross on the first day that this must be stopped by means of a direct approach to the captain; that such things must be pulled out by the roots; that it must be made clear to the captain that we can only recognise men of our own choosing, in whom we can have confidence, as our representatives. Gross is hesitating and wants to delay; we mustn't annoy the captain, he looks as though he could become very disagreeable; we must see to it that the matter sorts itself out somehow. But today it has gone so far that revolutionary groups are forming in all the streets. It is said – camp rumours travel fast – that Herr Störmann is a representative of the Gestapo. It is a fact that he is not a refugee but a German expatriate, and he is said to have played a part in the German societies organised by the National-Socialists. But he is probably no more than a busy-body. In any case the camp representatives must make up their minds to act, otherwise they will lose control; hungry people are too much on edge. Weissenberg and Gross have decided to take action tomorrow and first of all to request Störmann himself to lay down his misappropriated functions, as he does not enjoy the confidence of the camp.

23 May

The storm in a tea-cup has subsided, Herr Störmann has resigned. There was naturally a row with the captain. He eventually gave in, but declared that he would revert to his intermediary again if the representative we had elected proved to be incapable of running the camp efficiently (as if this were our business!). He recognised, reluctantly, our elected representatives, but rejected Gross, who had been recommended to him as a permanent intermediary, and chose instead Dr. von Künzberg,[9] a young Edinburgh doctor, who is likewise a 'Street Father', and therefore in a position of trust. This was accepted and it is to be hoped that we shall now at least have order and amity.

With the latest transport, last night, came an old friend, the painter Arthur Paunzen[10] from Vienna. He is oppressed and care-worn, his wife has stayed in Brighton without any means. He has always lived from hand to mouth, often from the hand of others, and that has certainly not been any better in exile.

He introduced me to his room-mate Höllering,[11] who is a theatre-director and currently a producer and script-writer with a film company in London, a fine, pleasant man with kind, clever eyes. And today I stumbled quite

---

[9] *Cf.* Appendix One: Personalia, p. 193, below.
[10] *Cf.* Appendix One: Personalia, p. 194, below.
[11] *Cf.* Appendix One: Personalia, p. 192, below.

accidentally into the arms of dear little Dr. Blumenau,[12] who was my dentist in Mainz and whom I have not seen since. All these unfortunate people were interned because they were – many merely on a Whitsun outing – inside the 'Protected Area'. People were interned who had a visa and ticket for America in their pocket and now had to let their ticket lapse. On that Whit Sunday people were even taken off the ship on which, a few hours later, they would have left. What a malicious and thoughtless procedure! Those who simply fell victim to a Sunday outing – we call them the 'Weekend Casualties' – have already formed a society and hope to obtain their release soon. Another group who hope for favourable treatment are those who were bound for America. Applications are being written and lists made, – but whether any of these applications will ever make it through the barbed wire of the commandant's office no-one can tell. We only know that all our post is still lying there. Although it first has to go to the censor in Liverpool, the commandant does not want to let it go without prior censorship here; but since none of the gentlemen has time for this, everything is just left lying; that is, from their point of view, the safest method that can be adopted.

26 May

This morning was parade. All the men had to line up in front of their houses, and the commandant of the camp, a colonel, who never appears – the administration is done by the adjutant, a friendly and intelligent-looking captain wearing a Scottish cap, and the camp is really run by Captain Tanner – inspected the company with his whole retinue. He was friendly, asked individuals about their personal circumstances, what their profession was, where they came from and how long they had been in this country. Eventually, after questioning a man from the neighbouring house, he turned to the adjutant standing next to him and said 'There seem to be many refugees here!' Dr. Blumenthal, the Berliner, whispered to me: 'He doesn't miss a thing!'

Since in this camp refugees and German expatriates, Jews and Nazis, are all mixed together, there is certainly a percentage of people who can be assumed to sympathise with the Germans. Recently a young chap, a newcomer, made a patriotic German speech in the street, quite uninhibitedly. He seems to have misunderstood the situation and was completely taken aback when he was eventually arrested. But was that really necessary? After the outbreak of the war tribunals were set up. Three categories were established, those designated A and immediately interned (there are some of those here), those who were given a B and, though free, had to observe a five-mile zone

---

[12] *Cf.* Appendix One: Personalia, p. 188, below.

and were subject to certain restrictions, and those who had the mark C, 'Refugee from Nazi Oppression', stamped in their passports and were free from all restrictions.[13] That applies to all of us who came from Edinburgh and to the majority of all genuine refugees about whom the Home Office is sufficiently, and often more than they themselves know, well informed. When it is now explained that it is difficult to separate the wheat from the chaff and that for security reasons the innocent must suffer along with the guilty, one can only respond that it was after all unnecessary to mix the wheat and the chaff together in the first place.

Yesterday a fairly closed intellectual group arrived from Cambridge, almost all people who are involved with the University there. There are teachers and students from all faculties, which will produce an excellent combination with those from Edinburgh, Aberdeen and St. Andrews. Plans are already afoot to establish a camp university. But there is initially opposition from above to everything. It is not allowed for more than ten people to assemble in one room. There are no books, no instruments or apparatus, not even blackboards and chalk. Whatever is suggested to our fat captain, the answer is 'impossible'. He finds things difficult enough as it is, and avoids anything that could create complications. But everything that is not foreseen in his 'regulations' creates complications. It is impossible to get any money from the sums that were taken from us when we arrived. This money is lying in a hut along with the other objects taken from us, none of the gentlemen has time to sort it out, and it is forbidden to let the internees do it. It is impossible to set up a camp canteen to supplement our meagre fare, as there is no money for it. The offer to do it by means of credit (many have bank accounts, and any amount could be obtained) is turned down, as an internee cannot have credit. It is impossible to have newspapers. It is impossible even to issue and post a news bulletin, at a time when we are all burning for news and everyone knows that the events at the front will determine their life and their future. The camp representatives, Professor Weissenberg and Gross, are completely powerless and without influence. They receive orders and are supposed to ensure peace and discipline in the camp, but they are not in a position to fulfil any wish, however justified. Every day I have a row with Gross, in all friendship. I point out to him that every rejection of a justified demand has the effect of further depriving us of our rights and spurring the captain on to further arbitrary acts.

Yesterday he went round the camp and confiscated musical instruments; he simply snatched the instrument out of the hand of one youth, who was sitting on a straw sack blowing his clarinet, from another a flute and from a

---

[13] *Cf.* p. 32, above.

third a concertina. Today he took an umbrella – it was pouring with rain at the time – from an internee. It is hard to work out what is in his mind. The most plausible explanation is that he is inebriated. In one respect, though, progress has been achieved, namely with regard to the food. The rations are more or less in order, the cooks have gained experience, the food is beginning to be more or less adequate and eatable, even if still very, very tight, and for young people absolutely insufficient. If here and there some fruit, chocolate or tobacco comes in, which we have been allowed to buy with the few shillings that we have left, that is praised as an immense success for the patient policies of our camp representatives. Gross thinks that all resistance is senseless, that he and Weissenberg would resign if there were a threat of passive resistance, hunger-strike or the like. He may be right; no one listens to us; we are completely without rights, there is no authority to which we could appeal. Even so, I consider the policy of meek submission to be mistaken. This buffalo knows only too well that he is in the wrong, and he is as cowardly as any other ranting fool. He will give way if he is confronted by an energetic will, because he is scared of responsibility and is conscious of his own incapacity.

He needs our co-operation to keep order, he himself knows that best. We spend half the night discussing these questions! I am often so aggressive to poor Gross that I am sorry for it afterwards; the poor chap cannot sleep for agitation, worry and scruples. A new worry has now come. Although our village has spread considerably – various branches have been added to the T as in dominoes, and we have had to take a third more people in our houses – it has become necessary to create more space, as large new transports have been announced in the next few days. So tents will be erected, and we ourselves will put them up. Tents are springing up everywhere between the backs of the rows of houses – they are small plots, partly uncultivated, partly sprouting with potatoes. They are painted with green and brown stripes as camouflage against air attacks, and look bright and bold in the sunshine. All young people under 25 must move into the tents. It is taking a lot of persuasion to achieve this, some of the youths are stubborn and refuse to move out of their good quarters, but for the most part it has been successful. In good weather it is no sacrifice to sleep in a tent. We have had to give the boys a promise, which will be hard to keep, that we will find shelter for them in the houses in front of the tents if the weather makes it unpleasant to stay in the tents. The terrain is uneven, the ground is tough clay; a period of bad weather would be a catastrophe. That, too, is now a subject of endless discussion between Gross and me. I don't understand how we can be made the instrument of a measure whose implementation must bring with it the most serious harm to the health of those involved at the first inevitable period of rain. It is explained that it is merely a temporary measure, space must be made for 1,000 people and there is no alternative. But if those involved do not themselves make it clear that they utterly and unconditionally reject such a regulation, no authority will ever have any reason to consider how it could be done differently and more sensibly; must one really wait until the first cases of pneumonia? The same arguments keep going round, nothing has happened, the boys are sleeping in the tents, and luckily the weather is fine.

28 May

I have met a good friend from Vienna, Otto Erich Deutsch,[14] author of a comprehensive Schubert biography, an excellent specialist in bibliography and archive research. He was one of those people who came from Cambridge. He is in his mid-fifties and seems not to have been able to cope with the hard deprivations of the first and worst days of imprisonment. He looks pale and distressed and is anxious about his sixteen-year-old daughter, whom he has left behind alone. We are together a lot, I love his noble, peaceful, wise and reflective way of assessing things and people, and we have a lot of professional interests in common.[15] Today he received a telegram; his daughter has also been interned and taken to the Isle of Man. As she was below the age-limit, she did not appear with her father before the tribunal which had classified him as C, 'Refugee from Nazi Oppression'. When she reached the 'dangerous age' she was automatically 'B', namely 'suspect', as she had not yet been before a tribunal, and couldn't have been – so to celebrate her sixteenth birthday she was arrested. The police authorities must be explicitly instructed to keep an eye on such cases, to make quite sure that they act at the right moment without delay. The same fate presumably awaits my younger son Peter. He is at school in Yorkshire, and safe for the time being. But he will be sixteen on 2 August. That is the moment when a person becomes suspect and therefore belongs behind barbed wire.

30 May

A pleasant enthusiast, Pastor Hansen,[16] has been to see me. A tall, blond man in his thirties, with a face like the young Brahms and shining blue eyes. He is a passionate amateur musician, a violinist and singer, and he

[14] *Cf.* Appendix One: Personalia, p. 189, below.

[15] Deutsch and Gál were both early contributors to *The Music Review*, in the very first issue of which (No. 1, 1940, pp. 123–43 and 255–78) Deutsch published an article, 'The First Editions of Brahms'; Gál's 'The Riddle of Schubert's Unfinished Symphony: A Contribution to the Psychology of Musical Creative Work' was published in *The Music Review*, No. 2, 1941, pp. 63–67.

[16] *Cf.* Appendix One: Personalia, pp. 191–92, below.

wants to organise some music in the camp. He has come with a list of instrumentalists, I supplement it with my Edinburgh people, and we have a splendid orchestra of over forty players. We just lack the most important thing: the instruments. But there is no stopping his enthusiasm. There are a few violins here, a clarinet, and two or three flutes. The authorities must give us permission to obtain instruments and music, and above all a piano. Everything else will follow as long as I am prepared to be the director. He knows about the instruments that were confiscated a few days ago. The adjutant has already promised him that they will be returned. He himself is very interested in music and will do everything to help us. I have declared myself ready to participate and for the moment have undertaken to sound out the players and find out which of them, given the opportunity, would be prepared to have his instrument sent. Hitherto we have been more or less cut off, and we can hardly predict how long it would take if we relied on the normal post. Our letters have apparently still not been sent and are piling up from week to week. Our camp-speakers are working with persistence and patience to get the post moving. There are still no newspapers, the wildest rumours are circulating, only to be replaced a few hours later by other, contrary ones.

Every mealtime is a trial of patience and of one's nerves. We are around a hundred and twenty, with eight to a table, in our low, badly ventilated mess-hut. Every hut has its distribution arrangements. In front of each table is placed a small bath-tub of soup or a vegetable-and-meat dish. The dishing-out, the clatter of spoons, the eternal shifting of benches makes an indescribable racket. You can hardly communicate except by shouting. There are always people dissatisfied with the quantity and the quality of what is on offer. In every hut there are offensive grousers, nasty noise-makers, revolting slurpers and slobberers. The mealtime is used to read out necessary camp announcements, which extends the delights. As extra spice, Herr Julius, an energetic Berliner who runs the kitchen, often appears, to explain why it is just today's food that is so bad or so little. He is a terrible wind-bag and loves to make speeches. I fear that he will end up getting thrashed.

31 May

The first female visitors were here, two women from Edinburgh. They got our address from kind soldiers in the Donaldson Hospital and quickly decided to move to Liverpool. They pleaded for admission at the camp entrance for so long that they were given permission. They are only allowed to visit their husbands twice a week. By this means we have received the first authentic news from outside, and, as far as the situation at the front is concerned, it is shattering enough. There was also an official visitor, the chief rabbi of Liverpool. He solicitously enquired about the kosher food and the Sabbath service, but carefully avoided listening to or passing on any requests or complaints, or even engaging in private conversations. He is exclusively a pastor.[17]

Brilliant summer weather. On the road it looks like a seaside resort, only less elegant. An elderly gentleman is walking there, dressed in nothing more than scanty underpants, which, like all underpants, tend towards an open-door policy. Pot-bellies, hairy chests, South-Sea Island manes, skin colours ranging from lobster red to sepia. Card and chess games are being played in the open air on blankets, sleepers and loungers are lying among the tents, in every available strip of shade. The continuation of Belton Road, beyond the T, divides. To the right it leads to the parade-ground, a large, well-trampled, gravelled square on which the soldiers exercise and where newly arrived troops of internees have to stand for hours on end with their luggage before they are taken to their quarters. But to the left is a piece of heath-land, uneven and overgrown with grass and nettles. There you stumble over tree-roots, rusty wire and half-overgrown ditches, but it is a piece of green, and if you can find a reasonably flat place you can roast there wonderfully in the sun. This meadow is, like all open spaces in our little world, restricted by the barbed wire, and there is an open corner-tower with a machine-gun at the ready and a guard who is constantly busy chasing off curious children who approach the barbed wire. We are well and safely guarded! Towards evening, when it gets cooler, Schneider and Sugar, my two friends and room-mates, rush along the less busy path by the parade-ground. They never go otherwise than at the double, and they are engrossed in a serious occupation: they are learning English vocabulary. They are both extremely assiduous in their language study. Sugar is skilful and linguistically gifted. But Schneider will never manage it. His intelligence and his memory are impeccable, but his musical hearing is deficient. He speaks with the singing, very characteristic German idiom of his homeland, the Ostrau-Karwiner corner of the Austro-Hungarian monarchy,[18] and he transfers this to his English. We weep with laughter when he practises quietly: 'daughter – because – because – 'he can't get this vowel, he sings it with a kind of musical mordent, but he can't produce the difference between

[17] In fact, the chief rabbi of Liverpool at this time was the Belarus-born Isser Yehuda Unterman (1886–1976), a leading figure in the British Zionist movement and normally a vocal champion of refugees. After his period in Liverpool (1924–46) he became chief rabbi in Tel Aviv and then (1964) chief rabbi of Israel.

[18] That is, the mining area around the towns of Ostrava and Karwina by the eastern border of what is today the Czech Republic, to the west of Kraków in southern Poland.

a closed and an open O. He is unshakably persistent and endlessly good-natured in his patience with us wicked mockers. Incidentally, he has a secret weakness: he likes to sing in the morning. His repertoire is limited. The first opera that he ever heard in his life was *La Juive* ('The Jewess'),[19] and he has remained faithful to it. He sings 'Rachel, quand du Seigneur'[20] – he rarely gets any further, because at this point I usually bring him to silence with a poke in the ribs – or he sings 'Laugh, Pulchinello'.[21] Sometimes he even sings 'Laugh, Rachel'. He invents the most unlikely melodic turns-of-phrase for it. He seldom uses the original ones; he has grown tired of them. His wife is an amateur singer and doesn't allow him to sing at home; now he can live it up. The two eager language-students have found a splendid, patient teacher, Dr. Guder,[22] an English specialist and teacher of German at the University of St. Andrews, who comes every day and gives lessons. He does this here in the camp literally the whole day, naturally without remuneration. I sometimes take part, because the instruction is so wise and stimulating and he is such a dear, touching man. When it is too hot outdoors, we sit on our straw sacks. Otherwise we are here in the meadow. There is reading and translation, and every phrase is the occasion for detailed grammatical and idiomatic investigation. Guder is a master of his art. He is an 'Aryan'; barely thirty, he emigrated from Germany because he couldn't stand it under the Nazis, he is religious and full of genuine trust in God, with a soul like a child's, so pure and innocent. The 'Aryan' concept, otherwise for us the most ridiculous of all pieces of nonsense, has assumed a fatal reality here in the camp: people whom the Third Reich sees as 'Aryans' are possible Nazis. One therefore has to take special care in meeting them. I have already been warned against Pastor Hansen; he is a 'German expatriate', he was active in the German cultural societies, just like our former disturber of the peace Störmann, he was interned immediately after the beginning of the war; one shouldn't trust him. Well, I've only spoken to him about music and he hasn't shown any interest in anything else. But I shall be careful.

Schneider and Sugar have remained true to their principles. Their beards are blossoming and flourishing. Sugar's promises to be an attractive one; his rather soft face gains relief and masculinity. But Schneider looks like King Thrushbeard.[23] He has a sparse, red, goatee beard that gives an indescribably

---

[19] A five-act grand opera by Fromenthal Halévy (1799–1862), first performed, in Paris, in 1835 and very popular thereafter.

[20] The much-recorded aria that ends the Fourth Act of *La Juive*.

[21] 'Ridi, Pagliaccio, e ognun applaudirà!' ('Laugh, Pulcinello, and everyone will applaud'), from Canio's aria 'Vesti la giubba' in Act One of Leoncavallo's *Pagliacci*, premiered in 1982.

[22] *Cf*. Appendix One: Personalia, p. 191, below.

[23] 'King Thrushbeard' ('König Drosselbart') was one of the fairy-tales collected by the Brothers Grimm; it is No. 52 in their *Kinder- und Hausmärchen*: an arrogant and proud princess 'ridiculed especially one

grotesque appearance to his otherwise sharply and characteristically cut face. Dr. Bien, the psychoanalyst, on the other hand, is getting a hermit's or prophet's beard. He wears nothing but a blue dressing-gown over his naked, brown body, and looks almost holy; I just call him Zarathustra, and that really flatters him.

A little game is giving me a lot of pleasure. The morning sun shines on the wall next to my bed. I am generally awake early – I still haven't been able to get used to lying on the hard floor, with nothing between me and it but a consumptive sack of straw – and watch the shadow of the window alcove moving slowly across the wall. That gave me the idea of drawing a sun-dial on the wall using the most primitive principle conceivable. It's enough to put a vertical mark where the shadow is now: half past eight. A quarter of an hour later I draw another line, quarter to nine, and so it goes on, every quarter hour has its mark, and it is nice to see how accurate my clock is. Every visitor gets to see it as the main scenic attraction of our room. But it only works from six to half past eight; at this point the shadow moves from my wall to the floor and the whole thing would get complicated.

Our furnishings are still not extensive. But Sugar, the inventive one, has constructed a table on which it is almost possible to work. You can't lean on it, and it often collapses when you just talk loudly. It is constructed like a drawbridge; a blackout-board is fixed just about horizontally to the window, propped up on the sill by means of a wire contraption. A leg made from a stolen fence-post completes the construction. The whole thing falls over a hundred times a day, but then we just put it up again a hundred times. We also have two seats: a box that held tins and the drawer from a cupboard which, when placed on its side, makes quite a solid stool. Schneider and I are usually awake early; he lies on his straw sack reading. At half past six he wakes Gross – the poor man is usually still fast asleep – as he has to attend the Street Fathers' Assembly, our parliament, early.

He spends the whole day rushing around with his brief-case from one meeting to another, always cheerful, always ready to help, always thinking of others and apparently completely content with this strenuous occupation. Persistent petitioners sometimes come into our room as early as seven in the morning, asking him something, imploring, demanding an intervention. He has unshakable patience. Never have I seen him turn anyone away. He is the first one in the bathroom, then Schneider and I generally arrive simultaneously, the one in the bath, the other at the wash-basin. This is the hour when he is irresistibly overcome by singing.

---

good king who stood at the very top of the row, and whose chin had grown a little crooked. "Look!" she cried out, laughing, "He has a chin like a thrush's beak." And from that time he was called *Thrushbeard*.

I sometimes allow myself to be infected by him, then we sing, as a dialogue, whole operas in *secco recitative* style. But his real pleasure doesn't begin until he can sing 'Rachel, quand du Seigneur'. Sugar is usually the last to come. He hurls himself like one possessed into the activity of washing, as with everything that he does. He rubs his face with cold water for minutes on end and puffs like a locomotive. But his real hobby-horse is cleaning the room. Every day the straw sacks and suitcases – since we have neither chests of drawers nor even sideboards, almost all our possessions must remain stored in our suitcases – must be dragged into an empty side-room. Then the sweeping takes place. It is horrendous! The dust flies everywhere, the floor is sprinkled with water, nasty woolly balls of dirt are cleaned out that were apparently not there before and were only produced by this pointless procedure. Then the blankets are shaken according to a quite specific ritual, four times on each side. And again the dust flies. A ghastly occupation! But he really flourishes in doing it. Today Sugar got a dangerous notion into his head: the whole room must be scrubbed. I bitterly opposed this, but it won't be any use. When he dictates something like this there is no veto; we shall have to go along with it.

2 June

At least twice a day Pastor Hansen comes to me in my room. He always has different musical worries. I must write down and arrange a tune that he composed for the birth of his child or when his mother-in-law had a tooth out, or when he saw his wife again for the first time after three months' separation. He sings such tunes – or what he regards as tunes – full of enthusiasm and with a quite pleasant tenor voice, and he beams with admiration when I put it down on paper almost as quickly as he can sing it. He is a very doting husband and father and showed me delightful pictures of his family. His wife is English and seems to be very pretty and his barely one-year-old baby looks like a little angel. I like him more and more, because there is something so genuine, so natural and inspired in the best sense of the word. We chat and philosophise a lot, he is good at giving conversational leads and he is a theologian of the pleasant, undogmatic kind.

I have got to know most of the musicians on Pastor Hansen's list. There are a couple of very good violinists and two quite decent flautists who have brought their instruments with them. The youth with the clarinet (he really did get it back) will not be of much use, as it is an E flat instrument and he is self-taught and in musical terms almost illiterate. I am wondering whether I shouldn't write a piece of chamber music for the available resources. The main difficulty is the lack of low-pitched instruments; there is neither a viola nor a cello, and it's still very doubtful whether Pastor Hansen will succeed in getting a piano – he has been promising one from the first day – especially as we would be in an embarrassing quandary over where to put it. In any case it will be some time before we are really in a position to make music. It would be nice to be able to have some music in the meantime. But composing music – how does one do that? There's not a spark of it left in my body, my brain is dry and dusty.

I have been approached repeatedly to give talks in the camp university that is now beginning to get under way. But I'm so unwilling to talk about music when I am not able to give examples on an instrument. I will rather become a student again myself and go to lectures. Two excellent people interest me especially, Dr. Elias,[24] a sociologist, and Dr. Liebeschütz,[25] an historian. The art historian Dr. Benesch[26] from Vienna is here, the curator of the Albertina and a great music enthusiast – we were together on the committee of the Vienna Bach Society[27] – and he manages to bring off the feat of talking in a stimulating way about art history without any visual material. All faculties are represented. It's strange that for all the innumerable unemployed doctors the hospital business refuses to work properly, in spite of the best intentions of the young, very friendly military doctor who has to organise it. There is a lack of instruments, medicines and above all of beds. Becoming ill here is a catastrophe. The one person who is unceasingly and constructively active is the medical auxiliary, a bespectacled young sergeant who can be seen at all times of the day hurrying through the camp, brandishing his sceptre. This sceptre is a stick with a rubber end. With this he pokes the blocked toilets and frees them.

For the youths who are preparing for the School Certificate examination a proper school has now been set up, there are enough teachers in all subjects. Idleness is a serious danger for the young people; I keep thinking of my son Franz, who is in the same position and in the same danger. He was right at the beginning of his career as a practical chemist, an apprentice with the City Analyst in Edinburgh; it had been hard enough to find this opening for him. I can think of nothing worse than idleness for him, with the whole way he is, and I fear greatly for him.

In the afternoon a youth brought me a piece of paper: a parcel has arrived! I immediately went to the post office, a hut in the parallel road, where a dozen volunteers are busy sorting and distributing parcels. The first despatches arrived a few days ago, skilful experts immediately organised a postal service and set up an address list. It is the first piece of organisation that the authorities have left to us, and the task was completed quickly

---

[24] *Cf.* Appendix One: Personalia, p. 190, below.
[25] *Cf.* Appendix One: Personalia, pp. 193–94, below.
[26] *Cf.* Appendix One: Personalia, p. 187, below.
[27] Gál had been a founder member of the Vienna Bach Society in 1912.

and effectively. The parcel contains underwear, clothes, washing materials, food – the first sign of life from Edinburgh! An hour later the postman came again and brought me two letters, written shortly after one another. Fortunately our address had long been known in Edinburgh before our first letters arrived, otherwise we could have been waiting a long time. The letters are from 23 and 24 May. Hansi writes that no news has been received from any of us (the 'widows' are in touch with one another), but that she has received news from Franz. He is in Lingfield, Surrey, asks for clothing, money, tobacco, and concludes 'keeping fine'. I am suddenly a new man; being cut off from my loved ones had definitely been the worst thing. Incidentally, our letters have apparently now gone off, after long and laborious negotiation. Once the news exchange is up and running the worst will be over. My friends have also received letters and parcels, Sugar three at once, enormously substantial ones. We shall no longer suffer deprivation!

4 June

Strange how it happened.

I had slept wonderfully well yesterday – the first time for three weeks – I had sung duets with Schneider, argued with Gross, allowed myself, in spite of valiant opposition, to be pressed into cleaning by Sugar, and then I sat down and started a quite decent piece of music. A flute and two violins, these are the only available instruments that are seriously worth considering. A problem to create a trio out of them! The idea gripped me as soon as it entered my head. At first a quite unassuming, march-like piece came. I had to see if I could still write music at all. But it developed delightfully and today I finished it. The reveille fanfare made a nice coda for it. One little movement is ready! I think it will become a sort of suite, three or more movements. A second one has appeared in its beginnings; I'm afraid it will turn out considerably more complicated technically, and I must be careful on account of my players. But the beginning is good, and the three parts are so intertwined with one another that no-one will know if he is on top or underneath. And why should he? I had better take it outside into the open, in order to hear more clearly, the concertina player opposite is playing like mad today and never stops at all.

It is a hot summer's day such as we are having now almost without interruption. The white walls are gleaming brightly and pleasantly. I have found a patch of shade in the green area on one of the camp-sites, where I am reasonably undisturbed; the nearest card-players settled on the grass leave me a space of perhaps two metres in diameter. For us that is so much that it almost borders on privacy. After an hour I knew considerably more about my second movement, and I also already know more or less how the third will look. It came along quite unexpectedly, as it should on a good, hot summer's day. I must be economical with my sketching, as I have only a few pieces of manuscript paper. What solved itself quite naturally, as if by itself, is the problem of the three high voices, the lack of a deeper foundation. With three voices and enough air between them there is always blissful music-making. I had the happiest day in a long, long time.

7 June

The trio is growing like an asparagus. I have nothing else in my head, I see nothing, hear nothing, do nothing else. My friends laugh that I don't allow myself to be either disturbed or even briefly interrupted even by the loudest conversations in the room, by visitors or controversies. Two movements are finished, the third begun. Of the last one, which is still to come, I as yet know nothing.

Sugar has carried out his threat: yesterday there was scrubbing. It was barbaric, he and Schneider were like men possessed. I tried in vain to exercise a moderating influence. It didn't help; I had to fetch water, one bucketful after the other. And so it went on, for two hours. Then came the command: let it dry. Regrettably I then caused a disaster. My jacket had been left hanging on a nail on the wall above my place, with a sketch that I absolutely had to have. Unfortunately, just before this I had walked over the camp-site behind the house, where the boys had showered, and had created a quagmire; I had brought in a little bit of this quagmire on my shoes. As I crept on tiptoe to my jacket and back, nasty marks were left behind on the floor. But that wasn't the worst of it. In the afternoon, as I was sitting at our improvised table, my fountain pen didn't work properly, and I carefully pressed down on the knob to gently stimulate the ink-flow. I don't know what went wrong – but suddenly a spiteful splash of ink spurted out, right onto the beautiful fresh floor. What an ugly, blue-black stain! I carefully placed the box, my seat, over it, but Sugar had naturally seen the crime and immediately identified me as the guilty party. And the foot-prints! Well, what was done was done; Sugar has decreed that tomorrow everything must be scrubbed again.

In the last few days I have not even read a newspaper. There are, indeed, newspapers! Not officially, of course, but smuggled in; no-one knows how it's done; soldiers are said to be helping. This newspaper service is the only one that really works perfectly in the camp, following the eternal economic principle that everything works if someone can profit by it. There can't be many copies – the Daily Chronicle, Daily Sketch, Daily Telegraph tend to appear – and you can only have it on loan, that is, you can withdraw with it to a discrete place for twenty minutes. Payment is rational according to the principle of diminishing value. At eleven o'clock one pays, according to the importance of the incoming news, one shilling to one-and-sixpence for the enjoyment of a loaned newspaper. Then the price falls rapidly, and after five o'clock the remaining fragments – it's usually torn by then – cost only a penny. No-one knows who is running this business. But it must be profitable. There is again rather more money in circulation, and something like credit is developing. Anyone who has no money borrows some. Mutual trust has not yet been disappointed; and the creditor is sure that his debtor will not run out on him. The authorities have at last (we have been petitioning for this since we arrived here) given permission for some banking experts, who have offered their services, to bring order into the deposits of the internees. The adjutant laughed and said: 'I wonder whether you will manage to find a way'. It immediately became apparent that the difficulties were not half so great as imagined, and today – it will be in alphabetical order – payments should follow. If we were allowed to run the camp ourselves everything could be organised easily and without trouble. But initially the authorities didn't even have a list of the names of the internees. To find someone, you turn to the Post Office that we ourselves instituted and which, in so far as someone has sent or received correspondence, possesses a reliable register of addresses. According to well-informed sources not even the number of internees in the camp is certain. There are always variations in the daily roll-call, but if the difference is no more than fifty or sixty it is not taken too seriously. This roll-call! Because it refused to work, new methods were always being dreamt up. Once we all had to go onto the parade ground, with the result that anyone who was compos mentis had predicted: there was such a crush and such chaos that the non-commissioned officers, who had to perform a sort of sheep-dog task, were not able, despite their indefatigable efforts, to round up the street- and house-groups in such a way that they could eventually be counted. The only sensible suggestion, to carry out the count during meals in the mess-huts, was only adopted after long hesitation, because it is so unmilitary. But since then the number has remained approximately stable, which is a tremendous step forward.

My friend Pastor Hansen left this morning with a group of four hundred internees who are to go to the Isle of Man. There was terrible disorder with this transport. First of all the whole kosher community was assigned to this group, for no other reason than that is was an existing group which could be easily overseen and registered. Naturally there were immediately dissidents; and friend Bien, too, the orthodox opportunist, immediately set every wheel in motion to leave the kosher club again. Others (they included Pastor Hansen) pleaded urgently to be allowed to go with this transport, as their wives are interned on the Isle of Man. Eventually it became evident that there are many more people here who would like to go than could be accommodated. At any rate the result was enormous confusion. Throughout the whole night lists were being compared, corrected, corrected again, rewritten, and there were still exchange operations in the morning. Friend Gross was woken as early as six in the morning to intervene for people who wanted to go or not to go. In the end all that could be concluded was that four hundred people have marched off; which of these was on the final list will never be able to be determined and presumably no-one at the destination will be any more interested in this than here. The departure looked pitiful, as the people had to carry all their possessions with them to the railway station about two miles away. In the middle, between two Whitechapel figures, marched Pastor Hansen, waving happily. He sat with me for a long time yesterday and told me all sorts of things about his life. Then he went, but on the stairs he suddenly turned round, came back into the room and embraced me with the words: 'May God safeguard you from serious harm!' A curious fellow! What with others would be a pose is with him so natural that one is quite moved.

His legacy is the concern for our camp orchestra, which doesn't yet exist. My beloved trio has so totally filled my head that there was no room for anything else. I will now have to attend to these things after all; nothing will happen by itself.

12 June

As is usual at this stage, it has grabbed hold of me more and more intensely. I have almost finished, tomorrow the conclusion must be there. It was a wonderful time; all the worries, the war, the barbed wire, the loved ones at home, were all as if blown away. I would most like to rehearse straightaway, the people are there and are just waiting for their parts. But they have first got to be written, and I must have my score ready before I can even begin that. In the meantime I have given a young music enthusiast the task of drawing music staves on paper, as I have no manuscript paper left. So it will take a few more days before we have reached that point.

I am very happy with this piece, it looks as if it were made of air, light and sunbeams.

In the last few days there have been all sorts of upheavals in the camp. The newspaper smuggling has been broken up, some soldiers are said to have been severely punished, and there is now the strictest control and not a scrap of paper comes in. Again there is a pandemonium of rumours every day. But it seems to be a fact that Italy has declared war.[28] It is now reported

---

[28] Italy declared war on Britain and France on 10 June 1940.

that our camp has to be evacuated to make room for Italian prisoners of war, and that we are all to go to the Isle of Man.

In sober moments it is clear to me that I am mad. Here I am, writing music, completely superfluous, ridiculous, fantastic music for a flute and two violins, while the world is on the point of coming to an end. Was ever a war more lost than this one now? What shall we do if peace is now concluded? What if none is concluded? Each possibility seems as hopeless as the other. I must, as so often in my life, think of the 'Man in the land of Syria' in the parable by Rückert. I hang over the abyss eating berries.[29] How wonderful that there are such berries! Never in my life have I been as grateful for my talent as I am today.

13 June

That went more quickly than one would have guessed! We will no longer play my 'Huyton Suite' (this is what I have called my trio) here, and who knows whether and where we shall ever play it. Tomorrow we are off, we are going to the Isle of Man. The camp appears to have been disbanded, the whole contingent is to depart in three transports, one after the other in quick succession. We are in the first group of about 1,000 men.

We four will naturally stay together. We have become friends, beyond conventional relationships, under no circumstances do we wish to be separated, as long as we are prisoners. Most of our close acquaintances are also of the party: our English teacher Guder, the smiling Julius Schwarz, Dr. Blumenthal, the little Dr. Adler, the physicists Fuchs and Kellermann, Béla Keresztesz, the neurologist Dr. Lewin, Dr. Bien, the psychoanalytical saint in the blue dressing-gown, the anxious ornithologist Auber, who now, with his little side whiskers, looks like a thistle, the painter Paunzen, the film-producer Höllering, my Mainz dentist Dr. Blumenau, the fine, serious, ever-interesting Otto Erich Deutsch, most of the professors of the Camp University, among them Dr. Benesch, Dr. Elias, Dr. Liebeschütz, and many of their students. Remaining behind is Professor Weissenberg, the Camp Speaker, who, like a good captain with his ship, will only leave the camp with the last of his flock.

The whole picture has changed in the last week. The group who had left for the Isle of Man was already replaced by newcomers on the same day, a further transport came shortly afterwards, and both transports consisted predominantly of Eastern Jews from the London ghetto districts. There are

---

[29] Rückert's 'Es ging ein Mann in Syrerland' (one of the 'Parabeln' in his *Bausteine zu einem Pantheon*, published in 1839) tells of a man who hides in a well to escape an attacking camel, only to find that there is a dragon in the well below him; trapped between the two, the man gratefully gives his attention to some berries growing in the well beside him.

sidelocks and caftans, and a mixture of German and English that sounds like neither of the two. They are all 'B-cases'. How anyone could come to classify these ghetto characters as B, that is, suspected of Nazi sympathies, can hardly be guessed at. The idea that Hitler would seek his helpers among such people is absurd in the extreme.

Amid the preparations for the journey, I have finished writing out my trio. I have now read it through again as a whole and find that the four movements are balanced and contrasted in the happiest way. *Alla Marcia – Capriccio – Canzonetta con variazioni – Fanfaronnade.* The reveille appears again in the finale, nicely closing the circle. I had to laugh when I suddenly realised that at the end even our burly captain with the whisky cheeks had slipped in without my being aware of it. The man has a favourite sport: he blows his whistle and all the soldiers who are within earshot have to run to him, line up outside the house in question, and two men rush in, brandishing their rifles, to arrest the supposed rebels. At least we assume that this is the point of the exercise. He sometimes repeats it for hours on end, in the dust and heat, and sometimes even at night, to make sure his men stay in training. I have a strong suspicion that he has composed his way into an episode in the last movement, but it will do no harm.

Yesterday another parcel arrived from my wife, which gave me a blissful night: a sleeping bag. One has to have experienced the repulsiveness of a dirty, bare, straw sack for weeks on end to understand how wonderful it is to crawl into a bag like this that can be closed on all sides and is soft and warm.

Right from the first week in the Donaldson Hospital I had developed a nervous itch on my head, from the feeling of discomfort caused by the smell of the straw sack, the hairy covers, the quite hideous surroundings, and this has now become continuous and disturbs me terribly, especially at night. Naturally one scratches and that makes it worse. I already have a lot of little scars and scabs on my head. Dr. Blumenthal is of the opinion that the intolerance of the body to some ingredient in the food tends to bring on such symptoms, and that one can't do anything more about it under the prevailing conditions.

It's hard for me to leave here. Who knows if anything better will follow, and we were almost beginning to feel comfortable here. I am most sorry about my sun-dial. I hope that the Italians who will occupy our room from now on will appreciate it.

The 5th Column

J. o. Feather

'How anyone could come to classify these ghetto characters as [...] suspected of Nazi sympathies, can hardly be guessed at': a cartoon by a fellow internee

14 June, on the high seas

A wonderful day and a wonderful crossing!

The departure from Huyton was really cheerful. We marched the two miles to the station easily and unencumbered, our luggage was sent on ahead in lorries. After so many weeks, to see an open road again for the first time, with women and children, dogs and cats, is in itself a pleasure. Some people waved to us in a friendly manner. When we arrived at the station we were immediately stowed in our train, which was already waiting. Unfortunately there was no opportunity to grab a newspaper or at least a glance at a poster; we are burning for news after so many days completely cut off from the world.

In Liverpool we went right through the station and immediately down to the harbour. It looks completely dead. A hundred cranes stand unused, the workers standing around appear idle, there are no ships to be seen. The enormous traffic of Liverpool seems to have been diverted elsewhere. Only around our ship, a large excursion steamer, is there any movement. There is an indescribable swarm of people; at first it looks as though there will hardly be standing room, but after a while everyone spreads out quite nicely. It takes quite a time to get out of the harbour. It is now out of sight, one can only see the sweeping lines of the blue mountains of Wales. The water is marvellous in the blazing sunshine, a cool breeze makes it almost too chilly in the shade. We sit in the sun and enjoy the view of the seagulls, who are quite close above our heads and seem to float along almost motionless with the ship. We had a few provisions and that was just as well, as the catering arrangements are bad. There is a frugal lunch, consisting of a piece of bread and a wedge of cheese, but the distribution is badly organised, if you don't have elbows you get nothing, while the real elbows queue up again and get another helping. I have just met my friend Otto Erich Deutsch, sitting distressed and hungry on his coat on the floor. He has had nothing. His only gain is a scientific observation. He hates seagulls because they shriek so obtrusively and are thieving, cheeky beggars, and because they have such ugly, evil eyes and beaks. Now he has discovered one of their unpleasant traits. 'There's a man over there', he says, 'who is feeding them bread – the bread that I didn't get – and one seagull after another flies in to get its piece. But I've observed them: they fly away in an arc around the ship, and come again from the other side to line up once more.'

The Isle of Man is already in view, a blue chain of hills. Where we will end up there no-one yet knows. We shall probably have to put up with weeks without news from home again. In truth all of us were more or less unwilling to leave. We had got used to our nice little houses, the camp administration had eventually been sorted out reasonably well, the post was slow but at least it worked. Now it will be a matter of starting from the beginning again, fighting against the same indifference, lack of consideration, incompetence, pedantry. Only those who have family on the island are pleased with the move, because they hope to see their loved ones again there soon. Deutsch is also one of these: his daughter is at Port Erin, and to judge from a letter she finds the stay there not unpleasant. An officer has just told us that we shall probably be landing in an hour. The harbour that we are approaching is Douglas. But he was unable to say whether we shall stay there or be sent on further by train.

Central Promenade Camp, Douglas, Isle of Man

16 June

If we hadn't had such a marvellous day and the wonderful voyage, I am afraid that the first impression of our new camp would have been depressing. For many it was indeed just that, and friend Gross was one of these. But there are so many tangible advantages compared with our previous situation in Huyton that it is better to stick to the positive aspects.

Our camp lies directly on the sea-front on a kind of quay which comes from Douglas and goes along the coast. We are outside the actual built-up area, but there is an uninterrupted row of hotels along the quay, with a hill covered with green vegetation rising steeply behind. We are enclosed in a barbed-wire rectangle like in a zoo. Inside this enclosure, which is about a hundred paces long in one direction and seventy in the other, lies a block of 34 small hotels of the London middle-class boarding-house type, divided by a road running at right angles. The main promenade by the sea, along the fronts of these palaces, takes up about half the width of the quay road. A tram-line, interrupted by this, leads across our promenade, which from the house-front to the barbed-wire is about ten metres wide. When, as now, there are a thousand people strolling about, it looks like a London tube station at rush hour. And another thousand will arrive today! Seen from outside, this human zoo must look grotesque, and there are naturally plenty of inquisitive people who have come to gaze at the new sight.

The view of the sea is certainly magnificent, and Douglas Bay, which can be seen on both sides, is enchantingly beautiful. The air is pure and wonderful. The accommodation itself – well, I have always had a violent hatred of boarding-houses, and I won't rid myself of it here.

Every house has to take an exact quota, albeit one that is sometimes calculated according to unfathomable criteria. In our house, No. 2, the second house on the sea-front, seventy-two inmates are crammed together like sardines in a tin. In each of the tiny rooms, with which a modest summer visitor might, if need be, make do as a cheap single room, there is a bed, a kind of wash-basin – presumably earlier an old-fashioned wash-stand – and a washing facility with running water. This last is a gratefully acknowledged luxury. But it is also the only one. Every bed has to take two occupants, and there is hardly room to accommodate belongings. There are few blankets in the house, just one per person; no sheets, but proper, well-sprung mattresses, and uncovered, but tolerably filled pillows. After all that we have experienced in the last few weeks, such a bed is glorious, and I really enjoyed the first night in it.

My room- and bed-mate is friend Schneider. Sugar and Gross have a room and a bed next to ours. We were unlucky with the allocation or, more accurately, others were quicker off the mark. The good, bright front rooms with a glorious view of the sea were taken by others. We have narrow little rooms with windows looking out over the yard, a yard which is as narrow as a shaft, lets in little light and which, it appears, retains smells better than it does air. The kitchen backs onto this yard and today is dried-cod day.

The furnishings in the house, the dining-room on the ground floor, the lounge on the first floor, all are as ugly and repulsive as only a boarding-house interior can be. One bathroom and two WCs in the whole house for 72 people. There will soon be another cause of resentment besides the present one of food. We have ended up with one of the worst and narrowest houses, but still it is on the sea-front, which is an advantage. Most of the Edinburgh friends are with us, Fuchs and Kellermann, Dr. Blumenthal and 'his Julius', who have stayed together again and are now bed-mates, Keresztesz, little Dr. Auber, Dr. Adler and Dr. Guder.

The most difficult and initially almost insoluble problem is that of the cooking. Every house must look after itself. Food is handed out daily by the suppliers outside the barbed wire, in exact amounts according to the number of people in each house. But for cooking you need someone who understands it. Happy the house that counts a gifted cook among its number! The only one among us who has volunteered to act as chef is nervous and rude, and what he has produced so far is pig-swill. He assures us that the kitchen appliances are unusable and that he lacks trained assistants. The porridge that we get for breakfast is a sticky mess; beans are as bitter as gall, rice uncooked and hard, the potatoes are swimming in water. And everything that is served up tastes burnt. This food is bad, but the resulting mood is much worse. If we don't get some order into the cooking arrangements it will get nasty. Even Schneider is grumbling, though in his own way, always from the opposite side. 'Here we are getting used to the good, burnt food', he says anxiously, 'and then we'll go home and make a scene with our wives because they can't produce anything so fine.'

One positive addition to our camp has so far given me little pleasure: there are a number of pianos available, uprights, of course, most of them miserable, hellishly clapped-out and out-of-tune instruments. Two or three of them are playable at a pinch and will do good service. But for the moment they are drawing attention to themselves from their most unpleasant side: an unholy racket has broken out, starved piano-lovers have thrown themselves on this welcome booty, there is a constant hammering, enough to endanger the ear-drums. Thank God there isn't one in our house, we get quite enough from the neighbours. The original group of players for the 'Huyton Suite' is unfortunately no longer complete, one of the two violinists has stayed in Huyton. But I hope to be able to replace him. I have already begun the work of writing out the parts. First of all the flautist must get his part, as he will have to practise.

18 June

The day before yesterday the second group arrived from Huyton, filling our camp up to the limit of its anticipated capacity. We are now nearly two thousand. The remainder of our comrades are either still in Huyton or they have been sent elsewhere, like the first group, in which Pastor Hansen was, which must be somewhere else on the island. Not far from us there are two further camps that are in the process of being constructed; we can see the barbed-wire installations, one further to the left along the sea promenade, the other on the hill, towards the north-east, and also the workers who are still busy with it. If only we could go bathing! The sea is just a few yards in front of our promenade. But they would have to let us outside the enclosure and that seems to be so much against the rules that no-one thinks of this possibility. What we feel most is the restricted space compared with the much more extensive grounds in Huyton, and the constant sight of the barbed wire, which is everywhere inescapably before our eyes. Even the view of the sea is spoilt by the ugly system of lines drawn across it by the barbed wire. Without any collusion, as if by themselves, two symbols of our condition of captivity have passed into our everyday parlance: porridge and barbed wire. Both of these expressions symbolise for us the state of being interned *per se*. Anyone who has ever experienced anything similar will comprehend the hideousness of continually seeing the world through bars: nature, walkers, children, bathers. But to understand our hatred of

'Even the view of the sea is spoilt by the ugly system of lines drawn across it by the barbed wire': a drawing by another fellow internee reinforces Gál's complaint

porridge one must have had this foodstuff, rightly regarded as nourishing and digestible, dished up as it has been dished up to us daily for breakfast and often also for the evening meal: as sticky as glue, with neither sugar nor salt, as there is a lack of both substances, served on a badly cleaned plate and often with a dirty thumb in it. These last two factors would be the easiest to remedy, but there is no hot water to wash up with, no dish-cloths, and in addition the most wretched scratched cutlery and damaged crockery imaginable. Keeping things clean, under these circumstances, is a problem. The only one among us who tucks into his porridge without raising an eyebrow is Gross. Either he is a hero or he has no taste-buds. He himself maintains the latter, but I believe that he is so absorbed by his activity and his duties that he simply doesn't notice what he is eating.

As in Huyton a small government has quickly developed here. As there, our self-administered constitution rests on the institution of the 'house father'. The house-fathers have elected a sort of senate, the 'Committee of Eleven', which runs the administration, and at its head stands the Camp-Speaker and his deputy. Gross, our house father, is again also the Camp Speaker's deputy. A man I didn't know before has replaced Weissenberg, who has stayed behind in Huyton, as Camp Speaker, Pastor Hildebrand, who enjoys the greatest respect among the Cambridge group. He was one of the disciples of Niemöller,[1] he is a protestant clergyman in his thirties, with grey hair, a slim, youthful figure and the great personal charm of a thoroughly cultivated and at the same time wise and interesting man.[2] No-one can help liking this man, but I would wish him, and Gross, to be a shade harder for the difficult task that faces the head of our self-government in the face of the military authorities. Both are completely honest, selfless, extremely intelligent, and tirelessly hard-working, there can be no doubt about that. From the first day onwards there have been the same problems as in Huyton: the suspicious reserve towards the 'enemy aliens' that first has to be overcome before one can expect understanding and helpfulness, and the incredible organisational incompetence in the face of the task of looking after two thousand people in a more or less proper and hygienic manner, feeding them and keeping track of them. As in Huyton there is no list of names here, no registry, no check apart from the daily 'roll call', at which the number usually doesn't agree with the one that is, for some inexplicable reason, taken to be the correct one. No post has come as yet, neither parcels nor letters, and we have tried in vain to get them to communicate with the authorities in Huyton about this. As we have sent a collective telegram to Edinburgh, we hope that new items at least will duly arrive soon. To establish links with family members in other camps on the island was flatly refused. That has caused many bitter disappointments. The only thing that gives no cause for complaint is the handing over of food by the suppliers. That is, mind you, looked after by civilians, local businessmen who have taken over the service and have organised it properly.

Our hopes of release have receded far into the background. Since the war has entered such an unhappy stage[3] this question has hardly concerned us at all, as it has become unimportant. Our life and our future depend for good or ill on the outcome of the war. If things go badly, we are lost in any case. And no news! Here we are indeed hermetically sealed off from all the world. We hardly come into contact with soldiers, they patrol around our camp in the narrow corridor between the two barbed-wire fences which surround it in concentric circles, and they are completely unapproachable, as they are under constant surveillance. It is impossible to engage them in

[1] Martin Niemöller (1892–1984) was a German Lutheran pastor and theologian who, as a conservative nationalist, initially welcomed the Nazis' accession to power but soon recanted and became a vocal opponent of the regime; he was nonetheless guilty of anti-Semitic remarks on occasion. He spent the years 1938–45 in the concentration camps of Sachsenhausen and Dachau and after the War became a leading campaigner for peace and nuclear disarmament.

[2] *Cf.* Appendix One: Personalia, p. 192, below.

[3] Gál is writing two weeks after 'Operation Dynamo', the evacuation of 340,000 Allied troops from Dunkirk; ten days later, on 13 June 1940, Paris had been occupied by German troops.

The camp 'house fathers' as seen by an internee called Rosenthal,
one of several of that name imprisoned on the Isle of Man

conversation. Apart from the roll-call, hardly any soldier or officer ever comes into the camp. Our food is thrown to us as to animals in a cage, and no-one takes any further notice of us. It has occasionally happened that a passer-by on the road has come near enough for sharp eyes to be able to catch sight of a newspaper headline. Authentic information of this sort then naturally passes on like lightning, but unfortunately tends to be developed and embroidered. One cannot be too careful in choosing what to believe.

I am busy writing out the parts of my trio. It is an irksome task but it must be done. I have already handed the completed flute part to the player for whom it is intended, a young, blond Hamburger, who is musical and keen, but regrettably considerably less skilful on his instrument than I had assumed. He will have to work hard if he is to succeed in his task.

21 June

The gentlemen in command are friendlier than they were at Huyton, at least we are getting along with them without serious friction for the time being. The post is still unsatisfactory, but parcels do arrive, and do not take very long. Where there is still a hold-up is with all the post that must have arrived in Huyton after we left; that is nowhere to be seen.

The camp university is up and running again. There are better facilities here, as there is at least one room in almost every house that can be used as a lecture room. That doesn't happen without tough resistance from the occupants, above all the card-players, who are thereby driven out of their regular haunts for hours on end. Another difficulty is the piano-playing, which is admittedly a noisy, disruptive business. In most houses certain hours have been set aside for the use of the piano. A kind of musical life is developing. Tomorrow I shall take part in a house-concert that is being arranged by two keen amateur musicians. Free tickets will be distributed, as space is limited; we don't want to allow more than fifty people into the lounge in House No. 5, which has relatively the best piano in the camp. Even it is somewhat decrepit with age and its teeth are already falling out, namely the ivory of the keys. I prefer it to all the others because it at least plays at normal pitch, which is important for the violin that is taking part. Violinists hate having to tune lower. The organisers plan to repeat such concerts there or in another house as often as is necessary to satisfy the demand. There is a pleasant young baritone here, with a still rather immature voice, but intelligent and musical. I will accompany him in songs by Schubert, Brahms and Schumann that we both know by heart, as there is no music. The music problem is for the moment the most pressing for our musical plans. There are a few more or less decent violinists available, but not much music. As far as piano music is concerned, that is not lacking at present, I have enough of it in my head.

We soon got used to the strange situation of two in a bed. Since he has become my bed-fellow, I have – this is natural – become a more intimate friend of Schneider's than before. We are alone such a lot together, we talk about all sorts of things and in fact hardly have a thought that we wouldn't share with each other. I had known him slightly in Vienna and often met him in company in Edinburgh. But in the camaraderie of internment no aspect of a person's character remains hidden, one has moved beyond the conventional screen. And now even a room-mate and bed-fellow! Schneider is a somewhat nervous, restless city-person, like the rest of us, with many-sided interests of an intellectual and scientific kind, an untiring worker, and fundamentally of a cool, sceptical disposition, not given to spontaneous expression. He is by habit a mocker and can never suppress a sarcastic remark, whatever the topic. But he is the truest, most upright soul in the world. I have only rarely seen him annoyed, but never unkind, he seems to be completely incapable of unkindness. There is no better or more selfless comrade. He has very firm views, tending in a socialist direction, with which I do not always agree. But it is stimulating to discuss with him, and we sometimes do that for half the night. Schneider is, incidentally, also a good comrade as far as sleeping is concerned. Occasionally he slips over to my side of the bed a little, and then I have to push his sharp elbow gently away from my stomach, into which he has been trying to dig it; but neither of us takes this amiss. We don't disturb each other much, especially since each is wrapped up in his own sleeping bag; the principle of 'omnia mea mecum porto'[4] has distinct advantages in this situation.

Gross and Sugar have their window adjoining ours in the right-hand corner. We can almost shake hands across the narrow yard. At our morning toilet we are always engaged in animated conversation from window to window. Sugar and Gross also get on excellently as bed companions, and that is a decisive test of genuine friendship.

Of the three, Gross had been closest to me before we were interned. We saw each other constantly at our orchestra rehearsals, and if one is to become friends anywhere, it is when making music. But Sugar, like Schneider, had been more of a formal acquaintance, a pleasant, intelligent, well-mannered man, but nothing more. It is only with the comradeship of internment that I discovered what I had not suspected before: that he is a personality. This epitome of the bon-vivant, well-groomed gentleman, pampered by women, always intent, like a real bachelor, on his own well-being, whom one would have considered soft, has a character of steel. I am convinced that the five years as a Russian prisoner-of-war that he experienced as a young man have decisively influenced his character. Sugar will never do anything rash, but when he sets his sights on a fully-considered goal, he will see it through with iron persistence. At the same time he is as good-natured as a Saint Bernhard, always attentive and ready to help, and he has that certain personal charm which one encounters among the best of his compatriots – he is Hungarian – and which is felt by everyone with whom he comes into contact. He had been a very successful doctor, as had Schneider, incidentally, had earned a lot of money and was accustomed to a good, comfortable life. Both are unsurpassably undemanding now that we are living like convicts. There is always a good atmosphere among us four at home, we have a lot of fun together, we are never bored, and no-one has ever attempted to be down in the mouth. Here we have been called 'the company of the four stalwarts'.[5] We are a good four-in-hand because we are so fundamentally different and because

---

[4] 'Everything that's mine I carry with me' – attributed to Bias, one of the seven sages of ancient Greece, by Cicero in his *Paradoxa Stoicorum* (1.1.8).

[5] Joachim Rohde's comic book for children *Die vier Getreuen* ('The Four Stalwarts'), GEG, Hamburg, 1937, was one of a series presenting the adventures of two children, Hanni and Fritz, a dog called Putzi and a raven by the name of Kolk; the illustrations were by Fritz Lattke.

each one has respect for the others. I just fear that they have less for me than I for them; although I am the oldest, I am the most impulsive of us four, and I have occasionally, in all humility, had to let them give me a thorough dressing-down. Each of them will under certain circumstances behave more sensibly than me. But that doesn't detract from our mutual love. My three comrades have yet another inestimable quality: none of them snores.

27 June

I have been inadvertently caught up in intensive work; musical life is flourishing, and for the moment I have to bear the main burden. There is no shortage of pianists and some of them are quite respectable. But the repertoire of what they know by heart is limited, and for none of them does it exceed one or two solo pieces. With my young baritone I managed in a short time to produce a whole evening of lieder and arias. He is musical and hard-working, and he quickly learns whatever I write down for him. My main difficulty is getting hold of the texts. Lots of Schubert, Brahms, Schumann and Wolf songs are musically completely present in my head, but I often have gaps in the text. Fortunately there are lyric memory virtuosos who can reproduce all sorts of things, and even some anthologies of poetry have made their appearance, and they do good service. My singer – his name is Hans Mayer – is from Cologne and he lived for six years in Rotterdam. When the Germans came, he fled to England with two friends in a lifeboat, leaving behind his wife and child. It was an incredible journey lasting 36 hours. They didn't actually get to see much of England; on landing they were immediately interned. Since then they have had no news of their wives.

One of the violinists has proved to be especially gifted: a young Viennese by the name of Kaufmann, who is a tailor's apprentice but has always taken his violin-playing very seriously and has benefited from a proper training. We play each programme four times, twice each in House No. 5 and House No. 14, and we would not lack an audience if we did it twice as often. But the artists would go on strike and I would not make an exception in this case. The people are starved of music. When I play Bach or Beethoven there is a reverence such as I have rarely experienced in music-making. In principle I play only good and the best music. Since the popular kind of music is catered for elsewhere, everyone gets what they want.

More for the sake of politeness, I tried inviting the authorities to one of our performances, and was almost embarrassed when the commandant of the island, a colonel, who was here in Douglas just for a few days, appeared with his staff of five officers, for a programme consisting of the C sharp minor sonata by Beethoven,[6] songs by Brahms and Schubert, and the Mendelssohn Violin Concerto, which Kaufmann plays very brilliantly. I hope the gentlemen were not too terribly bored; if so, they maintained the best possible composure. Afterwards the colonel made a very flattering speech, assuring us that he felt as though he was in Queen's Hall,[7] and the collection (we have a collection for the camp welfare fund after each concert) raised over a pound, thanks to the distinguished attendance.

As a matter of principle I have made sure that all concerts are free of charge, and I insist that the performers take no fee. As all work in the camp for the common good done by doctors, chemists, teachers and professors, as well as those who work in the postal, parcel, telegraphic and bank service, is carried out free of charge, I would find it contrary to professional honour for musicians to put themselves on a level with boot-boys, launderers, sock-darners and hairdressers, who are paid for their services. It is reasonable to pay for personal services, otherwise no-one would do them. But work that is for all must, in a community such as ours, be organised on a mutual basis. There are differences of opinion on this point, and it is especially the representatives of the lighter muse, who are incidentally almost entirely amateurs, who have been enormously enterprising in earning a gratuity for their 'artistic' activity, and have tried very hard to corrupt 'serious music' as well. It is quite extraordinary how inventive some people are when it is a matter of directing a few pence out of their dear fellows' pockets into their own. A camp café, where coffee and pastries are administered, was established after only a few days. The material is probably from appropriated rations. Recently, even a concert-café has been opened, run by the leader of the 'Wolf Band', consisting of a violin, a piano and an accordion, which makes a row there all afternoon. 'Heurigen'[8] singers squeeze out 'Wien, Wien, nur du allein',[9] and all the cantors in the camp – there are half a dozen of them – compete in singing the prologue from 'Pagliacci'[10] to a wrong piano accompaniment and with a dreadful amount

---

[6] That is, Op. 27, No. 1, the work known as the 'Moonlight Sonata'.

[7] Queen's Hall, built in Langham Place (immediately in front of where the Broadcasting House headquarters of the BBC now stands) and opened in 1893, was London's most important hall for orchestral concerts, renowned for its superb acoustic, until an incendiary bomb dropped by the Luftwaffe during the night of 10–11 May 1941 left the building gutted.

[8] A Heuriger is an Austrian wine-tavern that serves new wine – *heurig* means 'of this year'. *Heurigensänger*, usually two in number, wander from table to table, singing *Wienerlieder* and accompanying themselves on guitar and accordion.

[9] The first line of the song *Wien, du Stadt meiner Träume*, the Op. 1 of Rudolf Sieczyński (1879–1952). Written in 1912, the song was soon known around the world. In 1935 Richard Tauber recorded an English version (as *Vienna, City of My Dreams*) for the film *Heart's Desire* that was released on Parlophone.

[10] As *Pagliacci* (1892) presents a play-within-a-play, the Prologue opens with the baritone Tonio, in his character Taddeo, addressing the audience ('*Si può?... Si può?... Signore! Signori!*').

of vocal excess. So many people share in the benefits of this business that the camp leadership turns a blind eye, while other 'enterprises' are subject to strict control and are rendered more or less impossible. I absolutely want to keep this kind of enterprise away from serious music, and so far I have succeeded.

From this week one of the main evils of our camp, the lack of physical exercise, has been alleviated in an agreeable manner. Almost every day there is a longish walk outside the barbed wire, and half an hour of sea-bathing. I take part in both as often as I possibly can, and the bathing especially is real bliss. The beach is closed off by sentries at both ends for a stretch of about a hundred yards, and we are allowed outside the gate. At first the water seemed terribly cold to all of us, but we quickly got used to it; admittedly, only a minority take part in this pleasure. Many shiver with horror at the mere sight of it, and the soldiers seem to share this horror. There are usually quite strong breakers, with a constant breeze the air is on the cool side, and the sun much interrupted by fast-moving clouds. For me, the pleasure of just seeing the sea without barbed wire in front of it is a renewed joy every time.

The walk does not take place in exactly the most enticing outward form. Five to six hundred internees walk in twos behind one another, flanked to the left and right by soldiers with fixed bayonets. We move through the countryside, up hill and down dale, in an endless crocodile. The population moves shyly out of the way. Naturally we are ready to seize any opportunity to cast a glance at a newspaper bill-board or a newspaper carried past. Sometimes we even succeed in getting into conversation with a soldier. Yesterday a young Scot was walking next to me, a friendly chap who has just returned from Flanders. 'Maybe the Germans will invade this country', he says, 'and perhaps they will even occupy it. But Scotland? Never!!' But what one can learn about events in the world outside by such means is relatively little, even though it does sometimes help to correct the fantastic nonsense that circulates amongst us on a daily basis in the form of rumours, and from time to time induces one into believing it. Yesterday a 'nearly new' newspaper passed through many hands; it was only a week old and had been smuggled in as packaging in a parcel. From it we learned all sorts of things compared with which our rumours were harmless. That the surrender of refugees was demanded and granted in Hitler's armistice conditions to France let loose a full-scale panic. Telegrams and memoranda to government offices, committees and individuals in public life are discussed, debates are conducted for hours, there is no end to the disputes as to whether, to whom and in what form such steps should be taken. There is a 'house assembly' almost every day, and poor Gross is pale and wretched with worry, work and all the nonsense that he is bombarded with. Together with Pastor Hildebrand, he bears the main burden of responsibility; but the 'Committee of Eleven', the senate, which they both chair, is not constituted in the happiest fashion, as the election took place at a time when, as a result of a lack of mutual acquaintance of the house occupants, who had mostly only just been thrown together, the result very much depended on chance or on the pushiness of individuals. There are communists and Nazis among the 'eleven', who greatly impede productive working. Gross is very conscientious and always reports back to our house exactly what has taken place in the Council and between it and the authorities. A more fantastic caricature of a parliamentary debate than such a house assembly would be hard to imagine. It is a real Polish parliament.[11] Everyone wants to speak, no-one wants to listen; crazy motions are proposed, the stupidity of which is immediately clear when the proposer is asked to formulate his suggestion precisely. All the wisdom and patience of our friend Gross is needed to keep the discussion more or less to the point. There is naturally all kind of opposition to the cautious, diplomatic approach of our camp speakers. These gentlemen always deliberately choose the most moderate, most modest formulation, and this method has its drawbacks. My friends Fuchs and Kellermann (Fuchs is Deputy House-Father) are often in opposition, and there have already been sharp clashes. The real nuisances, though, as always and everywhere, are the fools, especially when they are presumptuous and puffed-up with a desire to impress. There are a couple of these in our house. A touchingly ridiculous figure is poor Dr. Auber, the ornithologist. Hardly has a word been uttered in conversation touching on issues which affect us than he is there, with head bent forward to hear and eyes filled with terror, his hand on his thistle of a beard. We are often cruel enough, Schneider, Sugar and I, to tease him by suddenly uttering loudly, in the middle of a conversation, catch-phrases such as 'Gestapo-Agent', 'handing over', 'will no doubt be shot', or similar crude expressions. Whenever he hears such a word, he jumps up with a start and is all ears. We should really be sorry for him, but he gets on our nerves with his eternal eavesdropping and his unspeakably naïve questions.

---

[11] The expression 'Polish parliament', found in a number of European languages and signifying procedural chaos, has its origins in the practice of the Sejm, the parliament governing the Polish-Lithuanian Commonwealth from the mid-sixteenth to the late eighteenth century. A rule known as *liberum veto* ('I freely forbid') allowed any member to nullify any legislation passed in that session by shouting 'Nie pozwalam!' ('I do not allow!'). Although the *liberum veto* was an important check on royal authority, it also brought political paralysis: of the 150 or so sejms held in the period 1573–1763, around a third failed to enact any laws.

The latest object of our worry is the news, this time it is authentic, that internees are to be sent to Canada. For many this eventuality would be the most welcome, given the prevailing panic after the collapse of France and the undoubtedly acute danger of a German invasion. But most are agreed that such a measure should not under any circumstances be allowed to be undertaken without due regard for the families of those involved.

From the start I have been of the opinion that one should leave the military authorities in no doubt that married men would not go willingly without their families. On the other side there are some – they are mostly those who are politically compromised – who are of the opinion that in case of a German attack it would be especially the men and much less the women who would be in danger, and that, if the government had the will to send internees abroad, one should not call this intention, which is altogether in our interest, into question by making demands that can hardly be met. The memorandum that is to be sent is therefore the object of endless debates. I very much doubt if such a memorandum would even be read under the present circumstances, let alone be given serious consideration. Whatever we did would be too late. But it calms people's minds somewhat if something is done and we thereby have the illusion that we might have some influence over our fate. So it is better to send such messages off, with the risk that it is pointless.

The cooking has greatly improved. The grumpy Prussian who did it at first gave up the job after a few days, and one of our Edinburgh people has taken over, Felix Adler, a trader from Vienna, a gifted natural violinist, who is now revealing unsuspected talents. He can claim the credit for the fact that the mood in the house is incomparably better. He succeeds not only in making the unvaryingly identical ingredients – porridge, rice, beans, potatoes, a little bit of meat, fish twice weekly – eatable but even in developing a relatively varied repertoire. Since he is constantly friendly and never affronts anyone, the kitchen staff, who naturally also consist of volunteers, stand by him, whereas previously a dangerous strike atmosphere had already prevailed. It is now apparent that the rations, though not plentiful, are nevertheless adequate for a moderate appetite, especially when one receives, as most of us do, some food parcels to supplement them. What is again developing only slowly and with difficulty is the canteen business. Tobacco and a little fruit and chocolate come in; apart from that it is impossible to obtain food on the 'free market', as that has apparently been forbidden by the Isle of Man government. One can get writing and toilet materials and even razor blades, after all of them had, apart from one single one, been rigorously taken away from the new arrivals. The setting-up of a kind of bank to administer our funds, which had started in Huyton, has been continued,

*The Camp Council is 'a real Polish parliament. Everyone wants to speak,
no-one wants to listen': cartoon by a fellow internee of Gál's on the Isle of Man,
unidentified beyond his surname on another drawing*

and this institution functions excellently as far as those occupants of the
camp are concerned whose deposits have been correctly returned after
their internment. Unfortunately that doesn't apply to everyone; many who
were brought in with us have not yet been able to receive a penny of the
cash taken from them, and no-one can say where this money has got to. For
the authorities the matter is in no way important enough to be energetically
investigated. Those affected have as yet no means of getting what they are
due, as no-one wants to take responsibility for it.

Letters from Huyton have at last arrived, a whole batch, and even the
sound of a long-frozen post-horn is welcome under these circumstances. My
wife has not the best news of the boy. A relative who lives in London visited
him in Lingfield. The forty-odd boys who were brought from Edinburgh
are an isolated group among a lot of Nazis. There is no question of any
kind of organised work, Franz smokes, loafs about and is bored. Just what
I had feared! Here amongst us he would have had the ideal opportunity for
work and study. So far fathers and sons have been separated, apparently on
principle, but now things are to change, and my wife will take steps to see
that the boy comes here; at the moment that would certainly be the best
thing for him.

A constant worry for us is the threatened internment of our wives, about
which much is being said again. That would be the worst thing! They have

recently been expelled from the protected area, and that does not bode well. My wife, like most of her fellow sufferers, has moved to Glasgow. She told me this, and gave me her new address, in a telegram, but I know no more details. The loss of her home in Edinburgh and of all her friends there is a severe blow; this nonsense is going on and on, without end! Such inconsiderate interference in the life and work of innocent people who are in no-one's way! Xenophobic attitudes have been encouraged and promoted for so long that it has become necessary to take measures which pander to these attitudes. Gross has brought the official report of a sitting in the House of Lords which took place on the 12th June, and in which the Bishop of Chichester made a remarkable speech about the internment of refugees and the conditions in the camps. It seems to be the first time that a man in public life has dared to intervene on our behalf. Our case could hardly have been put in a braver and more committed manner. Incidentally, he must have had direct information from Huyton, as he was fully informed about conditions there. But how did the noble lords receive this speech? There could not have been a more uncomprehending stance with regard to the injustice that has been perpetrated and which the bishop characterised in such a lively and moving way. 'Intern the lot' was the answer. It is terribly disheartening! Nevertheless, we are pleased about this courageous, generous advocate. If even one person recognises the truth, it shows that it lives on and can't be suppressed, as long as there are such men at work.

30 June

We have had agitated days. Tomorrow a transport will leave with a mysterious purpose. We assume with some certainty that the destination is Canada. A few days ago a strange list was drawn up; everyone had to indicate, alongside his personal details and his family status, whether he was a Jew, not a Jew, a socialist, a communist or a 'Nazi-sympathiser' – a question of unsurpassable naiveté – and it leaked out that this list had been made in order to provide a basis for the intended transports. But then came simply the order that all unmarried men between 20 and 30 had to be ready to travel, each with 40 pounds of luggage. No more information was given. The best of our young students and teachers are among them, including Fuchs and Kellermann.

The camp university will hardly recover from this blow. I began a harmony course last week, which was very well attended and of which at least half of the participants will also be leaving tomorrow. Most of the young people took the matter philosophically, many consider deportation to be the lesser evil under these circumstances. Apart from the young people there is another special group which is specifically destined for the transport, which apparently includes those who are suspect. Our suspected Nazis on the Committee of Eleven are, for example, among them. There is already talk of a second transport which will follow soon, and feelings are more than a little disturbed by this. Those who are most seriously disturbed are those like our friend Gross who have already put down roots in this country. Gross would be utterly miserable if he had to leave England, and he refuses with remarkable obstinacy to believe in the possibility of an English defeat. Nevertheless it is with dismay that I must conclude that even he is incapable of finding the one and only consistent answer to an unambiguous situation. If I was asked what I, as a married man, would do if I were ear-marked for the transport, I would say that I would refuse. If a mere hundred people were firmly resolved to let themselves be shot rather than go voluntarily on a transport, this fact would be sufficient to make the plan unworkable. I am resolved; who else? The answer is almost always anxious and evasive: if force were used one would eventually have to obey, military might is after all *force majeure*, and similar expressions. They are like a flock of sheep! Sensible men such as Dr. Blumenthal and 'his Julius', but also Schneider and Gross, are of the opinion that one would have to accept fatalistically whatever happened. To oppose bayonets would be madness. Well, I wouldn't oppose them either and I wouldn't know how to. But I know that they would have to drag me to the ship on all fours to make me leave here against my will. If, after everything that has happened, they intended to separate me from my family for an indefinite period, the reward for continuing such a life would have no attraction for me. Let them shoot if they dare! I am sure, absolutely sure, that they will not do it and that the only thing with which they can achieve anything is fear of the shooting, not the shooting itself. There are now some who have similar thoughts, but they are too few. How extraordinary people are! I have had debates on this question for hours on end, particularly with Schneider, but, as always with such discussions, they have been fruitless. The one who worries us most is Sugar. Although he is over forty, he is a bachelor. He is little concerned about his personal fate, but he would still like to stay with us if at all possible, and we would be unhappy to lose him. For the time being he has hit on a simple way out; he has suddenly discovered that he is married. Since it would be much too inconvenient for the gentlemen in authority to check the responses against the documents that are there, the particulars given by us are actually decisive. Even Gross, who is ridiculously conscientious in such matters, finds that this is, after all, a harmless means of resistance. At least in this way one can win time.

For the moment we have gained some personal advantage from the change: a splendid room at the front will become free tomorrow, with two double beds. We have already secured it for ourselves. Sugar will share the bed with Gross and Schneider with me as before, but the four of us will now be together in a relatively large, bright room with a delightful view of the sea, instead of the dark holes in which we had to live before.

As so often before, Dr. Bien, the psychoanalyst in the blue dressing-gown, has again provided the satyr-play to the tragedy. I met him the day before yesterday, when the list of those departing was being drawn up, skulking around deep in thought and with an anxious expression, and he confessed to me that he was suffering bitterly under the torment of a difficult decision: should he declare himself to be under 30 in order to go with the transport, or over fifty in order to be spared in any event, even from future transports? (It is assumed, rightly or wrongly, that no-one over 50 would have to go.) I gave him a piece of advice that was so bold and surprising that it immediately seemed to him to be the right one: to declare himself to be as old as he actually is and to leave matters to his lucky star, as no-one was at the moment really able to say what was the wiser choice, to stay or to leave. So he remains at 41 (the gods alone know whether that is his real age or not), and he will let come what may. How marvellous when a difficult matter of conscience can be resolved so honestly!

2 July

It was a bitter farewell. Many of our best, most active people have left. My flautist and Kaufmann, the gifted violinist, were among them. And others will soon follow them: a new list has already been put up today which now includes all unmarried men up to 40 and also the young ones under 20. So far, married men have been exempted. Our dear Dr. Guder, who was still faithfully and conscientiously giving daily English lessons to my friends, is on the list this time. He is, as ever, in good spirits and unshakable in his childlike trust that everything that happens must be for the best, otherwise it wouldn't happen. What will Sugar and Schneider do now, the ever-eager language students? I have rarely been able to take part in the lessons here, what with my many musical duties, but the two of them have been assiduous and have made noticeable progress. They have remained faithful to their habit of rehearsing vocabulary as they shoot up and down the promenade at the speed of an average express train. But the stretch is miserably short from one end of the promenade to the other!

The worry that married men, too, will eventually be designated for the transport has not diminished, especially since the news came yesterday that they have begun to arrest 'enemy aliens' in the Unprotected Area, above all in London. Further arrivals here have already been announced, the relief for our houses was therefore a very temporary one. 'Intern the lot!' They seem to be making it a reality.

The manner in which our comrades were treated has deeply outraged me. They had to assemble at the exit with their luggage and were then led out into the Palace Hotel, the seat of the authorities, and were there subjected to a thorough inspection in which, for example, all money, right down to the last penny, was taken off them. Then they had to spend the night on the floor in the large hall of the hotel, as they couldn't be let back into the camp again after such a painstaking examination of their luggage. That they received no dinner happened not because of any evil intent, it had simply been forgotten. In the morning they had to carry their luggage to the harbour themselves, the commandant could not be persuaded to approve a lorry for this. For the next transport we have suggested the simple arrangement that the comrades should get their evening meal delivered from their house, and that has now been graciously conceded. There is, as mentioned, certainly no evil intention behind such events; but I find the inconsiderate, insensitive, thoughtless negligence with which such things are regulated by a commandant who is responsible for two thousand men worse than deliberate malice. Anyone who does wicked things still has occasional scruples. But these people are full of a mind-blowing complacency which excludes any feeling that they could be wrong. A principle that, in all objectivity and sobriety, degrades people to cattle, whose feelings one doesn't consider, for cattle are not supposed to have feelings – such a principle that has seemingly been applied for centuries to people with lesser rights, namely non-Britons, makes comprehensible all the hatred that has developed towards this outwardly friendly nation everywhere where one has had to get to know them from this side.

My young baritone Hans Mayer with his two 'Dutch' friends has just flitted past me in full travel outfit. Another forty volunteers were added to the list, apart from the age-group of bachelors who were conscripted into the transport, and they quickly made their decision. 'We've had enough with *one* German invasion', he says, 'we have no desire to experience that again. Our wives are over there and we have no contact with them. Why should we wait?' I bade them a warm and very sad farewell.

Another volunteer has come: Zarathustra-Bien with his now quite impressive prophet's beard. The nervousness has infected him, and, sure as anything, they won't come after him in Canada.

Perhaps I would do the same if I were single, although I mistrust the whole Canadian business. No country has been as utterly hostile to immigrants as Canada;[12] I fear that those who are counting on relative freedom and employment possibilities there will be very disappointed.

3 July

The second transport has left; it has now been admitted that it is bound for Canada. Things were arranged better with this second transport than with the first, there was even approval for a baggage lorry. I can never understand that so gigantic an organisation as the British military does not possess something like a collective memory or collective experience. It appears that each responsible commandant has first to learn from his own mistakes before he is capable of coping with even the most commonplace problems.

At last I am ready to try out the Huyton Suite. I have given the flute part to Dr. Fronzig, an elderly gentleman, a Berlin doctor who lives in our house and with whom I made friends while peeling potatoes. This duty is allocated according to a rota, and since he is my neighbour in the alphabet we are generally assigned to it together. He is of a certain taciturn and extremely bright Berlin type that I like, and he is an enthusiastic amateur musician and incidentally a frequenter of my harmony course, which has been a terrible headache for him. His flute-playing has good tone but he has a weak sense of rhythm and is a poor sight-reader. I am curious to see how he will cope with the task, but in any case he is practising with burning enthusiasm.

There is still no music. Mrs. Dickins, the daughter of our host in Edinburgh, sent the commandant a parcel of music for me and a letter. The letter was forwarded to me, but the music has disappeared. It probably arrived before the explanatory letter and found its way into the waste-paper basket. What is a commandant supposed to do with music?

Hansi, the good and brave, has apparently had a hard time. The women, who were sent away from Edinburgh, have had all kinds of difficulties with accommodation in Glasgow, and have had to move constantly. They seem

---

[12] Pre-War Canadian immigration policy had been restrictive, with the effects of anti-Semitism and xenophobia exacerbated by the Depression: between 1921 and 1931 only 15,800 Jewish immigrants were allowed into the country; between 1933 and 1939 the number fell to 5,000 – the lowest for any western country (by contrast, the USA admitted 200,000 and Argentina, Colombia and Mexico each admitted 20–22,000). The blame can be laid largely at the door of Frederick Blair, Director of the Canadian Immigration Branch from 1936 to 1943, who made no secret of his anti-Semitism. The policy gained some notoriety through the case of MS *St Louis*, a German liner carrying 930 Jewish refugees (and seven non-Jews) who in May 1939 were refused entry first into Cuba and then the United States; when Canada, too, refused to allow the ship to dock, it returned to Europe and its passengers were dispersed among a number of countries; roughly a quarter of them died in the Holocaust. *Cf.* Irving Abella and Harold Troper, *None is Too Many: Canada and the Jews of Europe, 1933–1948*, Lester and Orpen Dennys, Toronto, 1982.

to have borne it with good humour. When Peter's holidays start, at the end of July, both of them are to go to Mrs. Dickins, who lives somewhere in the country in Yorkshire. The main sufferer is likely to be our dear old gentleman, Sir Herbert, who was clearly attached to my wife and for whom she acted lovingly and caringly. We are nevertheless happy that our wives have merely been sent away and not immediately interned, as happened to us on that Whitsunday – but that could still happen any day.

5 July

The appearance of our camp has changed radically yet again. Almost half of it has left with the two Canada-transports, among them many of our intellectual elite. They were replaced by a large consignment of newly interned people, unhappy, downcast souls, largely from the north-west and east of London, most of them elderly. Their arrival was a sensation, as we had again been without newspapers for at least two weeks. It had been a period of optimistic rumours. The war situation had changed considerably for us: France was fighting on courageously and successfully under a new alternative government; the Italians had been beaten and were retreating into the Po valley; the Italian fleet had been virtually destroyed in the Mediterranean, the whole of Libya and Abyssinia had been conquered by the British; Ireland had for security reasons been occupied by British and French troops; and yesterday even Portugal had been occupied, in a peaceful arrangement with the government there, in order to have a safeguard against any Spanish adventure. It was both cruel and amusing to see how zealously some people tried to protect their castles in the air against destruction; they didn't want to give credence to the newcomers when they declared all this to be fantastic nonsense, replacing it with the far less welcome facts of the previous week, the final and complete defeat of France. How do such rumours arise and spread? Hard to say. Whoever came with such news had always just spoken to someone who had managed to get hold of a secret newspaper, or the Medical Officer had told him, or he had heard a loudspeaker outside in the commandant's office. Since the same rumour was immediately confirmed from all sides, one eventually believed it – one is so willing to believe if it is something good!

Two hundred participants in the second Canada-transport have returned 24 hours after they left. The ship that awaited them in Glasgow was overfull, and there was no room for them. These 'home-comers' told us that they would have had to starve from the time they left until they returned if the soldiers had not taken pity on them and shared their rations with them, and if some of them, wise from bitter experience, had not taken supplies with them. It was nice and consoling, on the other hand, that there was a canteen on the transport ship in which one could get all sorts of food and tobacco for one's smuggled money (our people on the second transport had learnt from the fate of their comrades and had hidden their cash). Feeding a transport seems to be one of the most difficult problems to solve. What dreadful dilettantes! I keep asking myself: how can one conduct a war with such technique?

One of the bits of news that has been brought in has got me agitated: a ship called 'Arandora Star', filled with prisoners and internees and sailing without a convoy, was torpedoed and sunk last week in the Irish Sea. Seven hundred prisoners are said to have drowned. There were apparently wild scenes, as there were no life-saving facilities.[13] This news immediately went right through me, as a letter from my wife contained the news that Franz is no longer in Lingfield and his whereabouts are unknown. Since several fathers in the camp are anxious for the same reason, the commandant has posted a notice saying that according to official information only prisoners of war and A-category internees were on the torpedoed ship. That reassured us. But where has the boy got to? His last news from Lingfield was on 12 June and on 20 June he seems to have been no longer there. Gross advised me to request a personal enquiry to Lingfield and I asked for an interview for this purpose. But in the upheavals of the last few days, with all the departing and arriving transports, no interviews could take place, and so I put in my request in writing. I did it out of conscientiousness; I have no doubt that Hansi, the most concerned of all mothers, has done everything possible and has taken the right steps.

I must train new forces for my concerts. One of the cellists has at last had his instrument sent. He is called Dr. Ball and was a distinguished law-officer in Berlin and must have been an excellent cellist. His right hand became almost useless in a German concentration-camp through frost-bite, the fingers are crooked and incapable of gripping anything. It is a mystery to me how he can use the bow, but he manages it, although he is somewhat restricted and technical things can easily go wrong. He is a very valuable asset for our musical life and will be more so when we get a few piano trios that have already been ordered. Since we raise quite considerable amounts for the welfare fund through our collections, we can also occasionally afford to make a purchase; I have in the meantime ordered Beethoven and Schubert trios, but that goes by a complicated route and will take time.

The itching rash on my head has become an intolerable affliction. It has spread over my temples on both sides, there are horrible new outbreaks under

---

[13] In fact, the Arandora Star had fourteen lifeboats, although four of them could not be used. *Cf.* also p. 38, above, and note 20 on p. 112, below.

my eyes, and yesterday I was taken into the camp hospital for treatment as an out-patient. This hospital consists of two of the boarding-houses that have been set aside for this purpose. The Medical Officer responsible for the practice, a civilian doctor from Douglas, has probably not yet treated any patients here himself, as that is taken care of by our medical comrades, who have made themselves available for this. Even Sugar has offered his services as an ear, nose and throat specialist, but has not so far done any work because even the quite modest minimum provision of instruments that he asked for could not be obtained. The Medical Officer generally has to do only the medical administration, e.g., whether someone needs to be sent to the hospital in Douglas for an immediate surgical operation, or what medicines, instruments and materials are to be acquired. As far as the last point is concerned, his activity is predominantly that of refusal. Our doctors work as well as they can despite the impediment of lacking the necessary wherewithal. They lack sheets and blankets for the beds, they lack, as just mentioned in the case of Sugar, almost all the necessary instruments, and with regard to patient diet – since the hospital gets exactly the same food rations as the other houses, the only practicable diet is a starvation diet. The offer to buy whatever is needed at the expense of the welfare fund, that is, from our own means, was rejected, as medical material can't be acquired at the expense of the internees, that would be against the regulations. But the administration doesn't do it, presumably because it doesn't deem it necessary. My doctor, the sole dermatologist currently in the camp, has arrived from London only in the last few days. He is called Dr. Löwenberg and he comes from Düsseldorf. He gives the impression of being experienced and efficient, and is said to have had a great reputation in western Germany. Unfortunately he is nearly deaf; that makes his job more difficult. He began with an ointment for me which ate its way into my skin like poison, and now he wants to try out another preparation which, however, he has not yet been able to obtain.

Our new room, with its wonderful view of the sea that we are able to enjoy from the third floor, uninterrupted by any barbed wire, is a great source of well-being for us. And we look forward every day to our bathe in the sea. This pleasure of bathing on the beautiful, flat, sandy beach, with the sun, the wind and the waves in our face, is the only possible opportunity for an internee to forget for a few minutes that he is one. In such moments one is suddenly aware how pathologically our perspective has shifted, how terribly inflated this barbed wire has become in our consciousness. Being imprisoned means much more than the loss of physical freedom; it means a clamp around the brain, a pressure that does not leave one, even in one's dreams. I have been dreaming differently since I have been interned, and I have already become afraid of my dreams.

8 July

Yesterday we had a tragi-comic intermezzo. After the evening meal, as we were standing in front of our house discussing the latest implausible rumours, an orderly came with the message that Sugar and Schneider should go immediately to Headquarters, the commandant's office. What has happened? A secret. In two minutes the two of them were at the gate; we suspected important matters, the most likely was naturally release. Schneider, poor chap, could hardly hold himself up; he had got gallbladder cramps because of the excitement. I didn't find out what had happened until nearly ten o'clock at night, when the two of them came home, tired and annoyed. There had been all kinds of work to do in the office, still in connection with the reorganisation of the last few days and the indescribable disorder that had arisen in the already disordered arrangements for our administration. Some of our comrades had already been working there the whole day and one of these, the smiling Julius Schwarz, had in all innocence, when it was getting late, named a few friends who would certainly work willingly and well with them. Poor Schneider was still quite ill with the excitement.

Perhaps this episode will have important consequences. They were both horrified by the helplessness and the lack of any kind of documentation there in the headquarters office. From occasional questions by the officers some anxiety had arisen that telegrams that come to the authorities requesting information about some prisoner or other are, as a general rule, not being answered, or, if at all, are being answered wrongly because no reliable lists exist. A list was actually drawn up of those leaving, but whether it is correct, given the continual retrospective shifting and changing, is very questionable. The authorities are generally only interested in how many people are in the camp and whether the addition or subtraction caused by the most recent arriving or departing transports is correct. There is 'roll-call' twice a day. It was just like at Huyton. All kinds of methods were tried until the authorities got round to making it simple. The way it is done now, at our suggestion, is the simplest in the world. All occupants of the camp sit in the dining room, each on his appointed seat, six to a table. The number can therefore be determined at a glance by counting the tables and multiplying the number by six. But the executors of the armed forces will only rely on such risky methods in the most exceptional cases. The only arithmetical operation that the gentlemen seem to regard as safe is counting: one counts consecutively from the first man on the first table to the last man on the last

'Our doctors work as well as they can despite the impediment
of lacking the necessary wherewithal.
They lack [...] almost all the necessary instruments'

table, each one in turn raises his hand and calls out his number. The result has to tally with yesterday's, and tomorrow's will have to tally with today's, provided that no changes, which have to be notified by the house-fathers before the counting starts, have taken place in the interim. If one then adds the numbers of all the houses together there is a hundred percent guarantee that it is correct. How the gentlemen sometimes still manage to get it not to work out right is a mystery. That can only be because of the adding-up; one can see, therefore, that the scepticism about such a complicated procedure is not entirely unjustified.

After the terrible muddle of this last week, we four have now decided that something decisive must be done. Gross has suggested to the commandant – I have been saying that it was necessary ever since Huyton – that a card index should be created, and the suggestion has been accepted. It is clear that such a measure was originally intended, as piles of conveniently pre-printed registration cards have been available for ages, but have simply not been made use of. At my suggestion a second card-index, likewise strictly alphabetical, should be created for all those who have left the camp again, with the date of departure and the destination. Once we have these two card-indexes, one for those who are present and one for those who have left, every question will be able to be answered reliably. The adjutant shook his head over all these pointless measures, but he is allowing us to get on with it, and Schneider and Sugar especially are fired with enthusiasm and infused with irresistible zeal for the work. The learning of English has in any case come to nothing since Guder has left, and they have found a new occupation. A dozen colleagues were easily persuaded to help, and a kind-hearted house-comrade has even lent us a type-writer.

11 July

Again there have been turbulent days. Yesterday a third transport left and in the evening new additions came from London. We can't settle down in our houses any more, there are only strange faces to be seen now, and not the most pleasant ones. 'London C-case' is a kind of insult in the camp; as always happens, in a school, an office, a railway compartment, the 'oldies' form a closed bloc which observes the newcomer suspiciously and critically. The average intellectual level of the Londoners is for quite natural reasons lower, for in London the whole of the émigré proletariat settled densely together. Almost all of us have met people we know among the Londoners. I met Erwin Stein,[14] formerly employed at Universal Edition in Vienna, now with Boosey and Hawkes in London, Dr. Rosenzweig,[15] Viennese music-critic and a former pupil of mine, his colleague Dr. Ulrich,[16] who worked at the Neue Freie Presse, the composer Franz Reizenstein,[17] whom I got to know in London. He was a student of Hindemith's and I valued him as a very gifted musician and excellent pianist. He is in the same house as a young violinist, Hermann Baron,[18] a student of Rostal's[19] in London. I immediately recruited him for my 'Huyton Suite'. We had already had a rehearsal which was anything but satisfactory, as poor Fronzig produced considerably more beads of sweat than right notes and lost his place more easily than he could find it again. One of the two violinists whom I had enlisted left yesterday in the third overseas transport, I shall replace him with Baron. Fronzig continues to practise and swears that he will manage it, but I am not convinced. I would under no circumstances risk a public performance with him, but for myself I would at least once like to get some sort of impression of the piece.

This third transport included all the bachelors under fifty and a number of married men who put themselves forward voluntarily on account

---

[14] *Cf.* Appendix One: Personalia, p. 195, below.

[15] *Cf.* Appendix One: Personalia, p. 194, below.

[16] *Cf.* Appendix One: Personalia, pp. 195–96, below.

[17] *Cf.* Appendix One: Personalia, p. 194, below.

[18] *Cf.* Appendix One: Personalia, p. 187, below.

[19] Max Rostal (1905–91) was an Austrian violinist and violist who studied with Arnold Rosé in Vienna and Carl Flesch in Berlin. He himself taught at the Hochschule für Musik in Berlin from 1930 to 1933 but moved to Austria when the Nazis came to power; after the *Anschluss* in 1938 he moved again, to London, where he became an important teacher and performer. He had a professorship at the Guildhall School of Music from 1944 to 1958, was appointed professor at the Staatliche Hochschule für Musik in Cologne in 1957 and, a year later, at the Conservatoire in Berne, making his home in that city.

of a sudden, sensational offer by the camp leadership. This offer, which originated with the adjutant, Major Daniels, proved the optimists right. It consisted in a demand to the camp representatives to determine immediately how many married men would be ready to go 'overseas' voluntarily if approval were to be given for their wives who are interned here on the island to go with them, either on the same ship or, if this should be impossible, in the same convoy. In view of the short time available, it was not possible to consult the spouses, the wives would in these cases be immediately told to get ready. Gross was conscientious and asked the adjutant if he would be prepared to give this assurance in writing, and Major Daniels answered smilingly: 'One gets used to insults', but he answered in the affirmative. Following this, 23 people came forward who were prepared to go voluntarily under these conditions. The impossibility of consulting their wives and discussing it with them had stopped the great majority of those who were eligible from getting involved in the venture. We were all of the opinion that an agreement by the authorities in this form could be trusted; but those eligible were nevertheless faced with a difficult question of conscience with which I can sympathise. One man from our house, an otherwise rather rough fellow named Wessely, ran round from one person to another for the whole afternoon, to confirm again and again that he had done the right thing and that there could be no risk involved. The agreed written confirmation was not, in the event, given; in the hustle and bustle of that day no-one thought about it any more. It was in any case sufficient that the statement had been made before witnesses and that the whole business was communicated to the camp occupants in a public notice. I see no reason for mistrust, and would not have given the matter any further thought if Schneider had not brought up this case again today with a strange, sceptical question. Schneider is peculiar. When his view does not accord with the general one, he doesn't contradict but remains silent. And then at some time or another there comes an unexpected comment that makes one begin to wonder, as it is very thoughtful and shows that there is another side to the question. What makes him suspicious is the conditional form which the adjutant gave to his agreement by a small change in the wording, hardly noticed by Gross. 'Who would come forward, if...' Does this mean that the assurance has really been given or is it merely a possibility? The question would be worthy of a hair-splitting lawyer; at first I was speechless, then outraged at the idea. That would be a swindle of the worst kind. But he has put an idea into my head, and I notice that Gross has a rather subdued conscience in the whole matter. Well, the people have gone, that they could really have been deceived is such a fantastic assumption that I had rather not think about it.

Our card-index is for the most part ready. It was quite a job but the success was immediately apparent. The officers, who at first looked over our shoulders suspiciously and without much faith in the point of the undertaking, were enthusiastic when two dozen telegrams that had arrived at the commandant's office today could be answered immediately and reliably. The magic of being able to find every name in ten seconds, together with all the corresponding personal details, has made a colossal impression on them, as though this were a completely new invention. The adjutant beamed, there is no such order in any of the other camps! There is still a lot to do in sorting out the first two Canada lists, putting in the new arrivals, etc. I am already withdrawing from this office work. I have too many musical duties, and my pleasure in this work is too limited for me to be infected by Schneider's and Sugar's drive. The two of them are almost dangerous. They think of nothing else and talk of nothing else, and every day they invent new, sophisticated methods to improve their system. They are as if seized by a mania. If it were left to them we would work till midnight every day.

Incidentally, I am not very well. My face is a disaster. Dr. Löwenberg has received his new preparation and painted white patches on my face, so that I look like a pierrot. He has not yet attempted to apply anything to my head, which is behaving the worst. He thinks that the whole illness is of an 'allergic' kind, and therefore that nothing can necessarily or immediately be done for it with local treatment. But he is not in a position here to effect a suitable cure with injections, diet, etc. The old gentleman attends to his work with enormous dedication, and unfortunately he has a lot of patients. The change of the last few weeks has multiplied the work of the hospital, as it has raised the average age of the occupants considerably, and older people almost always have their major or minor complaints. But skin infections are rife in the camp, particularly barber's itch, and that is hardly surprising in the prevailing circumstances. Sleeping two in a bed, without sheets, with no disinfection when changing from one occupant to another, the impossibility of having a hot bath – where else should there be skin infections?

Among my friends is a patient whose condition I don't like the look of at all; Paunzen, the painter, contracted a lingering bronchitis following a kind of influenza, and it is keeping him in bed. He looks wretched and feels even more wretched. His room-neighbour Höllering assures us that half of it is hypochondria. Höllering is a refined, attractive person. He gave me one of his film scripts, which surprised me; it appears to be real cinematic art, which avoids all cheap effects yet uses sophisticated technical resources. It is evident that he is more director than writer, but in the case of films that may not be a weakness. I would like to work with this man.

13 July

Chindindindin, chindindindin, chindindindin - - - - This clatter wakes us up every morning at half past six: Uncle Löwensohn is raging through the house. He is hitting goodness-knows-what with goodness-knows-what, frenetically, for minutes at a time, and making an ungodly row. This is the wake-up call which he has taken over ex officio. I think he does it merely out of sadism.

Uncle Löwensohn is a relative of our Schneider. The latter likes to disown him but without doubt he *is* a relative of his and we lose no opportunity to make him take it as a silent reproach. 'Your relation', we say, and he is then quite small and guilt-ridden.

When the wake-up call has finished, every sensible person turns over and goes on sleeping. But when, half an hour later, I squint at the light with one eye, Gross is already at the wash-basin, cleaning himself thoroughly and carefully like a kitten. At half past seven it is roll-call, when he must officiate as house-father, fully dressed and shaved. The others mostly appear in more or less picturesque morning garb.

The most difficult thing is to get Sugar out of bed. In the morning he sleeps as soundly and deeply as a baby; I don't think he even hears Uncle Löwensohn. If he had his thumb in his bearded mouth the illusion would be perfect.

Gross has the patience of an angel. He warbles 'Sugar!' He calls 'Sugar, roll-call!' Sugar doesn't move. He shakes the bed, 'Roll-call! Roll-call!' Sugar sighs, turns over with an unarticulated sound and goes on sleeping. Today Gross has a drastic device. Last night Sugar put some clothes in the wash-basin to soak, the only possible receptacle for this. This morning Gross has taken them out and laid them carefully on a sheet of paper. Now he takes a soaking-wet sock and with it drips onto the sleeper's nose, slowly and deliberately. Sugar sits up, looks around him blankly, in a moment he is in his dressing-gown and slippers and is out headlong into the lounge, where the roll-call takes place. There he drops into an arm-chair and slumbers on for a while. Not until the officer enters to receive the report and count does he step back and take his place in the row. Now at last he is awake.

For breakfast we bring a whole arsenal of extras from our own stores: sugar, jam, margarine, condensed milk. That is above all in order to make the porridge eatable. But even this can't overcome its most unpleasant characteristic: that it is so sticky. Schneider mostly makes do with a few spoonfuls, Sugar prefers to skip it completely. But Gross is happy to eat a second plateful if it is put in front of him, and I try hard at least to finish mine. The first clients appear even during breakfast. Dr. Baer is the most persistent of them, breakfast would not be breakfast if he didn't come, pulling up a chair next to Gross and talking at him. Gross eats his porridge. That is the only thing one can do against Dr. Baer, for every word that is said to him provokes three times the torrent of verbiage.

There are already three more at the door. Gross picks up his briefcase and flees, with the clients after him. That's what it's like every day!

Sugar and Schneider have gone to work in the Registration Office. Today I am on house-cleaning duty. I can't say that I love this occupation, especially as its fundamental pointlessness annoys me. You sweep the dirt and dust with long, powerful strokes of the broom out of the top floor, down the stairs, and eventually out of the house. But you need a certain simplicity of mind to believe that. In reality you get rid of at most a quarter; the remainder is swirled into the air, where it lurks for a while and then settles again, to ensure that the person on house-duty tomorrow has something to do. The only positive result is that the staircase is impassable for half an hour. Meanwhile the partner on duty (there are always two assigned to it) has cleaned the dining room. That is also not pleasurable, but at least you get some gymnastic exercise in the process, as one must – so the ritual demands – put all the chairs on the tables before mixing the dust, food remains, cigarette ash and a little water together with the broom and sweeping it into the corners. Then everything looks clean again, the card-players take their places and diligently scatter cigarette ash again.

I have to be at the Post Office at 10 o'clock, as post has arrived for me. You get a strip of paper with the name, the exact time and a number on it. The time tends to be kept very punctually, our people have organised it brilliantly. A youth is sprawling over the window sill and calls out: all numbers up to 120! Then you go in and take delivery of your parcel, which is handed out from the back by the boss of the Office, Herr Moscari, cut open and finally checked by the officer present, before the recipient has it handed to him. The lieutenant is very conscientious and examines every piece, but he is adept and so the process takes place very quickly. The quickest of all, though, is Herr Moscari. Before the lieutenant has even looked at my parcel, his hand is already under the table, passing me a letter. Letters that are enclosed in parcels are confiscated, as they have not been through the censor. But Herr Moscari does his best to alleviate this hardship and we are all grateful to him for it, as parcels arrive much quicker than letters, and this is in reality the only way to get a message to us quickly. The parcel contains welcome things – margarine, brown bread, fruit preserves, chocolate – the letter is unfortunately short and formal; the success of this means of communication can't be predicted.

Our music rehearsals are mostly in the morning. Today I have one with Dr. Ball, the cellist, with whom I am playing in a house-concert on Monday. At half past eleven there is a meeting of the music committee. Dr. Ulrich, Professor Deutsch and I, who look after this department, have co-opted an enthusiast, Herr Hamburger, as a useful colleague, who writes the programmes and puts them on the notice-board in front of House No. 5; he manufactures and distributes the tickets, supervises the rehearsal arrangements, in short, does everything that an impresario would have to do. He is willing and hard-working and very talkative, and he is our good conscience, in so far as he is always after us with the whip, making sure that at least one new programme is started every week. And devising programmes under the present circumstances is not easy. Herr Hamburger is also tireless in tracking down new talents, though in that he does not have the happiest touch. I have learnt to fear it when he comes to tell me about a *wonderful* tenor voice, whose fortunate possessor is one of the newly arrived cantors. I have given up trying to make discoveries among the cantors. But what is to be done? I have to listen to the man, or Herr Hamburger will give me no peace. The man bellows like an ox. Herr Hamburger sits in the corner and smiles as if transfigured. 'Now, what do you say?' he asks eagerly, when the man has hardly left the room. 'Terrible.' 'A pity, I heard him singing in the synagogue yesterday, and he was really wonderful. But you must listen to another one, a bass-baritone, magnificent, I tell you!' 'Some other time, Herr Hamburger', I say, 'my ears are already hurting today.'

We have a late lunch. In our house it takes place in two shifts, because of lack of space and cutlery, and as Gross prefers the later time on account of his official duties, we generally don't eat until getting on for two. There is bean soup and potato stew. Schneider gazes gloomily in front of him and is silent. 'Why so care-worn, Herr Doktor?', asks one of the gentlemen on the next table. He is one of the new arrivals, otherwise he wouldn't ask Schneider such a question. It doesn't happen any more to any of our old comrades. 'How should one not be care-worn!' says Schneider. 'We are living here quite cosily, we have our comforts, get our daily good food, without having to concern ourselves with anything, we are gradually forgetting our profession and no longer know what it is to struggle for existence. That will go on year in, year out, we are getting older, we will finally reach sixty and then be cast out, into freedom, onto the street, and left to our fate.' The other man is really impressed. 'But listen', he says, 'the age limit has been raised to sixty-five.' He is really taking it seriously! 'Even worse', interrupts Sugar, grimly shaking his beard, 'what sort of profession can one take up then?' He likes nothing better than to second Schneider's tomfoolery with deadly seriousness. But then someone bursts out laughing, and the 'London C-case' realises that he has had his leg pulled.

There is no siesta today, as our table has been assigned to fetching the rations. We have to assemble at the gate by half past two, ten for each house. We are let out in groups and led to the two shops, where everything is already prepared for us, arranged by house. One carries five enormous sticks of bread, another a bucket full of milk and one full of herrings, a third a sack full of porridge; each one is laden with his allocation, and then we go in single file through the camp and back home, where we deliver the treasures to the kitchen. The group of walkers has already left, anyone who fetches the rations can't take part in the walk – and this morning I missed my bathe through my various musical obligations. Well, one can't have everything.

The British week-end has not been introduced here, Saturday is a working day like all the rest. We don't meet up again until half past six at dinner, which is mainly very frugal: tea, bread, cheese, margarine, rarely a hot course. Then we are free. We wander along the sea promenade or walk a few times round the quadrilateral of our camp, alone or in twos or threes, we see all our friends, listen to the latest camp news of the day, ease our minds by appropriate criticism of everything that has been done or not done. In the evening there is the house assembly, some people will have something to say.

At half past nine everyone has to be in his house for the evening roll-call. Then we usually sit for another hour at our window in the twilight, and have a small evening snack. But today is house-assembly immediately after the roll-call. I will skip it. Unfortunately, poor Gross can't, he has to give reports on everything that has taken place in the Committee of Eleven in the last few days, he must answer every relevant and irrelevant criticism and accept requests which he in his turn is to present to the Committee of Eleven. Such requests are generally superfluous, as it is not so easy to agree on a form of words, and when, around half past ten, it gets so dark that the chairman can no longer distinguish the raised hands of those who wish to speak, the assembly is then adjourned, and by the next time the request has already been forgotten or something else has become more topical.

Gross is not the chairman of the house assembly, as he is too often, as the main spokesman, at the centre of the discussion. He himself suggested for this honour the stupidest, most presumptuous person in the house, in order thereby to render him more harmless and to satisfy his ambition. But this measure did not prove satisfactory. Herr Frankenstein (that is his name) has finally reduced our house parliament to an operetta institution, and in the course of time it has become boring.

I sit writing until it is almost dark. That's how a day looks for us; in this way there passes one day after another, one week after another. It is, if you like, a quite tranquil life, one could get used to it as a matter of necessity.

If only it wasn't so idiotic, letting these valuable forces lie fallow, this senseless waste of time, resources and energy!

Now Gross, Sugar and Schneider will come, half annoyed, half amused and dead tired from all the nonsense.

And at half past six in the morning Uncle Löwensohn will rage through the house once more.

15 July

The latest sensation: we have received newspapers. We shall at last know again what is really happening in the world! The intervention of intelligent and well-disposed people has had the effect that the harshest and most ridiculous of all injustices, the withdrawal of newspapers, has at last been abolished. And it is in itself encouraging that the Chinese wall which the War Ministry has erected around us has been successfully breached for the first time.

From today every house will receive a copy of the most widely available popular London papers. There is a scramble for them, whole bunches of people sit and stand around the lucky man who first gets his hands on one; it is read out aloud, translated, debated.

We had already previously learnt about the most important event for us from a stray page of a newspaper: on 10 July a great debate took place in the House of Commons in which the internment question was discussed in detail for several hours. Speeches were made in which the injustice perpetrated on the refugees was openly described and condemned, and the answer given to it by the representative of the Home Office, Mr. Peak, bore out the justice of the sharpest criticism. One detail of his exposition caused agitation amongst us, because it was objectively untrue: he asserted that only 'dangerous classes of enemy aliens' had been shipped overseas. Our young people, almost all refugees belonging to class C, must now be regarded and treated as that in Canada! It is perfectly conceivable that Mr. Peak has received false information from his colleagues in the War Office, and once more no-one is prepared to take responsibility for the whole dreadful muddle of this ridiculous deportation. It nevertheless shows that there isn't a good conscience about the affair; so it is to be hoped that nothing similar will be repeated, now that the critical eye of the public has been made aware of it. But it now looks almost as though certain circles, for whom the immigration of German refugees was from the first a thorn in the flesh, have used this occasion as a pretext for getting rid of as many of these unwelcome intruders as possible in a simple manner.

Another passage in this report put me personally in deadly terror: the business of the torpedoed 'Arandora Star' still seems to be completely unsolved, and it is alleged that refugees of all classes were present on the ship.[20] And no news from Franz! My request to the commandant to investigate only met with nonsense and annoyance. I was recently summoned to the telegraph office and there learnt that an unaddressed telegram with my name on it was lying there waiting to be collected. What was the explanation? The contents were an enquiry to the commandant of Lingfield about the whereabouts of my son. As though I couldn't have done that myself ten days ago without the help of the commandant! I nevertheless paid for the telegram, since it was lying there, and had it sent off, and three days later came the reply: 'Apply to War Office'. The registration system in Lingfield seems to be just as accurate as ours was until recently. I have now, more out of conscientiousness than with any hope of a result, directed an enquiry to the War Office. If the boy has been sent to Canada that would not in itself be a reason for concern. But the 'Arandora Star'!! It is a nightmare. I have sleepless nights, and poor Schneider, lying next to me in the bed, his sharp elbows on his chest, must have been very disturbed by my restless rolling about, even though he never utters any complaint.

We have resumed work on the 'Huyton Suite'. We shall hardly get as far as a public performance, the good Fronzig is much too insecure. From another point of view it is no pleasure working with Baron, the young London violinist. He is a talented and cultivated musician, but he is a serious psychopath, with a wild need to assert himself. A rehearsal with him requires constant peace-making, he is self-opinionated, offensive to the other players, and at the same time over-sensitive himself. A few days ago we had to deal with a difference of opinion in which he had found a seconder in Reizenstein, namely on the question of honoraria for house-concerts. The two of them found that the great demand for music here offered an excellent opportunity to make money. The 'Arts Committee'

---

[20] When it was torpedoed, the Arandora Star is said to have been carrying 1,673 men: 479 German internees, 712 Italian internees, 86 German prisoners-of-war, 200 military guards and 174 crew (although these numbers, obtained from a variety of sources, do not tally). Most of the Italians, 712 in number, were already resident in Britain when Mussolini declared war on the United Kingdom and France on 10 June 1940. The death toll, either from the explosion of the torpedo or from drowning, was 470 Italians, 243 Germans, 55 crew (including the captain and twelve officers) and 37 guards. Gál's complaint about the indiscriminate nature of the embarkation was borne out by the wider reaction to the tragedy: the British Labour Party, for example, complained that there had been a number of Italian anti-fascists on board the Arandora Star. *Cf.* also p. 38, above.

which was formed some time ago, and to which I, along with O. E. Deutsch and Dr. Ulrich, belong, made an announcement that entry to all house-concerts was to be free, and only collections for the welfare fund, but no remunerations for the players, were permitted. That annoyed these two enormously. I put it to them, in all friendliness, to participate under these conditions or not; naturally, they will play. Reizenstein is a brilliant pianist, a musician through and through and with much more technical ability than I have today. I gladly leave him as much space and freedom of movement as he wants, and he enjoys great success and recognition with his performances among all serious music-lovers.

During the day, Schneider and Sugar are now only to be seen at mealtimes. They are working on the register with the same fanatical zeal that they developed in learning English. The registry is outside the barbed wire, in one of the shops built in front of the Palace Hotel, in which the various offices of the camp administration are housed. The two of them are already enjoying a certain popularity out there, and are well-known figures in their overalls; Schneider has blue ones, Sugar brown ones. Schneider has long since removed his thrush beard, it must have been a disappointment even for him. But Sugar's beard has developed splendidly, soft and luxuriant. He looks interesting and unusual. Both of them are always busy outside, always with new improvements and ideas for organisation. In the administration they have got used to them, and let them do as they like. Schneider has an inimitable way of making fun of everyone, including himself. One should see him outside, with a slight turn of his head and the gracious hand movement of a queen, waving to the soldier sitting in front of the sentry box and calling 'Sentry!' An internee must be accompanied by a guard to walk the twenty paces from the commandant's office to the camp entrance, and Schneider knows his duty. 'Sentry' jumps up obediently, picks up his rifle and accompanies Schneider to the gate, where the latter takes leave of him with another graciously dignified gesture. He performs this comedy at least half a dozen times a day, with a grave seriousness that no-one can imitate.

Something else in which no-one can emulate him: his coffee-making. Every day we have a cosy half-hour in our room after lunch, and it has become twice as cosy since we have had the 'black stuff'. Schneider has had his wife send him coffee and a coffee pan, and he has now discovered a live, that is, usable, gas tap in our room that must earlier have been the supply for a wall light fitting. Schneider stands at the wash-stand in his blue overalls, his head directly against the ceiling and holds his copper pan over the small gas flame. Anyone who comes into the room splits his sides laughing at this scene. But so far everyone has been thrilled with Schneider's mocha. We have many friends who arrange their visits around the coffee time, and they know why. And since Gross constantly has official discussions, a variety of department heads frequently assemble in our room.

Our organs of state have developed quite impressively. There is a law department, an accommodation manager, a canteen-master, a welfare office, a representative for 'Medical Hardships'. The last of these is the neurologist Dr. Lewin, our friend from Edinburgh. We like having little extra meals in our room, mostly in the evening after the roll-call, as we are amply provided with food; the parcel service functions splendidly. Lewin is a welcome guest, always with a good appetite and fully laden with amusing stories. He is an excellent observer and one of the most masterly story-tellers I've ever known.

We literally laughed ourselves silly over one of his stories. The hero of the episode is a man with multiple sclerosis, Herr Hayek from the Carmelite Market district in Vienna. Lewin presented him to the Medical Officer as a serious case, and arranged an application for release. Herr Hayek is enormously grateful to him for this and since then honours him with his particular devotion. Recently he came to Dr. Lewin again. 'What do you want now?' says Lewin, who is very busy at the time, 'I have no interest in released convicts. You're just about to go, anyway!' But Hayek very much wants his advice in an important matter. 'What is it, then?' says Lewin, who would like to get rid of him quickly. 'Look', says Hayek, 'you've filled in a certificate for me saying that I should be excused from peeling potatoes.' 'I have', says Lewin. 'My house-father says that he shits on your certificate'. 'If he really wants to', says Lewin, 'he should. But did you peel potatoes, then?' 'No', says Hayek, 'I paid sixpence instead, that is the rule in our house if you don't peel.' 'Then everything's fine', says Lewin. 'No', says Hayek, 'that's not all. Recently I was sitting in our lounge playing taroc. The house-father comes in and says: "Herr Hayek", he says, "anyone who doesn't peel potatoes is not allowed to play taroc in our lounge".' 'Unpleasant', says Lewin, 'so you haven't played taroc any more!' 'No', says Hayek, 'I haven't played taroc any more. But that's not all. Yesterday other people were playing taroc, and I just sat with them to watch. Then comes the house-father and says "Herr Hayek", he says, "anyone who doesn't peel potatoes can't watch in our lounge, either".' 'Too bad', says Lewin, 'so you haven't watched any more?' 'No', says Hayek, 'I don't watch any more, either. But that's not all. Now the house-father is demanding that I should apologise to him, otherwise he'll make a complaint to the law committee.' 'What should you apologise for?' 'That's just it! I don't know.' 'How come, Herr Hayek', says Lewin, 'there's something not quite right here. Something else must have happened, otherwise the house-father couldn't demand that you apologise to him. Have you not said something insulting to him?' 'As sure as I live and breathe, not the slightest!' says the man with multiple sclerosis. 'Now listen, Herr Hayek', says Lewin, "there must be a gap in your memory. Look, I'm from Berlin, but I have lived a long time in Munich, and Munich and Vienna have a similar atmosphere in some respects. Might you not perhaps have – now might you not have – now haven't you perhaps told him, for instance, that he should lick your arse?' 'Well', says Herr Hayek, 'I told him that, of course, but that was definitely all!'

Lewin tells such stories, and similar ones, and I even believe that they are mostly true.

17 July

Tovey[21] has died, Donald Francis Tovey, the English friend of mine to whom I am most indebted and who was really responsible for my staying in this country. I read an obituary in a London newspaper that made me very sad, because it shows how little one knows here – where in general people so grotesquely overestimate their own musical achievements – of a man who was in fact such a towering, extraordinary musician. As a personality Tovey was for me one of the most venerable phenomena that I have ever known. I don't believe that there is a musician alive today with so encyclopaedic a knowledge of the music of all periods. And I learnt to appreciate his own music more and more, as something genuine and significant, the more I concerned myself with it.

He brought me to Edinburgh, found work for me in the Reid Library, performed my music, brought about the issue of a work-permit for me by the Home Office. Since he had a stroke a year-and-a-half ago he has been wasting away. He was never the same again, it was a long, terrible agony. I often visited him in my last months in Edinburgh, he had better and worse days, but overall it was an awful spectacle to witness the gradual decay of this wonderfully rich, all-embracing spirit. I had no hope for him, and knew that the destruction could no longer be halted. But the news still hit me hard. It is as though one of the threads that has tied me to this country has been cut through.

But these clueless people don't know who they have lost. The nonentities are amongst themselves again and feel more comfortable.

---

[21] *Cf.* Appendix One: Personalia, pp. 195–96, below.

18 July

We are going to perform the *Huyton Suite*. A flautist has turned up among the new arrivals, Dr. Bergmann[22] from Halle, who is not perfect as a player, but is a good, well-trained musician. He has studied musicology, is a good pianist and is especially interested in the flute and the recorder. Dr. Fronzig has handed his part to him without any ill feeling, as he knows his own weaknesses. So at last we had a complete rehearsal and I was very happy with the piece as a whole. The main difficulty is really Baron, who can't stand it when someone else is leading. From the start he had been given the second violin part – it is just as important and difficult as the first – because the other player, a really good amateur by the name of Markowitz, had already been given the first part and had practised it. Baron can't get over that. Bergmann has studied the score and is considerably better informed than Baron, who has only seen his own part, and he therefore rightly lays claim to lead. I withdrew from the rehearsal today, as the gentlemen apparently prefer it. Meanwhile it has come to light that there is a much better flautist in the camp. He is called Draber, has come from the music college in Berlin and is a flautist such as I have not heard for a long time. If only I had known that before! I have known Draber for some time, he works in the headquarters and I had no idea that he was a musician. He has only just had his instrument sent. I heard him practising as I was passing, rushed hot-foot upstairs to see what sort of rare bird had suddenly flown in, and immediately acquired him for all kinds of collaboration. But I shall probably have to leave the *Huyton Suite* to Dr. Bergmann, he is a sensitive man, and in any case he plays his part very respectably.

My worries about Franz have taken hold of me like a disease. Hansi writes quite calmly and unconcerned about him; she does not seem to be worried, even though nothing has been heard of the boy for five weeks. Perhaps she doesn't know about the 'Arandora Star' catastrophe? The nights are the worst. I can't sleep, and when I then begin to slumber I dream about Franz. I almost always see him as a little boy – it is strange that he is much deeper in my memory as a child than as a grown-up, which he has long been. Then I wake up with my heart pounding and can no longer recall what it was that terrified me in my dream. But I am almost afraid to go to sleep, as this feeling of terror is so unbearable. My friends explain to me every day that there is no sensible reason to be alarmed. They mean well, but where is the boy? I open every letter shaking with agitation, but there are no developments. Our friends in

---

[22] *Cf.* Appendix One: Personalia, pp. 187–88, below.

Edinburgh and London are doing their best, the Scottish Council has also promised to look into the matter. And weeks go by! The War Office has not yet answered my enquiry, and I myself can do absolutely nothing more. Just wait, from one letter to the next!

My face is become more and more atrocious. The white coating that Dr. Löwenberg applied to me seems rather to have made the condition worse. There are now continuous sore patches on my forehead and cheeks, on which a thick scab is forming. He now wants to apply nothing but dry powder. And the itching has got even worse. I am given friendly warnings a hundred times a day: don't scratch! Don't touch it! But it keeps on happening inadvertently. *It* scratches. But once I have touched the itching spot, the itch is so terrible that I begin to scratch, scratch like a madman, so that bits fly everywhere. It happens mostly at night, when I am lying and thinking and can't sleep. This ship, this disaster ship! Many hundreds of prisoners are said to have been trapped under the deck, these were not let out any more. If Franz was among them! I sometimes have to bite my pillow in order not to scream out loud.

20 July

It is so despicable that at first we didn't want to believe it. Our comrades who went voluntarily with the third overseas transport on 10 July, trusting that their wives would join this transport, were deceived.

A letter from one of the wives in Port Erin, the women's camp on the island, led to this discovery. Even today, the wives still have no idea that their husbands were sent away. No-one has told them anything, they know nothing. Meanwhile it has also become known that the destination of this, the third transport, was not Canada but Australia.

So Schneider was right in his suspicion. The scoundrel who gave the promise at the time, Major Daniels, is no longer with us, but has in the meantime been transferred elsewhere. The gentlemen in command shrug their shoulders. They didn't know anything about it. They are 'sorry'.

We have the most agitated house assemblies that there have ever been here. Gross has drafted a memorandum to the camp administration, whose mild and moderate tone provoked dissent from me and many others. If we don't explain right now in the most unvarnished and undiplomatic form that such a breach of promise fundamentally endangers co-operation, that we must insist on an immediate communication about the incident being sent to the Home Office and on reparations for the injustice that has been committed, then no-one will take our protest at all seriously. Our Camp-Speaker's memorandum does contain the demand that the wives in Port Erin should be informed of what has happened, and that steps should immediately be taken to send those affected on. But it is certain that our commandant is not in a position to arrange for this. Major Daniels quite unscrupulously gave a promise that he was not authorised to give; he knew only too well that he had no possibility at all of keeping this promise, and it is just as impossible to keep it today as it was then. Our comrades are on their way to the antipodes and their wives are stuck here on the Isle of Man; for the time being that cannot be undone. The only positive thing we can do is to take a lesson to heart: not to believe a promise any more if it is only given by our authorities. The question has arisen again as to how we should behave if a further despatch of married men is attempted. I see no alternative to united passive resistance. After all the explanations that have been given in the House of Commons, the War Office has committed an act of despotism in sending away category C refugees, especially young people under eighteen and married men. If more such acts are attempted, unanimous passive resistance would have every prospect of success, since the gentlemen will not want it to come to scenes that would cause a furore; that would be extremely uncomfortable for them. If this were not the case they would not have induced our comrades to go voluntarily by means of a false promise. But how do you get sheep to have the necessary courage in such a situation? I had a discussion with Baron, who shares my opinion completely; if need be, we would quickly have to mount a kind of propaganda campaign to recruit heroes; but I am reconciled to the fact that the numerical outcome would be modest.

24 July

Sleepless and unhappy.

Today a letter came from my wife which was again so calm and confident that for the moment I felt reassured by it. I have learnt from experience to trust her instinct. She *couldn't* be so calm if anything terrible had happened to the boy.

I am alone a lot, mostly in my room, reading, if I can, but I don't normally get very far with it. I've had to give up bathing, as the sea-water stings. My condition is getting worse every day. Wind and sun also seem to do no good, so I no longer take part in the walk.

And I am so very ill-suited to being a hermit!

26 July

Still no news of Franz. I am in complete despair. I no longer know what peaceful sleep is. And I shall probably even give up eating.

Music can sometimes still make me forget, and there is always plenty of that. Now a concert on a grand scale is being planned. Over in the Palace Hotel, where the authorities have their seat, there is a large, beautiful theatre that holds about 2000 spectators. We have got permission to organise a concert there for the camp occupants. I don't want to make the programme too 'highbrow' on account of the very mixed community in our camp; on the other hand, I want to avoid all kitsch; the problem is not an easy one. And of course we want to present the best forces of our camp in as effective a way as possible, if only because officers will probably be present. Baron and Reizenstein will naturally take part. But in the first instance they are again the main obstacle; if it was left to them, they would do the whole programme themselves. I persuaded them against this with calmness and persistence. I want Draber, our excellent flautist, to take part. I also definitely want a vocal contribution, and finally – this is the sorest point – there is also another excellent pianist in the camp who I don't want to do without on this occasion. He is called Erwin Weiss,[23] he came from the Vienna Music Academy and is a genuinely talented pianist. Although not yet as mature a musician as Reizenstein, he is still more brilliant and plays virtuoso pieces in such a way that one really has pleasure in it. To get Reizenstein to see this would be quite a feat! Now the wild ambition of the pianist has grabbed him; he won't be content with anything less than Liszt. So Weiss wants to play two pieces by Brahms and the Abegg Variations by Schumann[24] (he does that excellently), and the big show-pieces are left for Reizenstein. My contribution will be limited to accompanying the flautist in short, pleasant pieces – Handel, Gossec, Mozart and Schubert – and the singer. I have discovered a new baritone with whom I have much enjoyed playing in the last few weeks, Hans Karg-Bebenburg. He graduated from the Academy in Vienna and had begun to be an opera singer at the theatre in Linz. He has long passed the beginner's age, in his mid-thirties, but I would give him excellent chances on the stage, as he is unusually gifted both vocally and musically, and in addition intelligent, cultivated and a very good-looking chap.[25] I already have a good repertoire with him from our house-concerts, most of it still without music, and I shall let him sing

---

[23] *Cf.* Appendix One: Personalia, p. 196, below.
[24] *Variations on the Name Abegg*, Schumann's Op. 1, composed in 1829–30.
[25] *Cf.* Appendix One: Personalia, p. 193, below.

'Wanderer' and 'Ständchen' by Schubert,[26] 'Mainacht' by Brahms,[27] my 'Drei Prinzessinnen'[28] and Löwe's 'Prinz Eugen',[29] all things that will suit him excellently. Baron will begin with a sonata by Mozart, accompanied by Reizenstein, and finish with brilliant virtuoso pieces by Elgar and Sinigaglia.[30] As the programme now is, it looks as good as it could be under such circumstances and conditions.

There's already been a row with my *Huyton Suite*. Baron and Bergmann, the flautist, could not agree about any tempo or nuance. Eventually Baron rudely affronted Bergmann and dispatched him. That happened in my absence and in spite of my best efforts I couldn't heal the breach. Baron is irreconcilable. Markowitz, who is playing first violin, is modest and peace-loving enough to tolerate Baron's arrogance, otherwise he would likewise have left long ago. Now we have invited Draber, for whom the piece is child's play. But it is difficult to get him for rehearsal, as he takes his office work very seriously and is therefore only available in the evening. We have fixed the first two performances for the 30th and 31st July and want to stick with these dates if at all possible, as Markowitz is expecting to be released soon.

I am deeply anxious about Paunzen. Almost every day I visit him in the hospital where he now is, and see a rapid, horrifying decline in his strength.

---

[26] Schubert's *Der Wanderer*, D493, the better-known of his two songs with that title, sets a poem by Georg Philipp Schmidt, was composed in 1816 and published (in a revised version) in 1821 as Op. 4, No. 1; the second song, D649, is a Schlegel setting from 1819. 'Ständchen', a setting of Ludwig Rellstab, is the fourth of the fourteen songs which make up *Schwanengesang*, D957, of 1828.

[27] 'Die Mainacht' is the second of Brahms' *Vier Gesänge*, Op. 43 (1866), setting a text by Ludwig Christoph Heinrich Hölty and first published in 1868; it featured in Vol. 24 of the complete edition of Brahms' music that Gál edited with Eusebius Mandyczewski, *Johannes Brahms: Sämtliche Werke*, Breitkopf und Härtel, Leipzig, 1926–27.

[28] Gál composed some hundred *Lieder* in pre-War Vienna but released only the *Fünf Lieder*, Op. 33, composed between 1917 and 1921; they were published by Simrock in Berlin in 1929. 'Drei Prinzessin', a 1917 setting of a Hans Bethge paraphrase of a Chinese original by La-Ksu-Feng, is the fourth in the series.

[29] The ballad *Prinz Eugen, der edle Ritter* is Loewe's Op. 92, a setting of a text by Ferdinand Freiligrath and incorporating elements of an earlier folksong; it was written in 1844 and published in Berlin in the same year.

[30] Leone Sinigaglia was born into an upper-middle-class Jewish family in Turin in 1868 and in the later 1890s studied in Vienna with Gál's teacher, colleague and friend Eusebius Mandyczewski (they often played billiards together) and in 1900–1 in Prague and the Vysoká with Dvořák. He returned to Turin later in 1901 and devoted himself to the collection of Piedmontese folksong while continuing to compose art-music; Barbirolli, Elman, Furtwängler. Kreisler, Mahler, Stokowski, Thibaut and Ysaÿe were among the musicians who performed his works. He was also a celebrated climber, with two first ascents in the Dolomites to his credit. Though Gál would probably have been too young to have known Sinigaglia in Vienna, he would probably have heard about him through Mandyczewski. Sinigaglia's end was tragic: he was a patient at the Mauriziano Hospital in Turin when, on 16 May 1944, German soldiers arrived to arrest and deport him; Sinigaglia dropped dead of a heart-attack as he pleaded with them not to hurt his wife (or his sister: accounts differ).

He can't sleep at night, dozes away during the day, doesn't eat and feels utterly miserable in his narrow, half-darkened little room, in a bed without sheets, in the whole wretchedness of this environment. I don't know the lung-specialist treating him, Dr. Marienfeld. But I often see the resident doctor in the hospital, Dr. Bauer, who is looking after him. I met him today on the promenade, and asked him what is actually wrong with Paunzen. He was reluctant to come out with it, saying that it is always difficult with patients who are of a nervous constitution, and one can hardly distinguish which of his complaints are subjective and which objective. But I noticed that he was embarrassed. And he eventually confessed to me, under the seal of secrecy (why this latter was unclear to me), that it was not a case of bronchitis but of bronchial pneumonia, a highly dangerous, inflammatory process which is hard to deal with. I was horrified: why is he not immediately transferred to a hospital where he can have the appropriate treatment, nourishment and care? 'That is hard to accomplish', answered Dr Bauer, 'only people who are in need of an immediate operation are taken to a hospital.' Apart from this it was not at all certain that he would feel better subjectively there; here he was at least among friends. I immediately went to Höllering, who was no less horrified. We must do something to get Paunzen into a private clinic in Douglas as soon as possible. Höllering will first speak to Dr. Marienfeld, the doctor in charge.

How indescribably remote those happy days in Huyton, of which every bar of my trio reminds me, now appear to me. I fear I have become a bad, unresponsive comrade in the last two weeks, as I have been too preoccupied with my own suffering. I notice that my friends are treating me like a raw egg, so gently and cautiously. Sugar has even stopped talking about cleaning. Two dozen comrades ask me every day whether I have heard any news, and then shake their heads in commiseration.

The intolerable thought that I can't get out of my head is not the fact that the boy is perhaps lying at the bottom of the sea, but rather *how* it happened. I have lived through the catastrophe hundreds and hundreds of times in my thoughts. How terrible this life is!

27 July

I have just behaved like a hysterical old maid. On the promenade, in front of all the people, in the presence of Gross, I had a crying fit when I opened the telegram, Hanna's telegram. God be praised, the boy is in Canada! No details, no explanation. But he is safe!!!

28 July

Last night I slept the sleep of the dead. Everything is all right again! Not even the grotesque mask that looks back at me from the mirror in place of a face can disturb me now.

Tomorrow we have the final rehearsal for the *Huyton Suite*, which is still in a very delicate state. Draber doesn't know the piece well enough, and Baron and Markowitz also know nothing except their own parts. A trio with three light, high parts will come unstuck if there is the slightest rhythmical instability, and if that happens it will fall apart irredeemably. Well, we are not in the Wigmore Hall; if that should happen we shall just start again.

The concert will begin with the concerto for two violins by Bach, followed by songs by Brahms and Wolf, sung by Karg-Bebenburg, and then comes the event that all my friends are eagerly awaiting, the *Huyton Suite*. The room only holds fifty people, so we shall repeat the concert on the following day and will then add another one or two performances in another, bigger room in the following week. Most of our concerts are held in this way, which has worked well. For the first two performances, veterans from Huyton are naturally given priority as far as the distribution of tickets is concerned. It is, incidentally, still doubtful whether more than the first two performances will be able to take place, as it is unfortunately likely that we shall lose Markowitz. The authorities are now actually contemplating sending families to Australia, even if the talk is as yet only of volunteers. For the moment it only applies to those whose families are also interned on the Isle of Man, and Markowitz is one of these. Yesterday the 'Australia men' were allowed to visit their wives in Port Erin for the first time since they were interned, in order to discuss things with them and make a decision. Markowitz has decided to go to Australia, and it is expected that the transport will already leave in the course of this week.

For me it was always one of the most incomprehensible of all acts of cruelty in internment that not only have family members living a few miles apart here on the island not been allowed to see one another occasionally but it has even been made virtually impossible for them to correspond with one another; a letter from Port Erin to Douglas took six weeks.[31] So yesterday two hundred husbands marched off in solemn procession, with a military escort, that goes without saying. They presented a comically touching picture, these mainly elderly gentlemen, many with a modest bouquet of wild flowers in their hands that they had picked on the last

---

[31] Port Erin and Douglas are approximately twelve miles apart as the crow flies and fifteen by road.

walk, full of the festive expectation of seeing their wives again for the first time after months of separation.

For this celebration even some coke had been approved for preparing the baths, as many had expressed this wish, and since a number of illicit bathers naturally slipped through, it was a celebration for the whole camp. There was also an illicit passenger on the trip to Port Erin: my friend Otto Erich Deutsch smuggled himself in among the husbands in order to see his daughter. That is admittedly a flagrant misdemeanour; the adjutant explained very seriously and emphatically to our people that this wasn't a pleasure trip but was for business. He couldn't resist adding a small threat: if there were not enough volunteers, then 'new measures' would have to be taken. The idea of compulsory deportation appears therefore, in spite of public assurances to the contrary, not to have been given up yet by the military authorities, and indeed the most uncomfortable aspect of our situation lies in the evident double game of the relevant government actions affecting us. The War Office and the Home Office, perhaps even different departments within the Home Office, are apparently in no way in agreement about the policy to be adopted, and what one party resolves is steadfastly sabotaged by the other. And all on our backs!

One fact that the visit to Port Erin brought to light did not in any way astonish me, as I didn't expect anything else. Our commandant had answered the memorandum referring to the deceived overseas volunteers by saying that all necessary steps would be taken without delay and the wives in Port Erin would be informed immediately. This undertaking fully satisfied our Camp Speakers, but it was not honoured. The wives in Port Erin still had no idea that their husbands were on the other side of the world. They came to the station assuming that they would find them among the visitors and one can imagine the scenes that followed. So, with wonderful lack of concern one goes from deception to lies, from lies to deception. This circumstance has, quite naturally, influenced the voluntary enrolment for the forthcoming family overseas transport very negatively. Only about eighty have enrolled, from over two hundred who initially expressed an interest. Our Camp Speakers are worried about this, as they fear it will result in compulsory measures. I believe that we must dissuade rather than persuade our colleagues, after all that has happened and the guilt which we have incurred by our gullibility.

A pity that we so often forget the delightful camp stories that the day brings us. Here is one that gave us much amusement. There are two 'kosher' houses in the camp, in which the food is ritually cooked and where the occupants are orthodox. With the arrival of the last transport, a newcomer was quartered with two elderly co-religionists in one room in one of the houses. The two of them were not exactly delighted by this – no-one is in such a case – and since the intruder was a younger man who looked somewhat Europeanised, the two old ones behaved in a doubly reticent and distrustful manner. At bedtime the first fundamental difference appeared in the customs of east and west. The two old ones merely removed their outer garments and went to bed in their shirts and woollen underpants, while the newcomer undressed completely and put on pyjamas. He then heard one of the old men whisper to the other: 'Gets into bed like a whore!'[32]

1 August

An experience like this performance is recompense for all kinds of hardship. I can hardly remember any chamber music piece of mine having such a direct impact and such an immediate effect as the *Huyton Suite* did. But then nowhere else can one find the audience for whom a piece was so tailor-made and dedicated as this was to my friends and fellow-sufferers. They see themselves in the mirror of this music, which reflects the feelings and life of all of us at that time; they feel this much more strongly in the supra-real, more general expression of music than they would feel it in a concrete utterance. The listener's own memory and imagination contribute creatively. All facial expressions are transfigured when the morning reveille sounds for the first time. The performance was unexpectedly good, it sounds like silver filigree in the small room. The conclusion was, however, interrupted by the intervention of a higher power. We had started a little late, and just as we were in the middle of the finale, at the place that I ascribe (but I told no-one about this) to the whisky-jowled captain, the whistle sounded, summoning us to roll-call. We could easily have played for the few minutes until the end, there wouldn't have been any danger in that, but the audience nevertheless became a little restless, and when a conscientious house occupant, whose duty this is, began to toll a bell wildly on the staircase, that was naturally the end. Everyone scattered in a strange mixture of humour, annoyance and enthusiasm.

The proper, complete premiere therefore didn't take place until yesterday, at the second performance. This time we took care to begin on time in order to avoid the unpleasant surprise of the first evening. The performance was even better and more secure than the first, the players are now properly on top if it. At the end there was never-ending cheering.

It is hard to say how much of this effect was extra-musical. I would like to see the reaction of an unfamiliar, objective audience. But it is good, that much I know.

---

[32] In the original, 'Legt sich ins Bett wie ä Chonte!' – 'chonte' being a Yiddish word for 'whore'.

Again there is a deluge of lists and applications. The Home Office has issued a 'white paper' dealing with the conditions for a possible release from internment. Eighteen categories have been set up for which release is foreseen. In general it is concerned with people whose services are useful to the State and the conduct of the war. From the point of view of a normal sense of justice, this white paper is a monstrosity. It means, objectively speaking, that an acknowledged injustice remains generally valid in principle, and is only suspended for those who are immediately and urgently needed. This criticism of it has already been made in the House of Commons; we hope that, after this first retreat by the government over the internment question, public opinion will work more and more towards putting right the injustice that has been committed. In the meantime we are dutifully writing applications. Anyone who doesn't belong to any 'category' is clutching at straws. We now address one another solely by category, e.g., 'Your Medical Hardship' or 'Your Key Position'. I am one of the few who will not apply. The only category that I could conceivably invoke is that of those conducting scientific research. But as even this is related to the war effort in the white paper, I would find it ridiculous to base an application on it. My musicological research can be of no interest for the conduct of the war. Artists fail to make it into the white paper at all, they are not needed.

The situation of the sick has now considerably improved; they are first and foremost to be released. Dr. Lewin, to whom this department has been entrusted, has taken on this task with gusto, and hopes to push through the first releases shortly. I have endeavoured to interest him in the case of Paunzen, for whom nothing has yet been done. He has promised me to intervene on his behalf.

My bed-mate Schneider is in a high state of excitement. Now it's his turn not to eat and not to sleep. His wife has telegraphed to him that his release is secured. He is the only one amongst us, as a dentist with a permit to practise, who will unequivocally be set free, according to the white paper. But his wife has been very efficient and has done the groundwork ahead of the white paper, otherwise the decision could not already be so definite. We are all happy at the news, even though we are sad to lose the best of all comrades. It will unfortunately be unavoidable that we who began this adventure together should depart singly. Who will be the last? It will be sad for him, and that already worries us all, without any egotistical thought behind it.

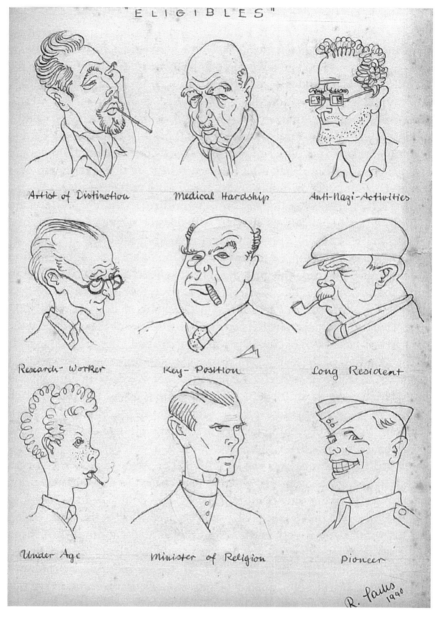

'We now address one another solely by category, e.g., "Your Medical Hardship"
or "Your Key Position"': cartoons by a fellow internee,
unidentified beyond his signature.

3 August

The diabetics, for whose diet provision can't be made here at all, seem to be given priority among the 'Medical Hardships'. It would be a miracle if there were *no* rumours, given the present circumstances. There is said to have been some string-pulling in the matter of 'Medical Hardship'. The names of doctors have been cited who are making a business out of it. The latest camp gossip says that there is a diabetic urine donor. He operates silently, no-one knows his name. It is said that one can only obtain a little bottle with the desired liquid through an intermediary for a corresponding fee. One gets to hear such stories when one is waiting one's turn in the hospital out-patients department. 'Look, sir', someone says to me in beautiful mock-Leopoldstadt[33] Viennese dialect, 'That's more than I can stump up; three quid a shot!' 'Then why doesn't this man go free himself?', I ask – the whole thing sounds much too ridiculous. 'Why d'you think, sir', says my informant, ''im go! While 'e's rakin' in the money! All his born days 'e ain't earned that much dosh. Just think – three quid a shot!'

Incidentally, my treatment is still making no progress. Dear Dr. Löwenberg, deaf as a post, mostly just shakes his head and says 'You are a real allergic'. That doesn't help me much, though. Today he tried to console me with a lesson that his teacher gave him at the University of Göttingen. 'If you want to establish yourself anywhere as a dermatologist, and the first case you get is eczema, then pack your suitcase and leave. You will never succeed in that city.'

He offers such nice comfort!

Sun is harmful, wind is harmful, sea water is of course harmful. What can you do? I usually lie on my bed. In any case, I look so dreadful with my encrusted face that I don't like to show myself, in order not to keep hearing the same sympathetically inquisitive questions and the good advice of all those who have also had that sort of thing. Tomorrow is the third performance of the *Huyton Suite*, I shall unfortunately have to show myself there after all.

A belated explanation has come for the flight to Canada of friend Bien, the psychoanalyst with the prophet's beard and the blue dressing-gown. It was contained in a letter from my wife and has amused us all enormously,

[33] Leopoldstadt was the main inner-city Jewish quarter, in the Second Bezirk, or District; it sits on an island bordered by the Danube to the north and the Danube Canal to the east. A ghetto existed there by the mid-seventeenth century, but the Jews were driven out by Emperor Leopold I in 1670. Proximity to the Nordbahnhof encouraged Jewish immigrants from eastern Europe to settle there again in the nineteenth century, only for the Nazis to eradicate the Jewish community entirely during the Second World War. With the fall of the Iron Curtain, Leopoldstadt has once again become the focus of Jewish immigration from eastern Europe.

because it's typical of the man. Hansi writes: 'I must tell you some little gossip. You know that Zarathustra had a very bad reputation in Edinburgh. All the ladies were furious with him. Now I have learned that one of his sweethearts was in the family way. She is on the Isle of Man by now, and they all think if he was not impotent like an honest citizen, he might have been more cautious at least. The sweetest Quaker ladies see red when his name is but mentioned. No good telling them that accidents may happen. I should just like to know whether this cuckoo has volunteered for overseas or had to go'.

One can see that spiritual healing brings with it certain risks.

5 August

Today is my birthday, together with Gross. How young he is! Today he was thirty-four. And how mature, how clever and self-controlled! Naturally we only celebrate in a culinary way. What else should one do? But we do it in style, having already started yesterday, and we shall have to continue it with all kinds of further celebrations, if only because we have far more eager co-celebrants than our room can hold, and because it has rained parcels for each of the birthday boys.

Hansi is already in Middlesmoor,[34] in the country, with our friends. And Peter is also there. They both seem happy to be there, and I am happy, too. Since I have been interned, not a day has passed without my thinking with gratitude of the fact that I am among good friends. This fact is more important for balance and well-being than anything else, and I know how enormously Hansi is dependent on this circumstance of a warm, friendly, domestic atmosphere. Now at least for some time she will be as well looked after as could be imagined.

Paunzen is in a dreadful state. I fear that he will not survive the week. Lewin has drawn his case to the attention of the Medical Officer and introduced Dr. Marienfeld to me, in order to discuss the matter with him. The latter would above all have to urge to have him transferred to a hospital. Dr. Marienfeld has now for his part spoken to the Medical Officer. The same result as before: 'Impossible'. The hospital in Douglas could admit him, but there is no possibility of it also accommodating four soldiers. — Yes, that's how it is. If an internee is taken outside the camp the authorities must ensure that there is appropriate security. I had a fit of rage. Höllering has promised to keep pressing; he will not slacken.

And he succeeded, too: this afternoon an ambulance arrived and took Paunzen away. He looked like a dying man, but he was very happy to be

---

[34] Middlesmoor is a hill village in Nidderdale, one of the Yorkshire dales, north-west of Harrogate.

told he was being released (which wasn't true). His wife in London has been informed by telegram, and we hope that she will be with him tomorrow.

As always, something drastic had to happen before something sensible, necessary and humane could be achieved. Yesterday a man died here in the camp hospital. He had a severe heart condition; the doctor had demanded a few days before that the patient's two interned daughters should be informed on the telephone and should be given immediate permission to see their father. This was refused. After his death they were informed immediately. The regulations state that in cases of death the next of kin are to be notified by the quickest means. But before that? Out of the question. Even so, somewhere a conscience must have stirred, since an ambulance was suddenly there for Paunzen, even without four guards. The M.O. magnanimously took personal responsibility for the patient not attempting escape. I only learnt later that someone else had also taken responsibility for something that was not quite so cheap: Höllering, that kind, helpful soul, guaranteed payment of the hospital costs, five guineas per week.

The third performance of the *Huyton Suite*, in a different room, twice as large, resulted in us having to give a fourth. But it can only be in the following week, as at the moment we are busy with the preparations for the concert in the Palace Hotel. There is now no urgency, since Markowitz will stay for the time being. The Australia transport has been stopped for unknown reasons.

We shall not be able to get more than a thousand people into the theatre, although there would be twice as many seats. There is a lack of available soldiers, whose number must be in an exact relationship to the number of prisoners that they have to guard. I have been a soldier myself[35] and I know that a certain system is part of military order. But I would never have imagined possible such a degree of inflexibility about regulations as there is in the British military. Any child will discover that one can guard five thousand men just as securely as a hundred by occupying the exits. There has never yet been an attempt to escape, the very idea is ridiculous. Where should one escape to? But the rule states: for a thousand men twenty soldiers, for two thousand twice as many. A conscientious officer keeps to this.

A well-captured group photograph of us four arrived today as a nice, improvised birthday present. Schneider brought the news one day that a photographer had been booked from Douglas to make passport photographs for some people who were travelling to America. Sugar had recently been incubating the idea of having his beard amputated. A letter

---

[35] *Cf.* pp. 14–15, above.

from Edinburgh seems to have been the decisive factor. A nice lady-friend there, whose opinion seems to be not unimportant to him, included in it a quite amusing 'ceterum censeo'. The sentence: 'Take that beard off!' kept recurring like a leitmotif, in ever larger letters. I must unfortunately confess that it was my fault that this beard became notorious and a topic of daily conversation in Edinburgh. I had mentioned it in a letter to my wife, and internee news spreads very quickly in Edinburgh among the small group of splendid people who take the liveliest interest in us. Sugar was now very much aware of the picturesque masculinity of his facial decoration, and he was reluctant to part with it. But 'que femme veut…', well then there's nothing to be done. He just wanted a souvenir first, and so it happened that he declared: 'First I shall have myself photographed. Then I'll remove the beard'. So when the photographer came, Schneider proposed that we should try to get a group photograph. So we went out into the Palace where the photographer was already waiting. I asked him if he could take a photograph of us four, at which he asked with a smile, 'Do you want it for a passport?' 'Of course', I answered. I had to poke Gross in the ribs at the same time, as he would immediately have vehemently denied it. He is incapable of letting even the simplest, most obvious untruth rest, the pedant! So, the photographer had understood, and as there was no-one near who could have objected, we quickly came to an agreement. He took the group photograph, and then a photograph of Sugar by himself. Both, as is now clear, were a great success. The photographer undertook to send copies to our families, it will be a nice surprise for them. But Sugar appeared yesterday as a new man, unknown in the camp. It is incredible how the beard changed him! We had the greatest fun with Baron, the violinist, who allowed himself to be persuaded that the unfamiliar man in our room to whom we introduced him was Sugar's younger brother, who had come to replace him in internment. He himself had already gone home. None of us was concerned about it, and the authorities wouldn't care what sort of Sugar was in the camp as long as the number was correct. Baron was beside himself about this incredibly daring feat, and spread it around, under the seal of secrecy, until someone who was acquainted with the facts of the case eventually enlightened him that his leg had been pulled. Today he came again to see Sugar once more without his beard: he would never have believed it, he wouldn't have thought it possible, but actually he is disappointed; he much preferred the bearded Sugar, who looked like a Russian general from the Crimean war. It is a fact that the camp has become the poorer by the loss of one of its most characteristic figures.

The 'well-captured group photograph' of (from left to right) Willi Gross, Max Sugar, Hans Gál and Hugo Schneider

7 August

Höllering had news from Frau Paunzen today. She is with her husband and he is noticeably better. With a condition like his an inner lift of the spirits means an immense amount for the possibility of recovery. That was above all what we hoped for him by freeing him from the barbed-wire enclosure; perhaps it was not yet too late.

In these weeks of common concern about our friend, I have become intimately acquainted with Höllering. He is a splendid person, the happiest combination of an artistic temperament, full of imagination and enterprise, and an orderly man, with strength of character. He has a new idea for a film that we have talked through together, and which might eventually result in collaboration. But that is music for the future. He is constantly busy with sketches, improvements, collection of materials, a man of the most active and positive kind. I admire him for his ability to work. I feel like a wreck with my ailing face, sticking to me like a foreign body. For tomorrow's concert in the theatre I shall have to powder myself like a plaster figure; with the harsh light of the stage, that will still be the lesser evil.

9 August

Paunzen died last night.

Miracles do not happen, we really knew that it was too late. And yet we are both as though thunderstruck, Höllering and I. He had, as is his lively way, befriended the painter deeply and directly, and I, who basically kept no closer than a respectful distance to him, saw his suffering, which was indescribably heart-rending. Murder has been committed on this man. We shall never be able to prove it in legal terms, but we know it: a murder, committed through indifference, thoughtlessness, heartless inertia.

It's just like Höllering to come to me on the day when Paunzen was transferred to hospital with the words: 'We've managed that. But now please do something for yourself; it can't go on like this with you'. Strange that I hadn't come up with the idea myself! I went to Lewin; he immediately placed me on his list; today I was presented to the Medical Officer. The procedure hardly lasted three minutes. I look so dreadful that no commentary was necessary. Dr. Löwenberg's certification stressed that effective treatment was impossible under the present conditions, and that there was a serious danger that the ailment would spread. I was therefore put forward for release as a 'Medical Hardship', and thereby have the hope that my turn will come 'in due course'.

First I shall no doubt have to undergo hospital treatment; I don't dare to venture out among people looking like this.

The concert in the Palace was a great success, and achieved a quite impressive level. Baron was noticeably better in the opening Mozart sonata than in the solo pieces that formed the conclusion of the programme. He is a good, cultivated musician, that is all. He completely lacks the virtuoso temperament, and a virtuoso piece is boring if it is merely played in tune and correctly. In addition he was from the outset put in an unfavourable position by an improvisation from his friend and accompanist Reizenstein. Reizenstein couldn't allow the laurels gained by his rival Weiss, who won rapturous applause in the first half of the concert, to rest. He just had to outplay him. And since, in spite of the Liszt Polonaise, he didn't achieve this so resoundingly with his group of piano pieces, he added as an encore a kind of variety number of his own composition, thereby extending the programme by an unwelcome quarter of an hour, by which means, however, he could count on a sure success: burlesque variations on the Lambeth Walk, in the style of the great masters.[36] It's not a new idea, but he

---

[36] Reizenstein's *Variations on 'The Lambeth Walk'* presents the song (from Noel Gay's 1937 musical *Me and My Girl*) in the styles of, successively, Chopin, Verdi, Beethoven, Mozart, Schubert, Wagner and Liszt. Along with the *Concerto Popolare* he wrote for the first of Gerard Hoffnung's music festivals in

did it with real wit and skill, and merely the popular theme, in a programme that must have been fairly serious and demanding for most of our listeners, was decisive in ensuring his success. So Reizenstein had his triumph, whose secondary effect however was to completely destroy the following finale by his friend Baron.

13 August

Our comrade Schneider left us on Saturday. It took almost two weeks from his wife's telegram, but one day the release order was there, for the very next day, and it was therefore in the end a hasty farewell. He had to get up early so we were all already up and about at six o'clock in the morning. He was happy and excited. We got it over quickly, but each of us suppressed secret tears, thinking that the others wouldn't see it.

My dear comrade! I won't be able to enjoy the bed that I now have all to myself ...

This bed has again become a place of torment. My condition is getting ever more intolerable. The rigid mask of scabs is getting closer and closer around the eyes. In the morning I can hardly open them. If, against doctor's orders, I attempt out of desperation to wash away some of these scabs, they grow back twice as thick. And my head! All the itching devils of hell – and I imagine that itching devils must be the worst of all – are concentrated on my parting, where a thinning in my hair has now made massive progress. If I touch this spot when combing my hair it drives me mad, and then the comb begins to scratch, whether I want it to or not. The wounds and the scab are getting worse from day to day.

This morning I went to Lewin and explained to him that I had reached the limits of endurance. I had to get proper hospital treatment immediately, and since this was impossible here, it had to be outside the camp. Lewin took me to the Medical Officer again and I presented my request to him. He is a nice, friendly man, and the hospital gentlemen, particularly Lewin, always assert that one can get along with him excellently. Well, he explained to me, in a friendly and gentle manner, that transfer to a hospital was out of the question. I replied that a man had been sent to the hospital the week before. 'Yes, but he was a dying man', was the answer.

I wasn't aware of it myself, but those present, Lewin and the medical staff, agree that I then behaved somewhat insanely. What I recall is merely that I expressed my opinion on this kind of medical care with frankness and candour, and assured him that I had so far always been of the opinion that

---

1956, the *Variations on 'The Lambeth Walk'* became Reizenstein's best-known piece of music, but he never took the work into his published catalogue and so it lacks an opus number.

A self-portrait by Arthur Paunzen from 1926, given to the Gáls by his widow after his death in 1940

a hospital was intended to cure the sick and not to receive the dying. Now my whole outburst was objectively pointless, as there is no dermatologist on the whole of the Isle of Man, and here in the camp there is at least a specialist in this field. To all appearances I again exploded at an inopportune moment, and the gentlemen reproached me bitterly when, in response to my angry outburst, the Medical Officer finally shrugged his shoulders and left the room. But you're supposed to maintain your patience and peace in the face of all that! If only one could! With the shaky nerves of many sleepless nights and with everything that the bitterness over recent events has bottled up inside one!

I am to play again tonight. It is the fourth, and for the time being the last performance of the *Huyton Suite* with the same programme before it. One of the English officers, the only one who is seriously interested in music, has announced his attendance. He is called Smith and is a grey-haired man with fine features and the only one among the officers who associates with us as with equals. He was especially pleased with my 'Three Princesses',[37] and so he is interested to hear some of my chamber music.

This little bit of music is still a consolation.

[37] *Cf.* note 28 on p. 120, above.

15 August

I am lying alone in a small, semi-dark little room, in a spacious bed. I have to lie a lot, I am allowed only a few visitors, and I have nothing but milk and fruit. The milk is delivered by my house, our old house number two; the fruit is brought from the canteen at my own expense. I am in the camp hospital, to where, after a bad night, I was led yesterday, like a half-blind man, by Gross. My face was heavily swollen and I could only see out of my eyes with a great effort. Today things are better, my eyes are free, I can read and write. I learnt to do this without my glasses some time ago, for several weeks I have been unable to tolerate glasses on my nose.

Last night!

Previously that evening there had been the fourth performance of the *Huyton Suite*. It wasn't completely without problems; there had been no new rehearsal and so there was some nervousness and a few accidents. But the effect was again extraordinary, and Lieutenant Smith, who was present, made such a warm, humane speech that we were all quite touched. We sat together for another hour at home; I was afraid of the night, and Dr. Blumenthal gave me what he said was a harmless sleeping pill.

I must have fallen asleep almost immediately. It was perhaps about two in the morning when I awoke. It afterwards occurred to me that I had been dreaming. A considerable part of the window panes in our room had been blackened with oil-paint for the purposes of the blackout. As we were not allowed lights, and the blackout was therefore in practice pointless, Sugar had the inspired idea of scratching the paint off with old razor blades. This gave us an occupation for a few days, but it was worth the effort. Since then our room has had twice as much light and sun. That is what I dreamt of now. I was in a gloomy room – it was, strangely enough, our bedroom in Vienna, in the last apartment that we lived in there – and I had to scratch the blackout from the window. I couldn't get it done, the window got blacker and blacker, and I *absolutely had to* get it clear. I scratched the black stuff with both hands, scratched, scratched. I could only rouse myself with difficulty, but I know that I continued scratching after I was awake, mindlessly, simply because I couldn't stop. Until a sticky fluid ran over my face. It was smooth and moist; I had scratched off everything, everything from my head, my face, my forehead, all the horrible scab, right to the last bit. Gross had woken up – he told me later that I had groaned out loud – and he woke Sugar, who did what he could in the dark. He laid my head between towels and handkerchiefs, put my hands into a pair of socks to keep them out of the way, and skilfully tied them with string to the bottom of the bed. This last measure was unnecessary, as nothing was itching now.

My face and my head were burning like fire. My comrades were incredibly good-natured, they didn't even scold me for disturbing their night's rest.

In the morning I noticed that I couldn't see out of my eyes. My face must have been swollen and distorted. In response to my question as to how I looked, Sugar replied in a friendly way: 'Like a monkey's behind, my dear friend'. He is always kindly, but he does not mince his words. He then went straight to the hospital and arranged for a room to be made available for me. He rightly believes that, under the prevailing conditions, the camp hospital is still the lesser evil, and Dr. Löwenberg had long been advocating this solution. I received poultices, and when the old gentleman came to me again in the evening he was by no means dissatisfied. 'You saved me a job', he said, 'as I would have had to take these scabs off eventually. But you shouldn't have done it quite so brutally.' He has now spread an ointment on my head, and a powder he has made himself, mixed with water like bricklayer's mortar, is painted onto my forehead and face. The swelling has quickly gone down. Since Dr. Löwenberg has above all prescribed rest, very short visiting hours have been decreed. To my not inconsiderable amusement I have learnt today from the 'Head Nurse' of the house, little Rosenbusch, that I am considered to be a 'mental case' and am therefore treated with special care. This is the result of my scene with the Medical Officer. That anyone in full possession of his mental faculties should be rude to this most important man in the camp is unimaginable. Again I see how careful one must be in judging what is mentally normal.

This Rosenbusch is an especially nice fellow and the real soul of the hospital. I don't know why he is called Head Nurse, as he is the only one here who carries out nursing duties. I don't believe he has a moment's rest from early in the morning till late at night. Someone is always calling 'Rosenbusch!' through the house. But he has time and patience for everyone, and the most skilful and intelligent hands that there are. He can make up the bricklayer's mortar for my face better than the doctor. He plasters me really thickly, laughs with enthusiasm at how comical I look, and enjoys it when, after a while, the stuff begins to dry and white dust rains down from me as from a badly whitewashed wall.

When I have a visitor, he must sit on my bed, as there is nowhere else in the room. A second one can stand, a third one has just enough room to lean on the door. But that is all that can be stuffed into my room. So my friends have to ration their visits. In the evening I get a sleeping pill and I sleep an enormous amount, the whole night and half the day. What I can't get used to is the fact that I now look out on the narrow, gloomy back of a house. No ray of sunshine comes into my room.

I really feel quite well, rather relieved. The itching on my head has greatly decreased. The doctor comes to me three times a day and is extremely kind and attentive. As far as my illness is concerned, he makes no prognosis. 'You are allergic', he always says meaningfully, and this observation seems to satisfy him enormously. I remember how once, many years ago, when Franz was a baby of a few months old, and was not recovering from an illness, we got a famous specialist on the advice of our doctor. He examined the child thoroughly, withdrew for a conference with the doctor and thereupon came with the momentous observation: 'The child is an exsudative person'. Having said this, he received his fifty shillings and left, conscious that he had done his duty.

To this day I don't know what an exsudative person is, nor do I know what an allergic person is.[38]

19 August

I have brought my blanket and my sleeping bag here with me. There are no sheets in the hospital, any more than there are in any of the other houses. A patient gets the bed just as the person before him has left it. Today Dr. Blumenau, my Mainz dentist, who works here in the hospital in the dental service, brought me a sheet. It now looks almost genteel here!

My house is touchingly concerned about me, our cook seems to be sending half his milk ration over in order to get me well quickly. I can't cope with even half of it, and have begged for moderation.

My head has got considerably better, but not much progress can be seen in my face. Dr Löwenberg is not dissatisfied with the results so far; he has always told me that eczema is a lengthy business. The strict milk diet has been relaxed a little, but the pleasure is not worth speaking of, since what is cooked here is barbaric. I have so little appetite that it hardly makes a difference. I'm already getting quite a few visitors. My closest friends visit me every day, and many others as well: the house-comrades from No. 2, the students in my harmony course, my musicians and singers.

It often happens that someone has to wait until there is room to get in. Dr. Ulrich and Professor Deutsch, my two colleagues from the arts committee, come almost every day. They have concert worries again. Following a justified general wish, we had intended from the beginning to hold a popular evening after the 'serious' concert, which was to be run by the representatives of the light muse. It was planned for a week today, the 26th, but it has now become clear from a rehearsal in the Palace Theatre

---

[38] Gál was right to be baffled. An exsudate is a liquid which seeps from the circulatory system into a lesion; a wound can thus be described as 'exsudative' but not a patient. And the medical term for someone prone to allergic reactions is 'atopic'.

that the level of offerings is too deplorable to risk in this demanding setting. None of these badly sitting voices carries, and something that can be quite pleasant and amusing in the lounge of a house sounds silly and impossible when produced on a large stage. There is disagreement among the 'artists' themselves, each of them complains about the others, but no-one has sufficient authority even to create a programme. Deutsch, who has the responsibility for this undertaking, declared himself powerless under these circumstances and with these forces. I now advised him to approach Höllering, he could at least give a few tips, contribute some good ideas, take over a kind of overall direction. There is a knock at the door: *lupus in fabula*; Höllering, who visits me almost every day, enters. The two gentlemen hadn't known him personally, and are very relieved to be able to hand over their unpleasant task to an expert, and Deutsch will assemble the 'artists' this very afternoon in the Palace Theatre.

Höllering came again yesterday. 'You've landed me right in it now', he says. 'It's not even worth talking about. Half of it is bad and the other half impossible. You can't really do anything with it.' 'So what will happen?' 'The evening has been cancelled and a serious concert will take place instead. Meanwhile I'll think it over, perhaps we shall find a way to get things into shape somehow, or at least part of it. The young people in the camp have a few pleasant, fresh numbers, the ensemble from the "Little Coffee-House" can contribute one or two pieces, a conjurer is there with a few nice tricks – but that's about everything that looks in any way tolerable.'

No sooner was he outside than the two arts committee functionaries came back. Now they have worries about the serious concert that is to be arranged. Deutsch has a concrete suggestion. There is another pianist in the camp, to whom astonishing things are attributed. He is called Alfred Blumen.[39] He himself maintains that he is one of the greatest living exponents in his field. If he can do even half of what he claims it would be a sensation. Now experience tells me that there is no reason to believe half as much of anyone as he himself says, a quarter is often too much. I don't know Blumen personally, but have known about him for a long time, and have never noticed that the piano had interested him in the slightest. He has never taken part in musical things, has never been seen in a concert, has only played bridge. He is from Vienna, and I remember having heard or read his name years ago. He has lived in America for a long time. I naturally have nothing against him playing in the Palace, quite the contrary. But what? Now comes the snag: Herr Blumen is very demanding. He will only play if he has the whole evening to himself. I find that out of the question;

---

[39] *Cf.* Appendix One: Personalia, p. 188, below.

one couldn't put an evening of piano music before an audience such as ours. If we did, it would be our last concert: we would have no audience for the next one. I suggest a chamber-music piece, perhaps a Beethoven trio, and a singer who has a large following in the camp, the bass Dr. Pick, cantor in the liberal Jewish community and former buffo opera singer. He is a ham actor but he has musicality, humour and knows how to perform. Deutsch doubts that Blumen will accept this. 'Then he should forget it', I say. But I see that it matters greatly to Deutsch to satisfy his Blumen. 'Anyway', I say, 'what's the point of me being ill? Arrange it in the way you think best. I can't be properly involved anyway. You know my opinion.'

This Blumen must have somehow made an impression on Deutsch. If he wants to take responsibility for him, he should do so.

An hour later, Höllering was there again, burning with a new idea. He wants to produce a revue, a real piece of theatre. With music. And naturally with my music! The performance will have to be in a fortnight's time, it couldn't be later, because the Italians from the neighbouring camp will need the stage for a performance that they are preparing.

I laughed. I am supposed to make music here in the hospital! The music for what? Where is the script?

There is no script yet. He still has to write it. But the title is already there: 'What a life!' It is to be a sort of photo-montage of our life in the camp, a series of short, lively scenes taken from everyday life. With two compères, one in German and one in English. And all the songs will likewise be performed bilingually, with two different singers. Here are two of the song texts, written by Hutter, one of our cabaret people, I should look at them right away. The two numbers worth considering from the planned 'Popular Evening' will be included. And he needs a grand parade march, to which the whole camp hierarchy, from Hildebrand downwards, is to walk personally across the stage, with emblems and a great razzmatazz. And he already has ideas for a whole series of scenes, barbed wire will appear on the stage, and the seagulls, and the double bed in which we sleep, and – and –

And then he was gone, he has to get working. I was half-dazed and enormously amused. We are to put a play on the stage in two weeks, when not a single scene is ready! What a fantast! I glanced at the two songs. These lines were originally hardly intended for music, they are really short and neatly incisive epigrams. The seagulls – the barbed wire – the women in front of it - well, the music had already come into my mind before I had finished reading. I can easily do him that favour. And while I was about it, I sketched a piece for the planned great triumphal march of the camp representatives. Höllering should be pleased with the prompt service.

26 August

That was quite a week! Work, work, work, from morning till deep into the night. And unfortunately it carries on buzzing around in my head during the night, it's all over again with a good night's sleep.

In six days I've almost finished writing the music for the revue, in tremendous haste, just as quickly as I could write the notes. And as that is still too slow, I have not even written a score, but just a sketch, and made the necessary parts from this sketch.

That it happened like this was admittedly my fault. That's what comes of prompt service! Höllering comes at least twice a day. He asks sympathetically about my health, how I have slept, how I feel, and then he pulls a few lines from his pocket that I am supposed just to compose, or he reads out a scene to me for which he needs music here and there. 'You'll do that right away, won't you? The people are already waiting for it.' Just like at the grocer's, and I was always prompt with the delivery. But that's just because it has grabbed me again. The liveliness of the whole idea has seized me in an extraordinary way, and the music comes as if by itself. Höllering's scenario – it is more a scenario than a script, dialogue parts are mostly only sketched – is really like a photo-montage; an improvised series of short scenes, which have an enormous appeal for me, because really there is nothing invented in it. It has all happened and happens daily with us, and yet, in the sequence of events, in the combination of these scenes and in the use of the available material, in terms of people and stage resources, there is such a supreme artistic taste and richness of ideas, that I was bewitched every time when he came with a new scene.

I have of course also had to start with the balance of available resources. There is a usable orchestra pit in the theatre, so it was clear to me from the beginning that I would have to improvise a kind of orchestra. I can get two first and two second violins, a viola and a cello. There is a quite able clarinettist, and of course Draber, the brilliant flautist. If this ensemble is supported and held together by a piano, we shall be able to do everything that we need. I will have the small grand piano that is now on the stage placed in the middle of the orchestra, and conduct from the piano, playing along just as much as is necessary, in the manner of a continuo, as was done three hundred years ago. I have written my music with this plan in mind. The songs are mainly only accompanied by the piano, but in each one there is also a solo instrument, a flute, a cello, a clarinet, or a violin. That will give colour, each of the players can enjoy a solo, and our unpractised singers on the stage will be reliably accompanied by the piano and not confused by an orchestral accompaniment.

Half a dozen of these songs are ready, as well as the overture (which is also the grand parade), an intermezzo and a finale. The parts have already been written out, I shall be able to hold the first rehearsal tomorrow. I anticipate that the main musical effect will come from the finale, which was my idea, and which needed a lot of persistence to get Höllering to agree to, as he had originally had a different idea for the ending. I was obstinate in this, because I am sure of the effect. The idea came from a gifted young man who lives in our house. He had painted a nice series of water-colours, and one of them depicts a soldier standing by the barbed wire and shouting at the moon as it comes out from behind a house 'Put that light out!' Like everything in our revue, this scene actually happened, though it wasn't the moon but its reflection in a window that had misled a sentry. We hear the call 'Put that light out!' a dozen times every evening, yelled, howled, bawled, barked. It is aimed at belated little lights that are still shining in a window, against the rules, after the blackout. Here in the hospital, where I go to bed early, this call has often woken me from my first sleep, and annoyed me intensely. It is now to appear in the revue in the form of the refrain to a song, and I hope to make it so popular in the camp in this form that the sentries will not be able to avoid making fun of themselves when they utter it in future. The scene of the finale is the double bed, with the two singers, German and English, in it. The above-mentioned song comes at the sentry's call of 'Lights out!' Then it gets dark and there follows a kind of dream vision: one of the sleepers gets out of the bed and walks like a sleep-walker up to the barbed wire which borders the stage at the front. The barbed wire falls, the man strides out, to freedom. It has become completely dark, so that the singer is able to get back to his bed again from behind unnoticed. Then a beautiful, smiling full moon rises at the back. A voice roars off-stage: 'Put that light out!' The moon disappears, the two sleepers jump up and embrace with the words 'What a life!' Curtain.

Höllering was unwilling to accept this until he heard the music to it, but now we are in agreement over it.

I shall go out in the evening today for the first time since I've been in the hospital. There is a concert in the Palace Theatre. It was a difficult time for poor Deutsch, he took on a terrible burden with it and received nothing but annoyance, protests and resentment in return. As the programme has now turned out, it is a compromise. It will again begin with a Mozart violin sonata, this time played by the two camp speakers, Gross and Hildebrand. Gross is a refined violinist, and Hildebrand a very musical, decent pianist, and it is naturally nice when the leaders of our community also show themselves to be able musicians. There then follows Dr. Pick, the buffo-cantor, with the Wedding Song by Loewe[40] and an aria by Lortzing. The second half of the evening is given over to Blumen, with what is really a whole evening's programme, containing the Schubert 'Wanderer-Phantasie', Schumann's 'Carneval', and a lot of Chopin. I would never have approved such a programme; what is certain is that it is much too long.

Since music has taken possession of me again, I have not thought much about my condition. But it has possibly got worse again in the last few days. I was given Luminal every evening throughout the first week, and now it's no longer effective. If I fall asleep at night I am awake again after an hour, and then I mostly lie awake until dawn. The nervous tension caused by my work has probably played its part, and Dr. Löwenberg shakes his head over my stupidity. But I must get through it, nerves or no nerves, and it is after all only another week to the performance.

One by-product of my sleepless nights has greatly pleased Höllering: I have translated the songs into English, as no one here could do it to the music. The English is probably bad, but they are punchy rhymes and the point comes over well. Both the English and the German singers are amateurs. The English one is musical, intelligent, and speaks a very genuine Cockney; the German one is unfortunately a blockhead, and I don't think that it will work with him, even though he's practising hard.

28 August

We have had the first rehearsals in the theatre. As far as the German songs are concerned, I have decided on Dr. Pick. It didn't work at all with the natural singer first intended for it by Höllering, and Karg-Bebenburg, who I would have preferred to have, has recently moved to the postal service, is very industrious there and is therefore not to be had for a rehearsal. Pick was for years on the stage as a bass-buffo and it will be an easy job with him. I loathe his hamming habits, but the public laughs at them. So if Höllering succeeds in keeping him more or less in bounds, the effect will be good. The day before yesterday he had an enormous public success over in the Palace, and I don't underestimate his qualities, above all his perfect sense of timing with speech. His voice is powerful, but very ugly.

Deutsch was right with his Blumen. The man is extraordinary. The 'Wanderer-Phantasie' left me cold, although unusual pianistic qualities were immediately recognisable. But Schumann's 'Carneval' won me over completely. I can't remember ever having heard this work with such a variety of colour, such magnificent overall shaping, such clarity of detail and such a healthy, spacious momentum. I didn't need the following group of Chopin

---

[40] Loewe's 'Hochzeitslied' is the first of his *Drei Balladen*, Op. 20 (1823), which set texts by Goethe.

pieces to acknowledge that we have a great pianist here among us. It is a long, long time since I had such pleasure from piano-playing, and I am grateful to him for it. And I have still more respect for Otto Erich Deutsch than before, not because he was proved right but because he stood up for something of which he was convinced with such composure and such dignified calm, even though it made his person the object of the bitterest enmity. Amongst the musicians he is at the moment the most hated man in the camp – this fine, restrained scholar, who never demands anything for himself and devotes himself entirely to the matter in hand. They will never forgive the one who caused Blumen to become the music sensation of the camp.

My little orchestra has started out well and we have got so far in one rehearsal that I can leave everything else to the coming stage rehearsals. We are so short of time that we have to arrange two rehearsals on Sunday, morning and afternoon, in order to leave Monday, the day of the performance, free of rehearsals and available for any necessary 'snagging'. If only Höllering were finished on stage! At the moment he changes things from one rehearsal to the next and there is hardly a scene where the dialogue, which, incidentally, there isn't much of, is fixed. The whole thing has a lot of Höllering's familiar film-technique; there is a lightning succession of tableaux and scenes, which in themselves, purely as images, express so much that there is not much room for words. Admittedly I don't yet have any conception of the overall effect. Many extras have been called in, anyone who likes can join in. Höllering is an incredibly active artistic medium. He seizes every idea that is presented to him, forming it in a trice and fitting it into his plan. And he is a masterly director. Today I saw him arrange a few scenes with his amateur actors; that was first-class work. There is a long dialogue scene, played by Herr Levi and Herr Mayer, two refugees from Berlin, who meet up again for the first time in this scene. Neither of them has been on stage before, Höllering picked them up on the promenade, because they interested him as characters. 'It would be unfair', he says, 'to expect such people to be actors. They could never act a "role". But they can play Herr Levi and Herr Mayer, since that is what they have been doing their whole lives, and I don't ask any more of them than that.' The two of them are a scream. I have occasionally seen acting like that under Reinhard in the Josefstadt.[41] This scene will be a show-stopper, every word is just right. And when fifty nervous, undisciplined Jews appear with their little suitcases, talk across each other excitedly – you could have nothing

---

[41] Max Reinhard (1873–1943) managed the Theater in der Josefstadt (in Josefstadt, the Eighth District in Vienna) from 1924 to 1933. Founded in 1788, the Theater in der Josefstadt was extensively rebuilt in 1822, when Beethoven's overture *Die Weihe des Hauses* was commissioned to mark its re-opening.

better in any theatre. The fun started even before the rehearsal, when the people assembled in front of the gate with their suitcases. Höllering has complete authority to take as many people as he likes out into the Palace. The sentries knew about it and laughed, but the rumour spread in the camp that a lot of internees had been released, and everyone came excitedly to see what was going on. At first the people didn't want to believe that this was just play-acting; only the empty suitcases convinced them.

29 August

For a day it thoroughly spoilt my mood again. Last night a sergeant came into the hospital to conduct me to the authorities. The first thought in such a case is that of release, for what else would they want of one with the authorities! Sitting in the office was the adjutant, Lieutenant Johnson, who is now the ruler of the camp, deputising for the commandant, who is on holiday; a simple-minded, pedantic tyrant, with whom there is some conflict or other almost every day.

'What have you got in your face?' he shouted at me. 'An eczema', I replied, somewhat astonished at his rudeness. I still get my face powdered white every day.

He leafed through a file that lay in front of him and put on the expression of an investigating magistrate. 'Why have you complained about the Medical Officer?' I naturally thought about the recent scene, but how did he get to this question? 'I am not aware', I answered, 'that I have complained about anyone to anybody.' 'You have complained in a letter to your wife that you have been given unsuccessful medical treatment here. The censor has queried this letter.' 'If I have written to my wife that my treatment has been unsuccessful, that was directed not against the Medical Officer but against the doctor who has treated me, Dr. Löwenberg. And that was not a complaint, but an observation; I have been under treatment since July and you can see the results!'

'Who is Dr. Löwenberg? What has Dr. Löwenberg got to do with me? Dr. Macpherson, the Medical Officer, is there for your treatment. If you complain about your treatment it is directed against him.'

It's difficult to talk to a person who has got stuck into something idiotic and can't be got out of it. He just can't get it into his head that our comrades work in the hospital, that Dr. Macpherson has nothing whatsoever to do with the patients and merely signs release papers. But he began with the more harmless point, the heavy artillery was still to come

'What did you have to do with Paunzen? How did you know him?'

'Paunzen has been my friend for twenty years.'

'I may or may not believe that. How can you prove it?'

'I would certainly have no trouble proving it, if it were necessary.'

'Your letter contains a sentence that will get you into court for libel. You write that the post-mortem diagnosis after Paunzen's death has confirmed rampant consumption, and that you don't believe it. That is libel, do you know that?'

'I didn't know that a private letter can be libellous.'

'You do not write private letters. Every one of your letters is a public statement, since it goes to the censor.'

This idiocy was just too much for me. I explained to him that a letter that I write to my wife is a private letter, and remains so, whoever opens it and reads it *en route;* that I expressed a private opinion about a case on which I believe I have a right to have a private opinion, as I have known the man for twenty years; and lastly that I am of the opinion that the censor is there to censor, and if he doesn't approve of my statement he can hold back the letter, as he has actually done.

'You have no right to write lies.'

'I have not written lies, but my opinion.'

'This is a very serious case, and I shall pass it to the colonel.'

The colonel is the commandant of all the camps on the island. I don't know him, but I hope that he is more intelligent than his subordinate, and that the file will end up in the waste-paper basket, where it belongs. The adjutant then threw the letter over to me, my letter, that had been the subject of this whole hearing. I read it on my way home: the ass could have saved himself half the trouble if he had read it carefully! That the doctor who is treating me here and the Medical Officer are two different people is as clear as day from the context. And since Paunzen's wife is simply addressed as 'Nelly', the reader can hardly doubt that they are friends of ours.

You hardly ever know with Johnson whether his actions stem from nastiness or merely from stupidity and pedantry. Since he has been in charge here, the relations between the camp representatives and the authorities have entered a crisis stage. Hildebrand and Gross, both true models of patience, are seriously thinking of withdrawing co-operation. There have been events recently which have caused the greatest bitterness, and the man is getting worse and worse, nastier and nastier. I went straight away to my friends and told them about my adventure. They took the matter with just as little seriousness as I did. But it is unpleasant as a symptom, and Gross intends to discuss it with the gentlemen in the legal committee, as it is not the first case of this kind.

It is just a pity that one loses peace and one's nerves with such nonsense, when one has more important things to do.

30 August

Dr. Pick, our buffo bass, has on the whole proved his worth. He learnt his part easily and he is a great support on the stage with his experience. But unfortunately he is getting worse with every rehearsal, as he keeps laying on more and more nuances to his hamming, the more he gets to know his part. Höllering is often utterly unhappy about him.

All the musical things are ready, there will be nothing missing, but on stage there's something missing with each and every thing. A gifted artist, Paul Humpoletz,[42] has turned up, who has some theatre experience and can achieve extraordinary things with a minimum of material. But next to nothing is ready. Tomorrow we have a full rehearsal and two on Sunday, as was decided a long time ago. Two performances are planned, on Monday and Tuesday. But so far not even the first, for which the initial application was made, has been approved by the authorities. Given the strained atmosphere that prevails between the adjutant and the camp speakers, it is not at all certain yet that permission will be given.

My condition has got worse again, the strenuous rehearsals may be to blame for this. Rosenbusch, the house factotum, now only calls me D.U. (*dauernd unterwegs* – 'always on the move'). I have literally had to do everything myself, as there is no repetiteur, no chorus director, not even a copyist for the music. The only one in front of whom I really mustn't complain is Höllering, as he is in the same position on stage, if not worse. He doesn't even have a reasonably reliable stage-manager. How he will direct the two hundred people who are to appear on stage is still a mystery to me. And with amateurs, who are curious to see something and are always somewhere else than where one needs them! His main task is still to come, mine is basically done.

In three days we'll have got through it, then I shall be happy to be nursed back to health.

1 September

I have known all kinds of bad, unprepared, nervous dress rehearsals, but I've never come across anything like the one we had today on the day before the performance. We shall need nerves of steel tomorrow, Höllering and I, if we are to hold this bundle of scenes and musical items together. A postponement is impossible, we only have Monday and Tuesday (both evenings have been approved), and the Italians will come into the theatre on Wednesday to prepare their own kind of variety programme. So we have to continue through thick and thin, and if everyone is on the ball and we

---

[42] *Cf.* Appendix One: Personalia, pp. 192–93, below.

have a lot of luck, it might even work. Höllering has been changing things right until the last moment. A few more groups in the big parade in the last tableau will make it longer; that means, for the music, that I shall have to agree some handkerchief signals with my musicians to indicate whether a repeat will be played or omitted, as we have to end at exactly the same time as the stage. Neither of us was satisfied with the final scene with the double bed, and tomorrow morning we shall change the scene. There are also still all sorts of unresolved problems that we shall have to leave to the fortunes of tomorrow's performance. But I have seen one thing, that it could be a delightful evening, and that the apparent randomness of this sequence of scenes is very clearly and felicitously structured. The whole thing has a distinctive atmosphere of artistic nobility; there is something wholesome and genuine in this blend of naturalistic and primitively expressionistic theatrical style, as only happens when such a style arises naturally from the conditions and the circumstances, as is here the case. The only vulgar bit in it, the scene from the 'Little Coffee House' with the Wolf Band on the stage and the music that goes with it, likewise has its place and its higher justification in the overall effect. I was very much won over to the 'Little Coffee House' for a practical reason: I have, with Hildebrand and Gross, a separate table on the stage and we get coffee and cakes. That is a pleasant interlude in a strenuous performance.

The feared crisis has arrived, Gross and Hildebrand resigned yesterday. It didn't come to the threatened withdrawal of co-operation, as the adjutant eventually gave way. But the disagreement was of such a kind that the two of them did not think it advisable to continue their activity as representatives of the camp, as it has resulted in an official complaint to the authorities in charge. In any case they were both tired of their office and have merely been waiting for a pretext. Both have had to neglect their own concerns and interests completely for months, so now it's someone else's turn. The final point of conflict, which was the last straw, was an occurrence which in itself was no worse than many recent events. The adjutant had one of the people working in the postal service arrested and sentenced him to detention, because he took some letters addressed to himself and his friends out of a post bag. It had already been approved for distribution, but its contents had not been vetted owing to the lateness of the hour. The adjutant calls such a thing 'robbing His Majesty's mail' – in all seriousness. The protest by the camp leadership, coupled with the threat of immediate cessation of all co-operation, had the result that the man was freed again. But further to this, the Speakers requested an interview with the colonel, the commandant of the island, and in response to the demand to give advance notice in writing of the subject of the requested interview, Gross drafted a memorandum which was equivalent to a formal complaint and left nothing to be desired in terms of clarity and decisiveness. The interview will take place today, but the Camp Speakers have handed in their resignation independently of the outcome and proposed as Hildebrand's successor our friend Sugar. I am in no doubt that he is the right man. The immediate result of all these events was that the adjutant suddenly became quite tame and friendly, just as he also approved, quickly and without asking too many questions, our two theatrical performances. With people of his stamp there is often nothing else to do but occasionally show them one's teeth. Even so, I doubt whether, in the light of the conflict, we shall have any officers attending our performance. Hildebrand will, of course, still have to appear as Camp Speaker in the great parade, and that will give a nice opportunity for farewell ovations. Gross has been excused from appearing on the stage, as he is indispensable to me as a first violin in the orchestra. But otherwise everyone will come onto the stage who has been active as a dignitary in the camp, in the university and the hospital, the bank and the post office, the canteen, the legal office, as house-fathers – provided always that Höllering succeeds in getting all his people in place when he needs them. His main concern is meanwhile to take the necessary precautions so that, apart from the two prearranged intervals of five and ten minutes, everything runs without a break and no 'holes' occur. This is a significant consideration in view of the unusual form, with a rapid succession of varied tableaux. The necessary time for each change of scene is provided by the intermezzos and scenes in front of the curtain, but we will not be able to make the final arrangements until tomorrow, as the changing times have proved longer than we anticipated.

3 September

We had a happy evening. I knew we would the moment I climbed into the orchestra pit and saw the theatre buzzing full with an excited, curious crowd of spectators. We had had a busy morning's work, got the last scene into the right shape, checked and sorted out all scene changes, and wrote out a checklist to lay down the complete order of the scenes, the music together with its cues, the curtains, etc. This checklist was really the only fixed link that kept the stage and the orchestra together, as much of it had been rehearsed in a different form or another order, and therefore none of the players, either on the stage or in the orchestra, could know what was going on. But my musicians were fully alert and attentive, and I saw with pleasure that the dreadful state of my nerves, brought about by illness and sleeplessness, did not in any way hinder me in my music-making. I was as calm as usual, and everything worked as if it were not improvised and actually put together in the right order for the very first time, but had always been like that and all the participants were familiar with it. The result therefore had all the freshness and directness of an improvisation, but hardly any of its shortcomings, and the effect was commensurate with this. I was in doubt beforehand as to how our public would react to episodes which are outwardly funny but nevertheless set against the background of our own tragedy, our own sufferings and disappointments. Internees come out of their cage, into the illusion of freedom, into the theatre. The curtain rises, one sees a barbed-wire fence, *our* barbed wire, our cage. And *we ourselves,* people like us, enter, poor wretched internees with their little suitcases. Resounding laughter! Two refugees tell each other about their experiences, how they fled from Berlin to Vienna, Vienna to Prague, Warsaw, Amsterdam, Paris and London. 'Join the refugees, and you will see the world!' Resounding laughter! How fortunate that with tragi-comic things it is above all the latter component that the spectators are conscious of. This morning one of the patients in the house who was at the performance told me how pricelessly he had enjoyed himself, and how he then cried half the night because it was so dreadful. So there are such sensitive people, but they are rare. The whole thing was after all nothing more than a true picture book of our own lives, transfigured by some music, elevated by the stylisation and colourfulness of the stage. This slight distancing is sufficient to let one's own life, with all its tragedy, appear as a farce.

The acting on the stage was splendid, and everything went like clockwork. Höllering told me afterwards that he sweated blood in rounding up his little sheep, that there always had to be half a dozen 'runners' on hand to get the necessary people in place backstage and in the auditorium for the next scene. But it worked! Our audience was intelligent, no points were lost on them and at the end there was never-ending applause. For me the whole thing was a pleasure of the sort I have rarely had; the magical freshness and lightness of these stage improvisations, which had an effect as natural as a bunch of flowers, richly repaid me for my work.

Today I have had another pleasure: I have taken a bath. There is a water heater in the house but its use is dependent on a doctor's prescription. Apart from that, the patient has to carry his bath-water by the bucketful two floors up to the bathroom. I managed that without difficulty – thank God I'm not yet an invalid – and as far as permission is concerned, Dr. Löwenberg wrote me an exemplary prescription which ran as follows: 'Dr. Gál may, should and must have a bath'.

It was my first hot bath for three and a half months, and another example of how one can obtain unusual delights by prior abstinence.

6 September

Very miserable, sad and dispirited. I have had another relapse. There has been a repetition of the fit of madness that I had before I came into the hospital. I have scratched and ravaged, my head is as raw as in the worst period and my face is worse than ever. Dr. Löwenberg has again made a careful attempt with an ointment, which, however, has failed. It is hard to say whether it is the fault of the over-sensitivity of my skin or the irritability of my nerves. The sleeplessness is certainly the worst thing. No sleeping pill has any effect. Three hours sleep is the most that I can achieve in a night. I mostly sleep for an hour in the afternoon, if I'm not disturbed, which, however, often happens. The faithful Rosenbusch has painted a sign with the words 'Patient asleep, don't disturb', which is put on my door in the afternoon. Unfortunately no-one can see it, as the corridor is pitch-dark.

Dr. Löwenberg is now going too, he has been released. Then I shall be completely delivered into the hands of the bunglers here, who do admittedly always insist that they know nothing about skin conditions, but come every day with new, infallible prescriptions to hand. Many of the 'Medical Hardship' cases have already been released, I am waiting eagerly to be freed. But nothing is happening, and I keep wondering whether the application has really been made for me. The adjutant, the Medical Officer – terrible when one falls out with the most important people! Here in the hospital they were surely right to regard me as mad.

I should be working again but I have no desire to. There are a few new pieces to write for the revue. The second performance did not, in fact, take place, as it has been postponed indefinitely; but this postponement is being used for a complete revision. The cancellation of the second performance was the result of a miscalculation. We had considered beforehand that a repetition would be necessary, as there was not enough room for the whole of the camp in one performance. But there were around two hundred and fifty participants on stage, and as a result of the present leniency of the authorities, and the turning of various blind eyes, it was possible to get significantly more than the otherwise permitted thousand into the theatre. As a result the sales for the second performance were pitifully bad. A seat only costs threepence (we had to charge an entrance fee this time, because the performance had cost quite a lot of money), but in the camp even threepence is a significant amount, and there were not enough enthusiasts who wanted to come again to the second evening. But Höllering was quite cheerful about the idea of a postponement: we will, he thinks, do the performance in about two weeks' time and improve and refine all sorts of things in it. The possibility of experimenting again has given him new gusto for work. Where else does one have the opportunity for such experimental theatre? For years always working on films, he has, through this opportunity, acquired irresistible enthusiasm for the theatre again. He would like to produce a revue with me in London in a similar style, and already has all sorts of ideas for it. But, by cutting out incidental and filler scenes, he would like to get our camp revue into a definitive, unified form, which could really have documentary value, so to speak, as the artistic expression of our life in internment. If we perform the piece in this new form after two weeks, the whole camp will come again, and we can then even attempt to ask double the entrance money and dedicate the profits to the victims of air-raids. This idea made sense to all of us, because there has again been a small conflict, in the face of which we have seen a good opportunity here for a demonstration. A suggestion came from the commandant of the island that we, together with the Italians from the neighbouring camp, should arrange a performance for the local population, the proceeds of which would go to charitable causes. We were naturally gladly prepared to do this, and to take over half the programme (we intended to use the musical scenes from the revue), but with the proviso that the programme should contain the notice 'Refugees from Nazi Oppression'. We were of the opinion that this notice was necessary, because we must not put ourselves in the position vis-à-vis the public of being seen as 'enemy aliens', which the Italians actually are, and with whom we must on all counts avoid being confused. The commandant answered very ungraciously: he saw no reason to mix a charitable occasion with politics, and under these conditions would have to do without our contribution. We are not at all sorry about this. We have noticed time and again that nothing is so embarrassing and annoying for the gentlemen as the observation that we are not *'enemy aliens'* but *refugees*. It is all the more necessary to instil this fact into them at every conceivable opportunity. In order not to put ourselves in the wrong with regard to the accusation that we have brought politics into a charitable occasion, we answered the commandant's letter plainly and clearly, making our position very precise and restating our willingness to put on a concert for charitable causes.

As far as the new revue is concerned, I can't easily get enthusiastic about it. I am feeling too unwell. If my release had come before the first revue, I would not have hesitated for a moment in requesting to be permitted to remain until the performance. The matter so interested me, and I would not have wanted to endanger it at any price by my premature departure. Now I feel that I would hardly be prepared to make such a sacrifice any more. But others who are taking part in the performance also have doubts, if we are to wait another two weeks. Höllering himself has been summoned by his film company as a 'key man', the tenor who sings the

English songs has applied for the Pioneer Corps, Dr. Pick also doesn't want to continue, as the main festive days are approaching and he has all sorts of preparations to do. Under these circumstances it is difficult to make such long-term arrangements, and even more difficult to approach a matter with enthusiasm when one does not really believe that it will take place – and I *cannot* believe that I should have to put up with this condition for another fourteen days, and fourteen nights – the nights are the worst. But this Höllering won't take no for an answer, and when he is so crafty as to have a good idea, he always wins me round. Yesterday he brought one that I found fascinating. Humpoletz, our set-designer, has painted a brilliant poster, which has been used on our programme as a cover picture: a grotesquely caricatured ballad singer sits on a crate of porridge, playing a harp with strings made of barbed wire. The harp is in the shape of a W and forms the first letter of the title "What a Life'. He now wants to put this ballad singer with the barbed-wire harp on stage in front of the drop curtain. He is to tell the story of our adventures and our imprisonment in several instalments in the manner of a street ballad, thereby replacing all the previous stopgaps that we used to fill the pauses during the scene-changes, and providing a kind of frame for the whole loose form. Wonderful! But who is to write it? Well, someone will be found. And who should play the ballad singer? He already has the person and is absolutely sure of his choice. I was at first surprised and then immediately convinced that he had chosen rightly. An actor called Baum took part in the revue. He had been at various provincial German theatres, seems never to have had a notable status and I could never stand him when I occasionally heard him recite, with his exaggerated emphases and wild gesticulations. That Höllering let him appear in the revue was an act of human kindness for which I gave him great credit, for he did it consciously, even to the detriment of the effect. Baum was one of the group in the Variety Evening that had originally been planned, and had prepared for it a scene in English from 'Macbeth'. He so implored Höllering not to take his number away from him that the latter gave way and found a solution by building him into a scene as Baum, the mad actor who has a rehearsal for himself. It was rather embarrassing, and we were often asked the question why this nonsense had not been cut; but the man saw his dream fulfilled of once more in his life standing on stage, and a few kind people even applauded. In the position in which we find ourselves here, to be able to make a man happy was worth a spoilt scene, thought Höllering. Now, in spite of the wild exaggeration of his acting, Höllering had found all kinds of qualities in Baum that were quite clear to me too; he is a good, technically irreproachable speaker, and he has the security gained from years of practice on the stage. He would be usable raw

Paul Humpoletz's poster
for What a Life!

material in the hands of a good director who knows how and for what he can use him. 'He will do it excellently', says Höllering, 'if I just sit him down with his barbed-wire harp in such a way that he can't move and can't play the fool. He is only allowed to speak, nothing more. And if he is given such a task in his present situation, we shall get the best out of him of which he is at all capable.' It is a magnificent idea! He will, of course, not sing, but only speak, and only intone now and then, if need be, like the ballad-singers do. He must be given a very strong, flexible tune that is so objective that it will adapt to any expression, and distinctive enough not to become boring even after fifty verses....

In short, the devil has got me by the collar again.

But now what about the poem? Hutter, the author of most of the songs in the revue, who occasionally has nice ideas, has experience and can be quite witty, was already released before the performance. There is no-one here who is really a professional. I think of Deutsch, who looks as though he might have written poetry in his youth. He is very skilled as a writer and has helped us with a lot of things, for example, he provided the first, German part of the *black-out song*. Höllering got hold of him straightaway;

he likes the idea and he will give it a try. As for the content, for the time being we three have three different opinions. But Deutsch will first deliver a sample.

7 September

I won't have to put in such a crazy amount of effort this time, since my music is, after all, ready, the musical scenes will remain and there will just be a few extra pieces to compose. But I am nevertheless in the midst of work once more.

I have implemented an idea that an admirer gave me through an undeserved compliment. One tableau in the revue is called 'The Camp Conservatory', and illustrates the opinion of many that music has become a major nuisance for us in the camp. Musicians – a violinist, a cellist, a pianist, a flautist, a clarinettist, a singer – sit on an architectural construction made of blocks and blow, fiddle, play and sing wildly and indiscriminately, until a peaceful newspaper-reader, sitting in their midst, leaves the uncomfortable scene with every sign of desperation. The scene presents a rather constructivist summary of what happens here every day. As we were standing together in front of the orchestra after the performance, an elderly gentleman came up to me, shook my hand and said: 'Your music is beautiful and interesting. And you know what I liked best? This conservatory scene, where they all play so beautifully mixed up together'. We laughed heartily at this, that someone took this pandemonium to be music. But the man put an idea into my head: why should one not actually compose the scene? Everyone plays something different, but together it can still make a piece of music. And so I have sketched a Quodlibet, in which the bass Pick is designated to provide the *cantus firmus*. He sings a very popular repertoire number, 'Auch ich war ein Jüngling mit lockigem Haar' from the good old 'Waffenschmied' by Lortzing,[43] and the instruments join in one by one with various well-known themes. The cello immediately gets hold of the popular second subject from the first movement of Schubert's 'Unfinished', the piccolo bleats the 'Tell' overture to it, the violin enters with the beginning of the G major sonata by Brahms,[44] the clarinet with Siegfried's horn call,[45] and the piano accompanies with the theme of the G major prelude by Chopin.[46] This continues with more and more thematic entanglements. There is a

---

[43] *Der Waffenschmied* ('The Armourer'), a three-act comic opera by Albert Lortzig (1801–51), premiered in 1846. Hans Stadler, the armourer of the title, sings 'Auch ich war ein Jüngling mit lockigem Haar' ('I, too, was a young man with curly hair') towards the end of the Third Act.

[44] That is, the First Violin Sonata, Op. 78.

[45] Siegfried's 'Long Call' occurs as an off-stage solo in the Second Act of Wagner's opera *Siegfried*.

[46] Op. 28, No. 3.

licentious moment when Beethoven's 'Fifth' comes right up against 'Dein ist mein ganzes Herz',[47] and as a pointed conclusion the piccolo bleats 'Du bist verrückt, mein Kind'.[48] Without letting himself be disturbed by all of this, the bass sings his 'Jüngling mit lockigem Haar', and all of this is neatly set and will sound splendid if it comes off; but it will take work.

9 September

Sugar has been elected Camp Speaker by an overwhelming majority. He always kept in the background, and even now didn't really want to put himself forward. But since his activity in the Registration Office he has been really quite popular, and also enjoys the confidence of the officers. What eventually won him over was an argument by Gross: 'I would like to know how it is to share a bed with the Camp Speaker'. Two Deputy Speakers were also elected, Dr. Fackenheim, up to now chairman of the legal committee, and Dr. von Simson,[49] one of the best and cleverest of the younger people in the camp. So now there is peace, and if anyone will know how to maintain it, then it's Sugar, who is an excellent diplomat.

The second revue will have to take place on the 16th, as the charity performance in which we will now not be taking part is fixed for the 19th, and the people need the theatre from the 17th. Every day, meanwhile, Höllering comes with a new scene, and if it goes on like this we shall again be pressed for time. I haven't yet seen anything of all the new splendours, but he tells me about them every day. He has found an artist in cardboard, and there will be concealed figures in the big procession and in various scenes, which are giving him a lot of fun. I have composed the barbed-wire ballad and think quite something of it, but I had to do it without the poem, and Deutsch will have to write his poem to my music. What he produced at first was unusable, not only in its content but also in its form and tone. Through my music I have now tied him down to a fixed form and rhythm – a long, ten-line stanza – and he is sighing over the difficulty of the task, but he has unshakable patience and works with obstinate zeal. I am sure that the form will give him no trouble once he has sweated through a few verses.

---

[47] Sung in English as 'You are my heart's delight', it is an aria from Franz Lehár's 1929 operetta *Das Land des Lächelns* ('The Land of Smiles') and was popularised by the tenor Richard Tauber, who made it a staple of his recitals.

[48] 'You are crazy, my child', sung to music from the 1876 operetta *Fatinitza* by Franz von Suppé (1819–95). In *Fatinitza* it is an untexted march; the words were added at some point between 1876 and 1906 (when the text is first recorded, in Adolph Stoltze's novella *Weltstadtbilder*) and 'Du bist verrückt' became a popular song. The implicit continuation of the song – 'Du musst nach Berlin / Wo die Verrückten sind, / Da gehörst du hin' ('You have to go to Berlin / Where the crazy people are / That's where you must go') – must have had an especial resonance for Gál's particular audience.

[49] *Cf.* Appendix One: Personalia, p. 195, below.

Where we have difficulty in agreeing is that he can't be got away from a tone of lamentation and accusation – and what I want is cool, objective statement, without lament, without complaint. The crueller and colder the observations, the greater their effect will be. Since the singer will speak in the rhythm, the form of the verse must be strictly observed, though the speaker will still have enough freedom so as not to be impeded in his expression. But whether Baum will learn that in a week? I am naturally leaning hard on Deutsch, as otherwise poor Baum has no chance of doing it, however hard he works.

Since the revue I have again kept to my room almost continuously, my condition is worse than ever. At the insistence of my two partners, the violinist Hans Meyer and the cellist Dr. Ball, I had announced a trio-evening and we had two rehearsals last week. We played Beethoven's 'Ghost' Trio and the Schubert E flat Trio, and with the two extremely enthusiastic and musical players it was a pleasure. We would have had no trouble getting the programme ready in one more rehearsal, but I have cancelled the event. It was not my blindness – I have already got used to that, being without glasses for weeks, and when I know the music half by heart the mere appearance of the music is enough – but playing these beloved pieces excited me too much emotionally, and I now shun all avoidable exertion. The sleeplessness continues, my face and head are in a desperate state, and it has now also spread to my back and arms. Dr. Löwenberg has left. I continue to apply my chalk white-wash, but without much conviction.

My friends are infinitely kind and solicitous. Dr. Blumenau comes to me whenever he is in the house, always with something kind, a small culinary treat, a newspaper. Gross comes every day. He is now a free man and is as happy as a king. You have to see him, walking along the promenade, with shining eyes, like a schoolboy on holiday! He is hoping to be released soon, his semester begins in a few weeks and the university in Edinburgh has taken all necessary steps to get him back in time. Sugar has become, though not a rare guest, certainly one in a hurry. Now the worries of state rest upon his shoulders, and you can tell by looking at him.

12 September

As expected, we have had to postpone the revue, having everything ready by Monday was unthinkable. As we have to wait until after the charity concert on the 19th before we can get onto the stage again, and Friday and Saturday are out of the question on account of the orthodox Jews, the next available date is the 23rd. So we would have plenty of time. But am I really going to have to stay here that long? I had a desperate night again yesterday with outbreaks of scratching, my face is swollen and horrible. I have emphatically explained to the head doctor in the hospital that something must be done, that the Medical Officer must, as has already happened in many serious cases, make an urgent request for immediate release. Sugar was here and has promised his help. As Camp Speaker and a doctor he now has overall charge of the medical service, in so far as it is independent of the Medical Officer, and that gives him a certain authority even with the latter. He prevented me from going to the Medical Officer again – after the scene last time he doesn't trust me – and I naturally prefer that he should get him to understand rather than me. The man has a tactic that makes you despair: he listens in a friendly and attentive way without replying, and if you press him he will say: 'Well, I shall see what can be done'. And then he does nothing, because the matter doesn't interest him in the slightest. Now a visit is expected tomorrow from the Bishop of Chichester, the ardent advocate of the internees, who had already visited us in July.[50] It was due to his interventions that our post, which had been building up for weeks with the censor in Liverpool, was finally released. Sugar will press my case on him for his urgent intervention, along with those of several others

15 September

I have got a new doctor, a youngish German dermatologist who arrived in the camp only a few weeks ago. He is called Dr. D'Amian; to judge from his name he is from a French immigrant family, and he comes from western Germany. In recent years he has been active in leprosy research in Cameroon. He makes a very intelligent impression, has that certain penetrating doctor's eye and is a remarkably monosyllabic, reserved person. Sugar had some trouble persuading him to see me; he seems to have no desire at all to involve himself with the medical service here. Since he looks completely 'Aryan', was working in Germany until 1937 and then moved to the former German colony, one can draw the obvious conclusion. But I like him, I immediately had contact with him and I have confidence that he can help me. To begin with he wants to start a damp treatment, boric acid compresses. My eyelids, swollen for weeks, are now so thick that I always need some time in the morning before I can get my eyes open. He expects the compresses to bring relief for this, but in general thinks that the wait-and-see approach must be replaced by a more energetic treatment, with the risk that there may be failures. Above all, the scabs, which have become thick and horrible again, must be removed in order to make any further treatment effective. He will come again tomorrow with everything necessary.

---

[50] *Cf.* also p. 94, above.

Deutsch is working at high pressure on his barbed-wire ballad. When he brings four verses, three are rejected and the fourth reshaped. But he doesn't get disheartened, keeps having new ideas and eventually manages what I want of him. The first group of four verses is now complete and it is extremely powerful. We tried it out with Baum, including the music. He does it excellently, and the effect is extraordinary. The fourth verse is about the leaders of the Third Reich. Höllering has had a series of life-size, terribly bloodthirsty caricatures painted, which will file past behind the ballad singer. That is just at the limits of good taste, but such things are excusable under the circumstances.

The ballad singer will come on three times, with four verses each time. The second entrance wasn't ready yet yesterday, but the content is clear and it will not cause much trouble. As I foresaw, Deutsch is already moving quite easily in the form imposed on him.

Meanwhile, Höllering is working on another scene, which is very close to his heart. It has broadened out into something altogether serious and demands a largish piece of music. Professor Elias, the sociologist, who, it now appears, also has a literary side to him, came with a very unusual and extremely interesting work, half in prose, half in verse, which is to be performed with music and illustrated with some kind of living pictures, 'The Ballad of Poor Jacob'. The Youth Group are to do this. I fought tooth and nail against any demand for a melodrama, as I basically hate the genre. But I was half won-over when I saw the first pages of the poem (which is extensive and will take at least a quarter of an hour), and I believe I have found the form which avoids everything that I find intolerable about melodrama. The music will start whenever the prose turns to verse, and will then accompany periodically recurring episodes with similarly recurring, clearly structured, formally complete intermezzi. The Ballad of Poor Jacob is the story of the Eternal Jew of today.[51] He has grown up among strangers, has always been beaten when his foster parents have fallen out with each other, and he is always and everywhere the innocent victim when others are involved in conflict. So he wanders through life, driven from one country to another, homeless, until he recognises that his home is humanity and has learnt to view his enemies without bitterness, as they too are after all poor, hounded people like himself. 'And if they haven't killed him, then still today he goes without money on his way.' Only parts of this poem are ready, Elias is still polishing the rest. There is a gifted boy here who will recite it, and Höllering will put group scenes, shadow back-drops and God knows what to it. I feared above all that the whole thing would not fit in on

---

[51] *Cf.* pp. 203–14, below.

account of its serious nature, but Höllering is unconcerned on this score. I suspect that the experiment as such is now of more interest to him than the overall effect.

Dr. Pick, the bass, must be replaced. He no longer wishes to go on stage. The great Jewish festivals are approaching, the liberal congregation to which he belongs is in any case at odds with the zealous orthodox one, and he seems to fear that he could lose dignity if he were to appear as a buffoon on the stage. Buffo and cantor are admittedly occupations that are hard to combine. Incidentally, I have learnt a detail about him that has inspired still more respect in me for his versatility. He is the chairman and chief priest of a Buddhist community that holds a devotional meeting every Sunday afternoon. The member of this community to whom I owe this information has assured me that he draws consolation and strength throughout the week from the wisdom which Dr. Pick dispenses to them. How varied in shape and form is our spiritual life!

I had already thought of Karg-Bebenburg before. Now he is really more or less the only one who could be seriously considered. He has agreed, and I am pleased about that, as I would have preferred him for it from the beginning. His ambition as a postal worker has now somewhat cooled, and the first revue whetted his appetite. He, too, is admittedly a candidate for the Pioneers, a sudden call-up can come any day and it would put us in an embarrassing situation. But this is a risk he shares with Rosen, the 'English' singer, and I, too, thank God, am in danger of recall. We must therefore take this eventuality into account. For the time being it is merely rehearsing that is a problem for him. We must find a repetiteur, as this time I can't take it on myself as I could the first time. I am glad if I can drag myself to the most important rehearsals that absolutely must take place. We shall see if we can get the young Weiss, who is willing and a good musician, to do it.

I have revised my original manuscript, which was a barely legible sketch, as best I could, and now everything is more or less written down. I would like to instruct Reizenstein as my successor to be prepared for any contingency. Some pieces, such as the overture, are sketched out as little more than notes to jog the memory. I then wrote out the parts straight away, and since I know what's in it I didn't need a score. It would be an imposition to expect someone else to find his way in something like that. Reizenstein is the only one here who could possibly do it. He has accepted in principle, but he hasn't yet seen my music, and I *can't* make a fair copy right now, neither the time nor my eyes will suffice.

There is, incidentally, a storm among the artists which Reizenstein and Baron have provoked. The object of their hatred is O. E. Deutsch, who crossed their path with the Blumen concert and who didn't bring about their own promised evening in the theatre. I have always warned Deutsch against luring people with promises when they are dissatisfied. It is an established means of getting peace for the moment but a sure way to difficulties later on. Reizenstein and Baron have now called a meeting of all 'artists', musicians as well as amateurs, all those whom they assume to be unhappy with the Arts Committee, and of these there are many. Some feel undervalued and underemployed, others grumble because they don't get enough time to practise the piano or have not been allocated the best instruments, another is puffed up with feelings of bitter resentment because he once didn't receive a complimentary ticket for a concert, and some, unfortunately, really do have reason to protest, as Deutsch has made promises to them that he can't keep. All this is directed against him, as he has represented the Arts Committee almost single-handedly during the last few weeks. I would expect to be able to deal with this storm in a teacup in the most amicable way, as I am on the best of terms with all these people and have the impression that they trust me. But to attend meetings now, listen to nonsense being talked, to talk myself and God knows what? No, they will have to sort it out without me.

Today there is a nice *bon mot* circulating in the camp: 'Nazi from Refugee Oppression'.

20 September

I have spent several days in bed, almost continuously, as I am half-blind. In front of my eyes there are thick swellings, which in the course of the day just now and again let in a little light. Then I do what I can't quite do without my eyes – keep writing 'Poor Jacob' – but otherwise I lie down with compresses on my face. As the direct result of my new treatment this is not exactly encouraging, but Dr. D'Amian sticks with it persistently and so I continually make my compresses, whereupon the oedema around my eyes has simply got bigger. Since the departure of Dr. Löwenberg, Dr. D'Amian has, after initial resistance, taken over the vacant dermatological clinic, and seems to be very successful. The numbers are greater than ever, and he has succeeded in building up, in place of the three bowls and bottles that his predecessor had to make do with, a whole arsenal of medical aids of all kinds. Always serious, always taciturn, he is one of those people about whom nobody knows anything, even remotely; but no one doubts that he is a good doctor.

Our performance is fixed for next Monday, but I don't believe it. We were held up in the end by my illness as well, although I twice went to rehearsals that were urgently required. We had to finish off the barbed-wire ballad with orchestra, and 'Poor Jacob' needed an ensemble rehearsal as there are various speaking choruses. A conductor with a compress over his eyes could be a novelty! But Dr. D'Amian insists that I must always keep my face moist with boric acid lotion, and since I couldn't open my eyes anyway, it amounted to the same thing. I have my music in my head, so it wasn't really a problem. Höllering reproached himself bitterly after the first rehearsal for being so barbaric as to drag someone to a rehearsal in such a condition, but when the necessity came yesterday finally to put 'Poor Jacob' on the stage, he reproached himself again and was barbaric again – and I must say that I didn't find it anything like as bad as he did. It least it passes the time and one doesn't feel quite so utterly wretched and useless. I've been alone a lot during the last few days, and didn't tolerate it well at all, with the necessity of lying still and doing nothing. The daily production meetings naturally took place in my room, and were always welcome as a pleasant change. Barbed-wire ballad and 'Poor Jacob' came a bit at a time, were read out, discussed, changed, and I have not yet let my friends down. The ballad is now ready and, I think, extremely successful. I had particular pleasure in seeing with what enthusiasm Deutsch dedicated himself to what was to him at first an alien task, and how perfectly we two fools, Höllering and I, succeeded in making him into a third one, one who works with the same absolute dedication towards a goal which is mere make-believe and play, and which only by such dedication and such seriousness can be ennobled to that which we call art – and which is only then fascinating enough fully to repay any amount of trouble, quite independently of its success.

Dr. Ulrich, our colleague on the Arts Committee, floats more on the periphery of all these things. He is always there, interested in everything, but doesn't let himself be as well and truly drawn in as we have managed to do with Deutsch. He has one personal trait that amuses me: he seems to find it hard to utter anything other than in the form of an operatic quotation. If he comes to me about something at eight in the morning, while I am still washing, he says: 'What does the early hour matter to persons of rank?'[52] If some visitors knock while we are having an urgent conversation, he can't counter it other than with 'Hang it, this eternal knocking!'[53] If he lowers the curtain at the wrong time – Höllering has temporarily and experimentally employed him as stage-manager – he excuses himself with the words: 'Can an apprentice be perfect?'[54] Wherever

---

[52] 'Was tut die frühe Stunde unter Personen von Stand?' – uttered by Baron Ochs in Act I of Strauss' *Der Rosenkavalier*.
[53] 'Zum Henker, das ewige Klopfen!', as Jaquino complains in the opening scene of Beethoven's *Fidelio*.
[54] 'Kann ein Lehrbub vollkommen sein? – David to Hans Sachs in Act III of Wagner's *Die Meistersinger*.

you tap, out come such things, he must know the texts of the whole opera repertoire off by heart.

From today my eyes have become usable to the extent that the lids, though thick, can at least be raised. Dr. D'Amian now wants to start treating me with an ointment which he considers will promise success after this preparation. We have arranged ensemble rehearsals for tomorrow and the day after, and Höllering wants to leave till then the decision as to whether we can risk the performance on Monday. He has become impatient and nervous as not everything is going according to plan. Today I had to make peace between him and Deutsch. He tends to vent his annoyance on those who in his opinion are there to make sure that all the technical things work and the right people turn up to the rehearsals, and Deutsch was again the innocent victim. It turned out that the extras had to be almost completely re-rehearsed, as the people in the first performance had partly left and had partly landed up in some other activities which were more important to them. Höllering now had to recruit new people; his former assistant, a capable youth, has left, he has to keep an address book, replace new drop-outs every day, think of everything – and if he does forget something it was always the fault of Deutsch, who really does think of a lot but can't have everything in his head, and also has the rare talent of just being there precisely when a whipping-boy is needed. It's time we brought on our performance, as even Höllering with his robust nerves can't stand another week. For all kinds of reasons the latest possible date is next Thursday, the 26th, as Friday and Saturday are not possible. The authorities don't want Sunday, and the Jewish festivals already begin the following week.

There is already some critical impatience abroad in the camp; we have postponed too often. Now a hitherto unprecedented high price, 6d., has been set for entrance, because of the charitable cause. Most of the tickets have been sold. We have declared with a good conscience that two-thirds of the revue will be new, as actually only the beginning and the end have remained in their original form. Unfortunately that has, for our circumstances, incurred high costs. I fear that there will not be much left to show for the victims of air-raids if we leave Höllering a few more days' time for new inventions. He came again today as calm as you please with a new tableau, for which he quickly needs a song. The text has been provided by the 'English' singer, who is to sing it. The tableau depicts the daily morning exercises on our promenade, behind it is a view with open windows; at each one there stands a man, shaving, and one of them is the singer of the song. As that is a nice idea, I'm afraid I immediately composed it. It can't go on like this, three days before the performance!

Sugar has made another approach to the Medical Officer. My left ear is in a deplorable state, the whole outer ear septic and swollen, shapeless like an elephant's ear. He considers it to be harmless, as eczema, he says, never spreads to the inner ear. But because this is his area as a specialist, and since the Medical Officer doesn't necessarily know that, he made a fresh attack and explained to him that he could not be responsible for any middle-ear septicaemia that might occur and the attendant danger, and that there must either be immediate release or immediate transfer to a hospital on the mainland. After protracted haggling the M.O. said that he was prepared to check the regulations to see if such a transfer was possible.

Meanwhile I have the same battle every night for a modest bit of sleep, which does not want to come, and the eventual scratching when I do fall asleep. My arms, legs and back are now also covered with sores. As far as the itching is concerned, Dr. D'Amian disclaims competence. 'It isn't itching at all', he says, 'It's just your irritated nerves.' I never doubted this fact, but it doesn't console me.

Gross comes every day and reads me the newspaper, tells me the latest camp stories and is always sure that my release will come tomorrow. Over there in house No. 2 I am already like a stranger. Many people have gone and come since I arrived in the hospital, and recently I have only been there very occasionally, just when I urgently needed something from the things I have left there. My place in the room has remained free, I would rather go back today than tomorrow, but in my current state that would be too great an imposition on my room-mates, and although the doctors keep stressing that eczema is not infectious, it is understandable that one doesn't want anyone in the house who looks like a leper.

Dr. Lewin, too, the successful advocate of the 'Medical Hardships', was released last week. So far it has not been possible to replace him completely. Dr. Ball, the fortunate possessor of the only cello in the camp, is leaving tomorrow. We will hire an instrument cheaply in Douglas, and since there are two quite respectable players here, the departure will be replaceable in the revue orchestra.

22 September

My eyes appear to be gradually improving, although I always have trouble in the morning getting them open. Today in the ensemble rehearsal I still had to rely more on my ears than on my inadequate bit of vision. The rehearsal was scenically completely unsatisfactory, but above all it was disrupted by various incidents. At one point Karg-Bebenburg, at another Höllering himself, were summoned to the commandant's office for an hour, God knows for what reason, the sets are more or less incomplete, a large number of the actors were not there. Höllering accepted it with humour, and I think he was quite content, as he did want a postponement. We have now agreed on this, namely to Thursday. But there it must stay, that is really the last possible date.

I have not actually seen any of the new scenes ready; even 'Poor Jacob', whose extended final part I only finished yesterday, is still a torso on the stage. Professor Elias held us up for a long time because no final fair copy could be got out of him. He, too, has been overtaken by the fascination of the theatre, he is full of enthusiasm. We all found this work of literature – for such it is – enthralling, but I am still uncertain whether it will not rather be harmed through the trivialisation of set-designs.

For me personally this whole creative process, this direct involvement with and in amongst the realities of the stage, this improvisation, experimentation, the immediate confronting of the conceptual with the living manifestation, has been something incredibly stimulating and refreshing. Through it I feel as though I have once more come closer to the essence of things, and it has been exactly the same for my colleagues. For our comrades we shall be giving a lovely performance, a nice, stimulating evening of theatre. For ourselves it is certainly more than that.

The musical parts will work, I have no worries about that. The new cellist went about it as well as the new violist did (our earlier one is ill), and the additional compositions have been rehearsed well enough that there is nothing more to fear. The most trouble has been given by the conservatory scene, composed as a quodlibet. I still have to change a few things and I shall hold a special rehearsal for it tomorrow. This piece promises to be huge fun, but it is more complicated than the listener suspects.

Dr. D'Amian has commenced the second stage of his more aggressive treatment. The result is that my face is now painted brown instead of the plaster-white which the camp had already got nicely used to. He has applied a silver nitrate ointment and is convinced that it will produce an improvement in the weeping patches on my forehead and cheeks. Meanwhile the itching in these places has really almost stopped. He has admittedly not been able to remove the worst evil: the sleeplessness. For over a month, since those days around the middle of August when I first came into the hospital and still reacted positively to the sleeping pill given to me, I have not had a single normal night's sleep. How I have coped with it, during almost constant, strenuous mental work, is a puzzle even to me. A symptom that concerns me is that I have become insecure in my movements, and my hands shake. Where I am still completely unhindered is when making music. I have the feeling that music would come out wherever one bored into my brain.

As far as 'Poor Jacob' is concerned, I am now at least completely in agreement with the speaker. The main problem was the finale, a self-contained, flowing piece of music that provides an independent, completely peaceful, quiet background, but is nevertheless expressive enough to give an adequate accompaniment at heightened moments in the poem. The task here was a kind of synchronisation, a finishing-together at specific points, and that is now completely successful. Reizenstein had a rehearsal with the speaker this morning – he is now interested in the whole thing, as he might have to take over the direction – and didn't manage at all, merely because he is not sufficiently familiar with the text, and doesn't yet have the right 'eye' to judge the movement and end-point correctly.[55] It is a technique that is directly opposed to that of the accompanying background music of the melodrama. The impression today in the ensemble rehearsal was immensely powerful and direct.

23 September

A bad night, and today in a bad state for work. Höllering, the scoundrel, has taken me for a ride yet again. I had to provide him with a couple of new verses of text for an old song of mine, at least the sleepless night was good for that. I had been incautious enough to play this song to him (it is from *Hin und Her*[56]), and he immediately declared that he needed it, with three or four new verses, for Karg-Bebenburg in one of his new scenes. I was unyielding: 'I'm not doing anything more.' 'I bet you'll do it.' 'And I bet I won't.' And we betted, with me quite serious and almost angry. 'If you deliver the song, I shall leave "Homeless" out completely.' 'You've won', I said, 'you'll get your song.' 'Homeless' is a song by Kurt Wolf, the man from the 'Little Coffee House', dripping with sentimentality, and a favourite with our English-singing tenor. None of us liked it, and I'm almost sure that Höllering had in any case intended to leave it out. Now he has offered it to me as bait! Afterwards we all had a good laugh over the fact that everyone can somehow be bought; one just has to name the right price.

---

[55] As the composer of four operas, of course, Gál was familiar with questions of dramatic pacing.
[56] Gál wrote the score to Ödön von Horvath's farce *Hin und Her* in 1933; it was first performed in the Schauspielhaus in Zurich in December 1934, conducted by Gál himself.

24 September

Every day for weeks one yearns for it to happen. And now it has happened, this unimaginable happiness – and it puts one in an embarrassing position.

As I was coming back from the post office with a telegram from my wife saying that a new, urgent application had been made on my behalf, Sugar rushed up to me. 'You have been released', he whispered breathlessly to me, 'You'll leave on Thursday. But don't tell anyone yet, it's not official. I have only seen your name on a list that has arrived.' I was so shattered that I didn't utter a word. He embraced me and went off.

I was still sitting on my bed as if numbed when Höllering arrived. I naturally had to tell him – I am to leave on Thursday! And the revue is on Thursday evening!

I was quite touched by Höllering's joy. 'The devil take the revue! The main thing is that you will at last get away from here!' But he is not quite serious about his devil-take-it wish, and nor am I. I explained to him that I am prepared to stay a day longer if that can be arranged. But I only know that there will be bureaucratic procedures; every postponement creates inconvenience and one prefers to reject anything that creates inconvenience. But he will immediately talk to Sugar and if need be go to the commandant.

I didn't really believe in this possibility and got Reizenstein to come to me. We took my rough manuscript and I explained everything to him for an hour. He is now prepared to take over the business if he can have tomorrow's dress rehearsal and if necessary another rehearsal on Thursday for it. If I leave on Thursday, I shall sit with him on Wednesday at the dress rehearsal and help out as much as I can. The rest must be left to his talent, and I think he will manage it.

While he was still with me the official notification arrived: I am to be ready to leave on Thursday morning.

But it turned out differently. Sugar has spoken to the commandant, arguing that the performance would be in question without me, that the charitable purpose must be taken into consideration as the whole camp has a deep interest in it. The commandant, Major Francis, who has been back here since last week, and, though no cleverer, is at least much more pleasant than his prickly adjutant, found it 'very sporting' of me and has approved my staying here until Friday, provided that I make the request myself. I immediately wrote the application, the matter is thereby settled.

Three more nights! As for the days, I really do have plenty to keep me busy, they will be filled up. In the meantime I have had hundreds of congratulatory visits and don't know whether I'm coming or going.

Karg-Bebenburg is also going on Friday. He has received his call-up papers for the pioneers and has to go to his company immediately, with no delay. But his wife will be waiting for him by the ship for the crossing to Liverpool. He will at least be able to be with her for those few hours!

And it is an extra bonus that he will be on the stage for his farewell to internment.

26 September

My release has caused a sensation, and still more so because I am staying a day longer on account of the performance. Following this, the last few hundred tickets have been sold, we are sold out again today. Endless congratulatory visits.

Last night, following the dress rehearsal for the revue, we had a small intimate farewell party in house No. 2, in our room, with just some of our best friends. It was rather melancholy. If one could only take one's friends with one! Gross hopes that he will soon follow me. Sugar's application has recently been turned down. He is a good illustration of one of the stupidest and most unjust conditions of the white paper. Foreign doctors who have studied here in this country and are still in the process of studying are to be released. Sugar was unfortunately one of the most hard-working, he had already completed his studies and obtained his British doctor's qualification. As a result the above condition does not apply to him and he must remain interned, in other words he must be properly punished for not having idled about for longer during his studies.

Our dress rehearsal was as we have now more or less got used to a dress rehearsal being. It looked like the first rehearsal might just about look at a good theatre: nothing ready, various sets still unfinished, missing participants, all the scenes in the wrong order, according to which of the performers happened to be there. Again several scenes had to be left out altogether because there was no time for them, and none of the participants has even the vaguest idea of the whole picture. Höllering continued rehearsing today undeterred, but my contribution was limited to a stage rehearsal of 'Poor Jacob', which also had short shrift yesterday. A checklist had to serve again, fixing the final order, curtains, gongs, etc. But this afternoon, when, following this checklist, I had drawn up a memo for my orchestral musicians and sent it to be duplicated, Höllering came with a new one; he has changed everything around again, moved scenes round, put in two new compères (the two very usable young men who appeared in the first revue are no longer here), and now everything has been turned on its head again. God knows what's going to happen! I have an even less clear conception of the whole sequence of events than at the first performance.

If that was risky, this is ten times more so. I have refused to let myself get nervous, and have merely asked Höllering, in case he intends to change things again and draw up a third plan, to let me know at least five minutes before the start of the performance, so that I know whether to start with the overture or the finale.

I am rather eager to hear the three more substantial pieces which have been added to my music in the new version: the Barbed-Wire ballad, Quodlibet and Poor Jacob. I am most sure of the ballad, it was incredibly effective at the main rehearsal. Baum, the reciter, is splendid, and the unusual nature of his whole appearance, the unity of style and execution, the general accessibility and vividness of the whole piece succeed in making it a hit of a kind that is rarely found. The effect of the Quodlibet is for natural reasons restricted to those with some musical culture; anyone who doesn't know the quoted music will miss the point. It aroused enthusiasm at yesterday's rehearsal. Dr. von Simson, Deputy Camp-Speaker, who is a very decent amateur musician and 'connoisseur', explained the effect in the following way: every musically experienced listener believes that he alone fully understands the whole joke. I am the least sure of Poor Jacob. The speaker is not bad, but colourless and dry, and the whole thing is too long and demanding for his capabilities; that is also probably the case with the majority of our audience. Something as serious and substantial is perhaps in principle out of place in this setting, but certainly only accessible at all to people of culture and taste, and they are in a minority among us as everywhere else. Karg-Bebenburg has learnt his new song as quickly as he did all the previous ones, but he is overall still insecure in his text, and that hampers him somewhat. Compared with Dr. Pick he is weaker as far as the direct comic effect is concerned, as that doesn't suit him. But his voice always sounds pleasant and he makes a fine, sensitive and warm impression. Tomorrow morning we shall leave here together!

I have packed and made a few farewell visits, much fewer that I should have. Tomorrow I must be at the gate at seven o'clock. I hope my friends will still be sleeping. I don't at all feel up to a farewell scene in public.

27 September, on the crossing to Liverpool

The outline of the Isle of Man is blurred in the haze. The sea is rough, the ship is rolling evenly from one side to the other; some people are already sea-sick, half an hour after leaving.

I have the feeling that I have become years older since we crossed over there on a wonderful, sunny day in June. Perhaps it is merely the physical weakness that is making itself felt, after the inner high pressure of the last few days which made me forget it?

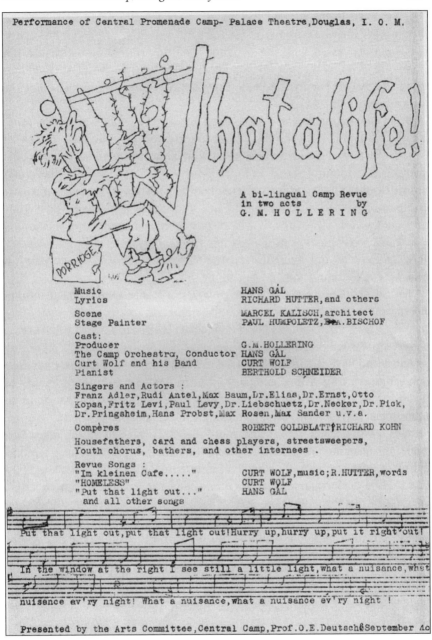

The cyclostyled programme for What a Life!

I lay down in the lounge and stayed there for almost an hour without moving. Next to me is a mirror. It shows me a strange, unpleasant face; one eye is almost closed with the swelling, the other one looks through a slit. I can only see this if I pull my head back to look through this slit. My face and forehead are besprinkled with brown spots. They've certainly made me look a pretty sight there!

But I am happier than I have been for a long time; I am even more happy about this last evening, which rounded off the whole adventure so beautifully and so gladdened my heart, than about being freed. I haven't yet succeeded in looking ahead, in looking forward to my regained freedom; I am still looking backwards to where my dear friends are, the many intimate companions who will continue to live and suffer in Douglas Bay. They arranged a farewell for me that I can't easily forget. But I have the feeling that I was a bad partner in the last few weeks: they were always the givers, they looked after me, helped me, cared for me, and I could do nothing but take and be grateful for it.

The beautiful moments of last night's performance keep going around in my thoughts. They didn't let me sleep last night and are still unwilling to leave me. We again had fabulous good luck; apart from some small hitches that the spectators will hardly have noticed, the performance went as smoothly as one could have wished. This time the whole staff were present, including some officers from other camps, and I think that we brought plenty of honour to Central Camp. If I compare it with the first performance, as an attentive and critical witness, I find that the effect of the first performance, seen as a whole, was fresher and more direct. It still had all the attraction of being spontaneous and the blessing that the most fortuitous groupings came out as successfully effective moments. The technical aspects of yesterday's performance were incomparably more refined, but precisely because of this the gaps and deficiencies were more noticeable. These were admittedly compensated for by moments of deeper, more original effect, which had after all taken up most of our efforts this time. The high point was – I hadn't doubted that it would be – the ballad with the barbed-wire harp. And one person certainly had an experience yesterday that he had never had before: poor Baum, who had never been so fêted in his life. His achievement was truly extraordinary, he rose above himself in a way that even the greatest optimist could not have expected. How marvellous such a Cinderella-experience must be! And how wonderful when a director is able to achieve this Cinderella transformation!

'Poor Jacob' was scenically not ready and therefore thrown back still more on its inner effect; but this was more powerful than expected, and the finale was profoundly moving. What I hardly expected was the

197

Geschlafen habe ich wenig, nach all dem. Um sechs Uhr morgens
weckte mich der getreue Rosenbusch, und ehe ich noch mit dem Zu-
sammenrichten meiner Sachen fertig war, kamen Höllering und Deutsch,
um zu helfen und mich zeitgerecht mobil zu machen. Beim Gate war
schon ein Auflauf, trotz der frühen Stunde. Etwa zwei Dutzend wurden
zusammen mit mir entlassen, alle Freunde waren noch einmal da zu
einem letzten Händeschütteln und Glückwünschen. Sugar stand oben
bei seinem Fenster und winkte herunter; zeitig aufstehen haßt er;
aber heute ist er doch früher als sonst aus dem Bett gegangen, und
eine Viertelstunde später, als wir schon draußen, außerhalb des
Stacheldrahtbezirks, vor dem Kommandogebäude warteten, kam er mir
nach zu einem letzten Händedruck. Weiß Gott, wie ich das gemacht
habe, aber es ging ganz ohne Tränen. Dann kam der Autobus und wir
fuhren los, hinunter zum Hafen.

Die Insel ist längst hinter dem Horizont verchwunden. "What a Life!"
Mach einen dicken Strich drunter, nun ist's vorbei.

Das Schiff rollt gleichmäßig auf und ab. Drüben steht Karg-
Bebenburg mit einer schlanken, jungen Frau, die er umfaßt hält.
Er ist glücklich.

Was wird Hänschen sagen, wenn sie mein Gesicht sieht?

'The island has long since disappeared below the horizon':
the last typescript page of Gál's diary

hurricane that broke loose after the conservatory scene. It was provoked by the compère, who used the occasion for a special improvisation, and announced this piece as my contrapuntal farewell to the camp. When, after the end of the performance, Dr. von Simson then came onto the stage and, after the usual words of thanks to all the participants, directed the applause to me, the one saying goodbye – the prop for this was an enormous bouquet of chrysanthemums evidently stolen from the garden of the Palace Hotel – I, with my spotted brown face and swollen eyes, had to submit to endless ovations.

After the performance there was a celebration in house 7, where Otto Erich Deutsch lives, with the usual speeches and replies. None of us said what we were really thinking: that through the community our life here had acquired a new, nobler meaning; that all of us, family men as well as single men, have discovered something new and beautiful; that there is something more universal and higher that transcends family and individual existence. We have replaced the book-keeping of civilised life, where giving and taking are always scrupulously calculated and balanced, by a new principle, according to which each one gives what he can and takes what is offered, without thinking about it, because it is taken for granted. And all of us have felt enriched by it, have enjoyed the warmth, the atmosphere of friendship and comradeship such as we have never known before.

I didn't sleep much after all this. The faithful Rosenbusch woke me at six in the morning, and, before I had finished getting my things together, Höllering and Deutsch came to help me and to get me mobile in time. There was quite a crowd at the gate, despite the early hour. Around two dozen people were being released with me, all the friends were there again for a last handshake and well-wishing. Gross was as tender as a brother. Sugar stood by his window and waved down to me, he hates getting up early; but today he got out of bed earlier than usual, and a quarter of an hour later, as we were waiting outside in front of the administrative building, beyond the barbed-wire zone, he came out to me for a last handshake. God knows how I managed it, but there were no tears at all. Then the bus came and we drove off, down to the harbour.

The island has long since disappeared below the horizon. 'What a Life!' Draw a thick line under it, it is over.

The ship is rolling evenly up and down. Over there stands Karg-Bebenburg with a slim young woman whom he is holding close to him. He is happy.

What will Hansi say when she sees my face?

Postlude

Gál in Britain

EVA FOX-GÁL

The biographical introduction[1] dealt largely with Gál's life before the Second World War – in all respects, his formative period. But 1938, marking his exile to Britain, where he was to remain until his death in 1987, more or less splits his life down the middle. He chose to stay in Britain and turned down the offer of a job in Vienna after the War, having finally obtained a permanent position as lecturer at the University of Edinburgh. More than half of his published works were composed in Britain; during the War years alone he produced his Second Symphony (the most substantial of his four numbered symphonies), his Concertino for Violin and String Orchestra, the Concerto for Cello and Orchestra, *A Pickwickian Overture* and *Lilliburlero* for orchestra (variations on the popular signature-tune of the BBC World Service), as well as numerous chamber, piano and choral works.

Astonishingly, Gál escaped the BBC ban on Austrian and German composers during the War and immediate post-War years, and there were frequent broadcasts, particularly by some of the conductors of the BBC orchestras, Guy Warrack, Ian Whyte and Trevor Harvey. *A Pickwickian Overture*, for instance, enjoyed eight broadcasts on British airwaves between 1940 and 1949.

Gál's own music-making in Britain began almost as soon as he came to Edinburgh in 1939, with a newly founded madrigal ensemble and refugee orchestra already underway before his internment. As a pianist he was extremely active as a performer in all manner of war-time charity concerts; he also participated, as pianist or composer, in a number of concerts in London, under the auspices of various political and cultural refugee organisations. A concert of the 'Council of Austrians in Great Britain' in February 1941 included the first public performance of the *Huyton Suite*, the trio composed during his internment in Huyton; and the piano suite from the music for *What a Life!*, the internment revue from the Isle of Man, was given a first public performance at the Austrian Centre, London, in May 1941, and subsequently in a concert of the 'Free German League

---

[1] *Cf.* pp. 13–24, above.

of Culture'. For a British-Austrian rally in London in March 1943, with the banner headline 'Five Years Hitler Over Austria – 1943 – Austria will be Free', Gál composed the music for an elaborate pageant, '"Immortal Austria": Highlights of Austria's History', written by Eva Priester and Erich Fried. In a programme of 'Austrian Music banned by the Nazis', presented by the Anglo-Austrian Music Society in the Wigmore Hall in June 1943, and including music by Berg, Grosz, Krenek, Mahler, Schoenberg and Wellesz, Gál's contribution was three of his *Four Madrigals on Elizabethan Poems* (the last of them by Queen Elizabeth I herself), composed in 1939, shortly after his arrival in Edinburgh, presumably for his new madrigal ensemble.

In Edinburgh, Gál was also a frequent performer at the weekly lunch-hour concerts at the National Gallery of Scotland, presenting programmes that included contemporary works by some of his compatriots banned by the Nazis as well as the classics of the 'core' repertoire – much of which would have been new to the Edinburgh audiences of the time. In a special 'Recital of Music Banned in Germany' in Edinburgh in March 1943, Gál included works by Mendelssohn, Mahler, Hindemith, Schubert and Schumann (songs set to poems by Heine), as well as his own Viola Sonata from 1942, adding a footnote to the programme:

> The 'Reichsmusikkammer' set up by Hitler as an institution for the supervision of musical life in Germany has thoroughly eliminated all music regarded as not in accordance with the Nazi creed. Thus not only has music by composers of Jewish descent been prohibited, but also music by 'Aryan' composers of a marked progressive attitude, such as Berg and Hindemith. The ban extends further to musical works written on subjects from the Old Testament, and therefore most oratorios by Handel are banned. Even many songs by as popular German masters as Schubert and Schumann because written on poems by Heine, the great German poet, who was of Jewish extraction, were eliminated from musical life in Nazi Germany.

During the war, as 'caretaker' of an evacuated school, he started a 'collegium musicum', a regular meeting of musicians who would rehearse a work, such as the 'Trout' Quintet, or a Bach motet; this work would then be presented to a small audience with an illustrated talk by Gál, followed by a full performance. Hanna's teas on these occasions, with her Austrian-style open sandwiches and cake (in spite of food rationing) were the stuff of legend.

As a much-loved teacher, performer and conductor, Gál influenced generations of musicians and music-lovers. His sphere of influence as a pedagogue was extensive. Not only was he a full-time lecturer in the Music Department at the University of Edinburgh from 1945 until his retirement

THE ANGLO-AUSTRIAN MUSIC SOCIETY

presents a programme of

AUSTRIAN MUSIC BANNED BY THE NAZIS

arranged by the

AUSTRIAN MUSICIANS GROUP

WIGMORE HALL

Wednesday, June 16th, 1943, at 7 p.m.

Programme

ADAGIO for Violín, Clarinet and Pianoforte - - - - - - *Berg*
MARIA LIDDKA, R. SAVAGE TEMPLE AND PETER STADLEN

SONGS "Rheinlegendchen"
"Um schlimme Kinder artig zu machen" } - - - - *Mahler*

From the Cycle "Africa Songs": - - - - - *Grosz*
"Elend"

From the Cycle "Liebeslieder":
"Aus dem Magyarischen"
"Aus Tunis"

From the Cycle "Reisebuch aus den oesterreichischen Alpen," Op. 62 - *Krenek*
"Friedhof im Gebirgsdorf"

Fiedellieder, Op. 64
ERIKA STORM
At the Piano: MOSCO CARNER

PIECES for Pianoforte, Op. 23 - - - - - - *Schoenberg*
PETER STADLEN

THREE POEMS by Angelus Silesius (translated by Hugh Ross)
for a Capella Choir for Four Voices *Wellesz*
"Where is my dwelling place?"
"Unfold, thou frozen Christian"
"Man, be from God reborn"

THREE MADRIGALS on Elizabethan Poems for a Capella Choir for Four Voices - *Gál*

"True Love" (*Sir Philip Sidney*, 1598)
"Cradle Song" (*Thomas Dekker*, 1603)
"Youth and Cupid" (*Queen Elizabeth*)

THE FLEET STREET CHOIR
Conductor: T. B. LAWRENCE

TICKETS: (Reserved) 10/-, 7/6, 5/-; (Unreserved) 2/6 and 1/6; from Wigmore Hall Box Office
(WEL. 2141) or Usual Agencies.

BAINES & SCARSBROOK LTD., PRINTERS, LONDON, N.W.6   [P.T.O.

Poster for Gál's 1943 Wigmore Hall concert of music banned by the Nazis

Gál with his daughter, Eva,
photographed outside their
Edinburgh flat in 1944

in 1955, continuing part-time for another ten years, but he also taught extra-mural classes, both in Edinburgh and further afield, and always had private pupils. Whether in Vienna, Mainz or Edinburgh, he had always involved himself in music-making in the local community. From the 1950s he conducted the Edinburgh Chamber Orchestra, an amateur string group, again introducing little-known repertoire. Soon after his internment he was a regular performer at the Edinburgh Society of Musicians, a venue that over four decades saw first performances of many of his own works. Indeed, he premièred his 24 Fugues for piano there in 1981, at the age of 91. For many years he was President of the Society of Musicians; he also served as President of the Edinburgh Society of Recorder Players from its foundation in 1957 until his death, and wrote a good deal of music for the instrument, particularly in the 1960s.

Furthermore, as a founder member of the Edinburgh International Festival in 1947 and committee member for decades, Gál had an inestimable influence, not least through his personal connection with its first director, Rudolf Bing, and with the great musicians, such as Bruno Walter, Furtwängler, Ernst von Dohnányi and Fritz Busch, who played such an important part in the early years of the Festival and gave it its truly international stature.

During the late 1940s and early 1950s his orchestral music was performed and broadcast in Britain principally by Rudolf Schwarz,

Gál was one of the co-founders of the Edinburgh Festival in 1947
and remained actively involved for over three decades;
here, in 1952, he stands between the baritone Horst Günter and contralto
Kathleen Ferrier on the left and the soprano Irmgard Seefried and tenor
Julius Patzak on the right – he and Clifford Curzon had just performed
the Brahms Liebeslieder *with these four singers.*

who had been his pupil in Vienna and was to perform all four of Gál's symphonies and every new orchestral work, including the Cello and Piano Concertos. In Germany, during roughly the same period, the conductor Otto Schmidtgen, a former student of Gál's from his time in Mainz, gave the first performance of the cantata *De Profundis* in Wiesbaden in 1948.[2] Schmidtgen was also instrumental in commissioning another major choral work, the 'symphonic cantata' *Lebenskreise*, which was premiered in Mainz in 1956. He continued to provide a platform for new Gál works in virtually every concert-season until his early death in 1964.

As a pianist Gál performed his own works, live and on radio, in Britain, in Vienna, in Mainz, until well into his eighties. But what he lacked was a major champion amongst post-War conductors and, indeed, instrumentalists, both in Britain and on the Continent. Moreover, as a result of the dislocations, both historical and geographical, of his life, his music was scattered amongst many different publishers, with immeasurable repercussions on the promotion, distribution and availability of his works.

---

[2] This large-scale choral work had been composed, with no prospect of performance, in Vienna in 1936–37, between expulsion from Nazi Germany and exile to Britain.

The poster for the premiere of Gál's cantata De Profundis *in Wiesbaden in 1948*

In spite of spending just over half of his life in Britain, his first language remained German, as did his musical language. What he communicated in his every utterance – not least in his music – were the enduring values that sustained him and the culture which he embodied. But post-War developments in contemporary music and the prevailing cultural climate, not only in Britain but internationally, became less and less tolerant of the Austro-German style and values in which Gál's music was so deeply rooted, and he became an increasingly marginal figure.

At the same time, in common with a number of other refugees from central Europe, Gál was valued and revered as a musicologist, and published a number of articles in music journals, especially in the 1940s and '50s, as well as his first book in English: *The Golden Age of Vienna,* which appeared in 1948 in a series[3] co-edited by Otto Erich Deutsch, fellow internee on the Isle of Man. Gál is probably most widely known, to this day, for his co-editing, with Eusebius Mandyczewski, of the complete works of Brahms and for his A*nleitung zum Partiturlesen*, published by the Philharmonischer Verlag in Vienna in 1923 (who also published an English edition, *Directions for Score-Reading*, a year later).[4] His monographs on Brahms, Wagner, Schubert and Verdi, all first published in Germany,[5] enjoyed considerable success, as did his *The Musician's World: Letters of Great Musicians*[6] and his edition of Brahms' letters.[7]

Recognition as a distinguished musician and scholar came on numerous occasions: from Edinburgh he received a doctorate in 1948, in appreciation of his entire *œuvre*; from Vienna the ceremonial renewal of his doctorate from the University of Vienna, on its 50th anniversary in 1963; from the University of Mainz an honorary doctorate in 1977; in 1964 an O.B.E. awarded by Her Majesty the Queen; and his native Austria honoured him with the Austrian State Prize for composition in 1958 and the 'grosses Ehrenkreuz, Litteris et Artibus', the highest medal of honour for services to the arts, in 1981. But despite these honours he never regained anything

---

[3] 'The World of Music', Max Parrish, London.

[4] It continued to be published even during the Third Reich, but under the name of Leschetizky and with the expurgation of 'non-Aryan' examples, such as Mahler.

[5] *Johannes Brahms. Werk und Persönlichkeit*, S. Fischer Verlag, Frankfurt am Main, 1961 (transl. Joseph Stein, *Brahms: His Work and Personality*, Alfred A. Knopf, New York, 1963); *Richard Wagner: Versuch einer Würdigung*, S. Fischer Verlag, Frankfurt am Main, 1963 (transl. Hans-Hubert Schönzeler, *Richard Wagner*, Gollancz, London, 1976/Stein & Day, New York, 1976); *Franz Schubert oder die Melodie*, S. Fischer Verlag, Frankfurt am Main, 1970 (transl.Hans Gál, *Franz Schubert and the Essence of Melody* , Gollancz, London, 1974/Crescendo Publishing, New York, 1977); *Giuseppi Verdi und die Oper*, S. Fischer Verlag, Frankfurt am Main, 1982.

[6] Thames and Hudson, London, 1965.

[7] *Brahms: Briefe*, S. Fischer Verlag, Frankfurt am Main, 1979.

Hans Gál photographed in 1962 by his former fellow internee, Ernst Blumenau, who had been his dentist in Mainz

approaching the position he had enjoyed before 1933 and, as a composer, he was largely forgotten, both in Britain and internationally. That ground is being regained only in the 21st century, with recordings of his orchestral, chamber and piano music that have at last put his music before the public once again.

Gál's personal life was also not without its traumas, above all the tragic loss of his two sons, both from suicide, in 1942 and in 1967. But unlike many of his fellow refugee composers, who all endured grievous loss and similar neglect, Gál never sank into depression and remained creatively active throughout his life. *Music behind Barbed Wire* gives some insight into the inner qualities that enabled his survival.

Appendix One
Personalia

A. Members of the Gál Family

EDITH (DITTA)– elder sister. Born in 1888, Edith stayed behind in Austria with her mother after the *Anschluss*, and in 1939 she and her mother left Vienna for Weimar to live with the latter's sister, the grand-ducal *Kammersängerin* Jenny Fleischer-Alt ('Tante Jenny'; 1863–1942), who had been a celebrated opera-singer under Richard Strauss at the Weimar Theatre before her marriage. But conditions under the Nazi regime became increasingly repressive and life-threatening, and Edith and her aunt took their own lives in April 1942, on the eve of their deportation to Auschwitz. Her mother, who was suffering from a heart condition, had died shortly before, following an accident.

ERNESTINE (ERNA) – younger sister. Born in 1899, Erna left Vienna for Norway in autumn 1938, following an invitation by the radical Austrian psychoanalyst Wilhelm Reich; prior to the invasion of Norway in 1940, she escaped to England with the help of A. S. Neill, a close friend of Wilhelm Reich and founder of Summerhill School, where she first taught music during the War and immediate post-War years, subsequently working as a répétiteur at Glyndebourne Opera. She was an excellent pianist and taught piano for most of her life. She lived in London, dying in October 1995 at the age of 96.

FRANZ – elder son. Born Vienna, 19 January 1923, the first child of Hans and Hanna Gál. In December 1929, when Gál took up his appointment as director of the Municipal Music College, the family moved to Mainz. Franz spent happy years in primary school, spoke the local Mainz dialect, was well integrated socially and a friend of the mayor's son. It came as a profound shock, therefore, when at the end of March 1933 Gál lost his director's post, which had just been renewed for a further three years, and in a short space of time lost all his civil rights; the Mayor had been dismissed from office on the same day. Subject to Hitler's racial laws, the family were reduced to the status of 'sub-humans', so that the children's previous schoolmates were no longer allowed to have dealings with them.

The return to Vienna in autumn 1933 was a difficult adjustment for all members of the family, and the school environment proved considerably harsher than it had been in the Rhineland. Franz was fifteen and his brother Peter thirteen, when, in March 1938, immediately after the *Anschluss*, their mother fled alone to London in order to find out whether the borders were open for her husband and the children. Gál followed a week later; the children could not follow until August.

At a college in London Franz studied towards the necessary qualifications for university entrance, but shortly after the start of the War the family moved to Edinburgh, where he took up an apprenticeship as a chemist in the laboratory of the City Analyst. In May 1940 he was interned and deported to Canada. From July 1941 until February 1944 he served in the Pioneer Corps and then in the British army until 1946. After that he was able to continue his chemistry studies as a student at the University of Edinburgh, where he was a member of the Student Representative Council. In July 1947 he acquired British nationality and naturalised his birth-name 'Franz Seraficus Gál' to the completely English 'Frank Paul Gall'.

Professionally he worked as an industrial chemist, mainly in the London area. He was a very talented photographer and had a lively interest in jazz. He remained a bachelor.

Franz Gál took his own life on 2 June 1967, at the age of 44.

HANNA, *née* Schick – wife. Born in Prague on 18 March 1902. Hanna's father, Alfred Schick, was director of the Steyr motor company and an influential industrialist, holding a number of honorary positions, including Vice-Presidency of the Styrian Steelworks, the Upper-Austrian Water Works and Electricity Works. Her mother, Margarethe Schick, *neé* Jerusalem, came from a highly cultured Prague Jewish family: her youngest brother was the philosopher and psychologist Wilhelm Jerusalem, a well-known professor at the University of Vienna and friend of Sigmund Freud; an ancestor was Karl Wilhelm Jerusalem (1747–72), whose suicide became notorious as the inspiration behind the depiction of suicide in Goethe's *Die Leiden des Jungen Werther*. Margarethe Schick was a keen painter and her house was frequented by artists and musicians, amongst them Hans Gál. Hanna, aged eighteen, kept him company while her mother was painting his portrait, and they became engaged soon after. They married in 1922 and had two sons, Franz and Peter, in 1923 and 1924, followed twenty years later by a daughter, Eva. It was a marriage that was to last 65 years.

Hanna studied at the *Akademie für soziale Verwaltung* (Academy for Social Administration) from 1919 to 1921 and obtained a diploma in *Jugendfürsorge* (youth social work). Interestingly, from November 1921 until February of the next year she had worked for a committee organising hospitality in England for children in need after the War (*Aktion Kinder nach England*). But by April 1922 she was married and turned her energies entirely to being a wife and mother. She took over all domestic responsibility and supported Hans with total devotion to the end of his life. It was she who first fled from Vienna in March 1938, leaving alone in order to test whether the borders were safe for Hans, who then followed a week later, but the boys could not join them until August.

Between the Wars she had trained as a speech therapist, so as to have some means of livelihood if circumstances should require it. By autumn 1938 she managed to get a work permit, enabling her to work as a speech therapist at a London clinic, but that job came to an end with the outbreak of war in 1939. She then acted as housekeeper for Sir Herbert Grierson (*q.v.*), enabling the family to find a comfortable refuge in Edinburgh until 1940, when Hans and Franz were interned and she, too, had to leave the 'coastal area', but was able to stay with Sir Herbert Grierson's daughter in a cottage in the Yorkshire Moors.

Her teenage years had already been considerably darkened by the First World War and the experience of losing so many of her own generation. She shared with Hans the irreparable loss of his career after 1933, the vicissitudes of exile and the tragic loss of both sons, but she was sustained by her love for him and his music, as well as for their daughter, Eva, and her family, and by immense courage and resourcefulness. She was an excellent hostess and the Gál household was a focus for many of the Edinburgh refugees. She maintained a lively interest not only in music but also in literature and the visual arts, attending extramural classes right up to the end of her life.

She died in Edinburgh in December 1989.

MARGARETHE (GRETL) – younger sister. Born in Vienna on 21 March, 1896, she was the middle one of Gál's three sisters. Like her elder sister Edith she worked in a bank until 1938. Being of Jewish extraction, they were summarily dismissed following the _Anschluss_. When Hanna and then Hans fled to England, Gretl and her sisters took over responsibility for the two children, Franz and Peter, until the boys received the necessary exit visas to be able to leave Vienna and come to England. She herself did not leave Vienna until March 1939.

Gretl obtained her residence permit for Great Britain as a cook for a family in the north of Scotland, where she was also to assist as a masseuse for the lady of the house. On her arrival in Edinburgh she was asked by the Relief Committee for Refugees whether she could actually cook. In fact, she had never cooked, as in the Gál household the cook alone reigned in the kitchen (Gretl and her two sisters lived in their parents' house until they emigrated). She could, however, type and take shorthand, whereupon she was employed as secretary to the Relief Committee, which was headed by Hedwig Born, wife of the atomic physicist Max Born; Gretl was accommodated in Edinburgh, and the Scottish laird presumably obtained a more suitable cook.

When in 1940 Edinburgh was designated a 'protected area', she was evacuated to Glasgow, where she spent the rest of her life. She obtained a position as secretary and book-keeper, built up a large circle of friends, played bridge regularly and was an excellent and enthusiastic accompanist on the piano.

Gretl Gál died in Glasgow in August 1984.

PETER HERMANN – younger son. Born in Vienna on 2 August 1924. The two sons of Hans and Hanna Gál were only eighteen months apart, and their lives thus ran more or less parallel until 1938. But when the boys left Vienna in August 1938, Peter was still in secondary school and had to continue his schooling in England. He went to boarding school at Ackworth, in Yorkshire, from September 1938. It was for that time an unusually liberal, co-educational school, based on Quaker principles, and provided stability and a good education at a time when the family were basically homeless, moving between boarding-houses and occasional hospitality. It must nevertheless have been hard for the extremely sensitive, uprooted boy to come to terms with life in an English boarding-school. Secure in the boarding-school, he was at least able to escape internment and could complete his formal education in July 1941, with the necessary qualifications for university admission in nine subjects.

From autumn of that year he was matriculated as a student of engineering at the University of Edinburgh, and, like his brother, he was a member of the Student Representative Council. Outside his studies he was much involved with music and was an enthusiastic and very competent chamber-music player – he played violin and viola. But he was emotionally vulnerable, and took his own life on 7 December 1942, at the age of eighteen.

*Hans Gál's wife, Hanna, née Schick
(1902–89), and his sons Franz
(1923–67), below left, and Peter
(1924–42), below right*

B. Others

ADLER, DR ERNST – medical practitioner. Born Vienna, 11 March 1899. Studied medicine in Vienna, graduated in 1924 and worked at Hospitals in Vienna. From 1930 he was a general practitioner in Vienna. Both Adler and his wife lost their positions after the *Anschluss* and emigrated to Britain in January 1939. Adler was one of only fifty Austrian doctors to be allowed by the British government to work as a doctor in Britain, after obtaining a British qualification. After his release from twelve months' internment he established a practice in Edinburgh. He was official doctor to the German Consul and honorary doctor to the Vienna Philharmonic Orchestra on their visits to the Edinburgh International Festival. He was active in the Edinburgh Jewish community. He died on 24 October 1970.

AUBER, DR LEWIS (LUDWIG) – zoologist. Born Vienna, 24 June 1899. Studied zoology at the University of Vienna. To escape the German occupation of Austria he transferred to the University of Edinburgh in 1938. In 1946 he became Senior Scientific Officer at the Wool Industries Research Association in Leeds, where he was mainly concerned with the histology of wool follicles. His major passion was bird feathers; he wrote over 25 articles on aspects of feather growth and was a recognised authority in this field. He died in Edinburgh on 16 September 1974.

BARON, HERMANN – music antiquarian bookseller and amateur violinist. Born eastern Germany, 21 April 1914. A violin student of Max Rostal in Berlin, he followed his teacher to London in 1934 and played in a number of orchestras; in the later 1940s he founded an antiquarian booksellers in north-west London, specialising in music manuscripts, scores and the like – although 'he maintained his deep love for violin and viola, and played chamber music until he could no longer hold the instruments'.[1] He died in London on 29 December 1989.

BENESCH, PROFESSOR OTTO – art historian. Born Ebenfurth, Lower Austria, 29 June 1896. Worked as an assistant at the Albertina in Vienna. He emigrated to England and from 1938 until 1940 was a professor of art-history in Britain. Afterwards he lived in the USA. In 1947 he returned to Vienna and worked there as the director of the Albertina. He died in Vienna in 1964.

BERGMANN, WALTER – musician and lawyer. Born 1902. Was trained as both a musician and lawyer, and pursued both activities until he left Germany in 1939. After supporting Jews from his law firm who were arrested by the Nazis, he was imprisoned for three months and kept in solitary confinement. He finally left Germany on 21 March 1939 and emigrated to Britain with the assistance of the Germany Emergency Committee of the British Society of Friends and the eminent musicologist Edward Dent. On 9 July 1940 he was arrested and, after a short stay at Kempton Park transit camp, interned on the Isle of Man. He became an editor for Schott, with a particular interest in the recorder, which he saw as an excellent vehicle to teach music to children. He became a leading figure in Britain's

---

[1] *The Beethoven Newsletter*, Vol. 5, No. 1, Spring 1990.

early-music movement and a popular teacher at Morley College, London. He died on 13 January 1988.

BLUMEN, ALFRED – pianist. Born Vienna, 17 March 1897; enjoyed a glittering international career during the 1920s. He was still a youth when in 1923 he toured South America with the Vienna Philharmonic Orchestra under the baton of Richard Strauss. By the late 1920s he had left Europe and was performing and teaching in the United States, with numerous prestigious recital engagements in Boston, Chicago and New York. In November 1926 he performed the Beethoven Triple Concerto with the Chicago Symphony Orchestra and Jacques Gordon and Alfred Wallenstein as fellow soloists and Frederick Stock conducting.[2] In a 1926 recital at Jordan Hall in Boston, Blumen gave the American premiere of the Sonata in C minor, Op. 2, by Karol Rathaus, and championed this work in subsequent American concerts.[3] He also promoted other contemporary *émigré* composers in his recitals. He gave many highly successful solo recitals in 1926–28, appearing in such prominent venues such as Aeolian Hall and Town Hall in New York and Jordan Hall in Boston. In these concerts, Blumen was praised both technically and musically. On 2 February 1928, when he returned to New York for a Town Hall recital, his ambitious concert programme, as advertised in *The New York Times* concert-listings pages, was situated between a Boston Symphony Orchestra concert conducted by Serge Koussevitzky and a Fritz Kreisler recital and features a large photo of Blumen, situated squarely in the centre of the page. It is unclear precisely what chain of events led to his being interned in Central Camp in 1940. The concert that Gál found 'won me over completely'[4] was given on a piano found in the foyer of one of the hotels and included Schumann's *Davidsbündlertänze*; fellow internee Michael Kerr, later a prominent jurist in the UK, recalled that 'many of the older men were crying uncontrollably'.[5] He apparently remained in the UK after internment.[6] In London in October 1947 Richard Strauss conducted a festival of his own works and he again chose Blumen as soloist in the *Burleske* for piano and orchestra, apparently to ensure that he received a soloist's fee.[7]

BLUMENAU, DR ERNST (ERNEST) – dentist. Born Cologne, 28 February 1890. Studied medicine in Frankfurt. Until 1938 he worked as a dentist in Mainz. From 1938 until 1940 he practised as a dentist in Southsea, Hampshire, and from 1941 until 1963 in Bletchley, Buckinghamshire. He died in North Buckinghamshire in 1982.

BLUMENTHAL, DR JEAN – medical practitioner. Born 4 May 1892. Studied medicine in Berlin, Munich und Rostock. He worked as a general practitioner in London. He died in London in 1975.

---

[2] Felix Borowski, *Christian Science Monitor*, 10 November 1926, p. 12.

[3] Anonymous review, *Christian Science Monitor*, 10 December 1926, p. 4B.

[4] Diary entry for 28 August 1940; *cf.* p. 142, above.

[5] *As I Recall*, Hart Publishing, Portland, 2002, p. 74.

[6] Alan Sanders, booklet note for *Strauss conducts Strauss: The Last Concerts*, Testament STB21441 (live concert recording from 1947)

[7] *Ibid.* This performance can be heard on YouTube at www.youtube.com/watch?v=E0tlOLuw8cQ.

BORN, PROFESSOR MAX – physicist. Born Breslau (now Wrocław, Poland), 11 December 1882. Studied mathematics, physics and astronomy at the universities of Breslau, Heidelberg, Zurich and Göttingen. After a short stay in Cambridge he returned to Breslau and worked intensively on the theory of relativity. From 1921 until 1933 was professor at the University of Göttingen. In 1933 he emigrated to Cambridge. From 1936 until his retirement he was Tait Professor of Natural Philosophy at the University of Edinburgh. In 1953 he was made an honorary citizen of Göttingen; in 1954 he was awarded the Nobel Prize for Physics. He died in Göttingen on 5 January 1970.

DEUTSCH, DR OTTO ERICH – musicologist. Born Vienna, 5 September 1883. Studied art history and literary history in Vienna and Graz. After the First World War he worked as publisher and librarian at the Anthony von Hoboken music-collection from 1926 to 1935. His first documentary Schubert biography *Franz Schubert: Die Dokumente seines Lebens und Schaffens,* was published in three volumes in 1913–14. In 1938 he emigrated to Cambridge, intending his stay to be only temporary, as he had the offer of a post in the New York Public Library. In 1947 he received British nationality. In 1951 his famous catalogue of Schubert's works – *Schubert: Thematic Catalogue of all his Works in Chronological Order,* with D. R. Wakeling – appeared in English, initiating the 'Deutsch numbers' which now identify Schubert's works. In 1952 he returned to Vienna. *Handel: A Documentary Biography* appeared in 1955; in 1954 he published *Franz Schubert. Briefe und Schriften, mit den zeitgenössischen Bildnissen,* and in 1957 *Schubert: Die Erinnerungen seiner Freunde.* He devised the system of Music Publishers' Numbers, which are indispensable for dating printed music. In 1959 he was honoured with the Austrian 'Ehrenkreuz 1. Klasse für Wissenschaft und Kunst'. The manuscript of *Admiral Nelson and Josef Haydn* was found in his estate. In 1961 there appeared two large volumes: *Mozart. Die Dokumente seines Lebens* and *Mozart und seine Welt in zeitgenössischen Bildern.* His studies of the sources of Mozart and Schubert are today still of seminal importance. He died on 23 November 1967.

NICOLO DRABER – flautist. Born in Ostendorf, Germany, on 12 April 1911. After working as a freelance musician in Berlin, he left Germany in 1933 and worked as a flautist in Russia from 1933 to October 1937. While in Russia he married a German woman who held Russian citizenship from a previous marriage. A son, Thomas, was born in 1936. A year later the Russian secret police decreed that all foreigners were to be expelled, and Draber was forced to return, alone, to Germany. His wife and son, who were Soviet citizens, were not permitted to leave. Draber, who was half-Jewish, fled Nazi Germany in 1938 and emigrated to the United Kingdom in 1939. His wife and son were allowed to leave the Soviet Union only in April 1940, but Draber's internment prevented the family from reuniting, and his wife and child returned to Berlin where her family lived. The final blow came when the Gestapo forced his wife to divorce him. By early 1942 this coerced letter requesting a divorce arrived via the Red Cross. Draber was 29 years old when he arrived in Central Promenade camp. He was a gifted flautist and performed in both the *Huyton Suite* and in *What a Life!* He eventually joined the British Pioneer Crops, and did translation work for British intelligence. After his release from internment, Draber took the anglicised name of Nicolas Frank Debenham. By 1943 he had risen to the rank of corporal in the Pioneer Corps and was transferred to a special intelligence unit based in Germany, where he translated Nazi documents. On 10 November 1943 he remarried, with the permission of his commanding officer, during a brief 'home-leave'; his second wife died a few years after their marriage. By February 1946 he was released from the British Army. Debenham eventually gave up music as a profession and became a successful accountant, but he remained connected to music throughout his life, and also became a close friend of Peter Pears and Benjamin Britten. He died in 1987 and is buried beside Pears and Britten in the Anglican cemetery of Aldeburgh.

ELIAS, PROFESSOR NORBERT – sociologist. Born Breslau (now Wrocław, Poland), 22 June 1897. Studied medicine, philosophy and sociology. Taught at the universities of Heidelberg and Frankfurt. After the Nazis' seizure of power he first fled to France and in 1935 moved to England, where he stayed until 1975. He adopted British nationality. He taught at the Universities of Leicester (1954–62) and Ghana (1962–65). After his return from Ghana he lived in Amsterdam and a number of German cities. He was an important sociologist; one of his main works is the book *Über den Prozess der Zivilisation*, which was first published in Switzerland in 1939. Further important works are *The Established and the Outsiders* (1965), *Die Gesellschaft der Individuen* (1987) and *Studien über die Deutschen* (1989). In 1977 he was awarded the Theodor Adorno Prize of the city of Frankfurt, the first public recognition in Germany since his exile. He died in Amsterdam on 1 August 1990.

FUCHS, DR KLAUS – physicist. Born Rüsselsheim on 29 December, 1911. Studied physics and mathematics at the Universities of Leipzig and Kiel. From 1930 he was a member of the German Communist Party. He fled from the National Socialists to Britain and studied at the University of Edinburgh. He completed his doctorate under Max Born. He was interned for a short time but was released early in order to work on the development of the atom bomb at Birmingham University. Was a British citizen from 1942. In 1943 he went to the USA to work on the atom-bomb project at Los Alamos. After the war he returned to England and worked as director of the Physics Section of the Nuclear Research Establishment at Harwell, near Oxford. He recognised the importance of his work and began to pass information to the Soviet Union, his espionage shortening the time it took the Russians to develop the atom bomb by about a year. He was arrested in 1950 and sentenced to fourteen years' imprisonment, but released in 1959 for good behaviour. He went to East Germany, where he received GDR citizenship and became deputy director of the Central Institute for Nuclear Research at Rossendorf, near Dresden. He remained a committed communist and received many awards. He died in East Berlin on 28 January 1988.

GOMBRICH, SIR ERNST – art historian. Born in Vienna on 30 March 1909. Studied Art History in Vienna and worked as scientific assistant to the museum curator Ernst Kris. From 1936 he worked for the Warburg Institute in London. During the Second World War he worked at the BBC for the monitoring service. After the war he returned to the Warburg Institute in 1946 and shortly afterwards became its director. From 1956 until 1959 he was Professor of Art History at the University of London, and from 1959 until 1976 Professor of Ancient History. He was one of the most respected art historians of the twentieth century and one of the most distinguished scholars, receiving various honours for his works, among them the

Goethe, Hegel and Erasmus Prizes. His best-known works include *The Story of Art* (1950), *Art and Illusion: A Study in the Psychology of Pictural Representation* (1960) and *Aby Warburg: An Intellectual Biography* (1970). His last book, *Preference for the Primitive*, was published shortly before his death, which occurred in London on 3 November 2001.

GRIERSON, PROFESSOR SIR HERBERT – professor of English literature. Born Lerwick, Shetland, on 16 January 1866 and studied English Literature in Aberdeen and Oxford. He provided the Gáls with a home in Edinburgh when they arrived in 1939. From 1894 to 1915 was Professor at the University of Aberdeen, and from 1915 until his retirement in 1935 Professor of English at the University of Edinburgh. He was one of the best-known literary figures in the country. He studied the works of John Donne, publishing *Poems of John Donne* in 1912. He contributed to the Cambridge History of Literature and was co-editor of *The Oxford Book of the Seventeenth Century*, published in 1921. Further publications include *The Background of English Literature and other Collected Essays* (1925), *Lyrical Poetry from Blake to Hardy* (1928), *Letters of Sir Walter Scott* (twelve volumes, 1937), *The English Bible* (1944) and *And the third day* (1948). He was knighted in 1936. He died on 16 June 1960.

GROSS, DR FABIUS (WILLI) – marine biologist. Born Krosno, Galicia, Austria (present-day Poland), 5 August 1906. Studied biology at the University of Vienna and worked with Professor Max Hartmann at the Kaiser-Wilhelm Institute in Berlin. After the Nazi take-over he emigrated to Great Britain. With support from the Academic Assistance Council he was able to continue his research, at first in London, then in Plymouth. He was mainly concerned at this time with micro-plankton and their importance as food for fish-larvae. For twelve years from 1937 he taught at the Zoology Department at the University of Edinburgh, continuing his research alongside his teaching. In 1939 he had the opportunity to collaborate with Professor Hans Pettersson of the Oceanography Institute in Gothenburg on the use of plankton. From 1940 onwards he planned various experiments to test the effect of chemical fertilisers on fish growth. The results of these important tests, carried out by the Zoology Department of the University of Edinburgh and Millport Marine Station, were published shortly after his death. In 1949 he had just accepted the post of director of the newly established Marine Biological Station at the University of Bangor in Wales when he was taken seriously ill. He died in Edinburgh on 18 June 1949.

GUDER, DR GOTTHARD – University teacher. Born Krombach/Siegen 1910. Emigrated to Britain from Nazi Gemany out of moral conviction, without racial or political compulsion. Before his internment he had taught German at the University of St Andrews in Scotland. In 1947 he was appointed to the German Department of the University of Glasgow, where he was a Senior Lecturer until his retirement in 1975. He was an extremely gifted and committed teacher of language and literature and published several pedagogically oriented articles, as well as, in 1966, a monograph on the Jewish lyric poet Else Lasker-Schüler. He died in Glasgow on 27 April 1978.

HANSEN, PASTOR WILHELM – Protestant minister. Born 1899. In 1933 he was a minister of the German Protestant Church in Manchester and from 1936 until

1940 minister of the German Protestant Church in Bradford. Like most of the other pastors working for the German Church in England, he joined the Nazi party (October 1934). He married in England, but went back to Germany for several years. From 1949 he was minister of the German Evangelical Free Church in Manchester.

HILDEBRANDT, PASTOR FRANZ – theologian. Born Berlin, 20 February 1909. Studied theology at the Universities of Berlin, Tübingen and Marburg. Ordained as a minister in Berlin in 1933. When the Protestant church accepted the Nazis' racial laws, he gave up his post (he was of Jewish descent) and lived for a short time in London, but was recalled to Berlin by Martin Niemöller and he taught for a time at the illegal Church University there. In 1937 he emigrated to Britain and was until 1938 assistant to Pastor Julius Rieger, a staunch opponent of the nazification of the German church, at the St George's Congregation in London. From 1939 until 1946 he was Pastor at the German Exile Community in Cambridge. From 1948 was a member of the Methodist Church, and worked in Cambridge and later Edinburgh. In 1953 he went to the USA where he was Professor of Theology at Drew University (Madison, New Jersey), and returned to Scotland in 1969. He died in Edinburgh in 1985.

HÖLLERING, GEORG – producer, director, film scriptwriter and editor. Born Baden, Austria, 20 July 1898. At the beginning of his career he worked mainly in Germany, Hungary and Austria. In Germany he produced the left-wing film *Kuhle Wampe* in 1932, for which Bertolt Brecht wrote the script. After Hitler's take-over he first returned to Austria, and in 1934 began working on the important Hungarian film *Hortobagy* (1936). In 1937 he became director of the Academy Cinema in London, which was completely destroyed in the war and had to be rebuilt afterwards. In 1951 he directed the filming of T. S. Eliot's *Murder in the Cathedral*, which received the award for the best costumes and art-work at the Venice Festival. It was his last film. He then worked exclusively for the Academy Cinema, for a total of 36 years. He was mainly concerned with obtaining and showing continental films, bringing works by, among others, Ingmar Bergman, Miklós Jancsó und Andrei Tarkovsky to London. In the 1960s he extended the Academy Cinema and introduced the late-night showing. He died in Norfolk on 10 February 1980.

HUMPOLETZ, PAUL – painter, illustrator, cartoonist and caricaturist, and publisher. Born 1889 in Austria. After the First World War he was politically active on behalf of the Austrian Social Democratic Party and a leading caricaturist for the socialist weekly *Das kleine Blatt*, published in Vienna. He published the satirical political magazine *Die Muskete*. Later he left the Party and became a freemason. After the *Anschluss* of 1938 he remained at his desk at *Das kleine Blatt*, opposing the Nazis, but it became clear that under the prevailing political conditions he could no longer stay in Vienna. Secret contacts with freemasons and Quakers enabled him to escape to England in 1939. During his internment (1940–41) he created a series of drawings and caricatures, including the set for the camp review *What a Life!* After his release he returned to London, and from then on worked regularly as an illustrator for the well-known family magazine *The Leader*, but was also a freelance illustrator for various other publications and children's books. In 1947 he became a British citizen and changed his name to Paul Hubert. He returned to Vienna with his wife in 1968 and remained there until his death. Drawings and sketches for his stage sets can be found in the collection of the Museum of Jewish Heritage in New York. He died in Vienna in 1972.

KARG-BEBENBURG, HANS, FREIHERR VON – singer. A graduate of the Musikakademie in Vienna, before the Second World he had appeared as a baritone in Linz and was also the author of two published collections of poetry (*Wandern im Sturm*, Gerold, Vienna and Leipzig, 1933; *Flammen*, Gerold, Vienna and Leipzig, 1935). A member of a famous aristocratic family – the equivalent of a baron – he went on to have a distinguished career as singer and teacher in post-War Vienna.

KELLERMANN, DR WALTER – physicist. Born in Berlin in 1915. After being denied a place at German universities after 1933, he studied at the University of Vienna, graduating just before the *Anschluss*. He came to Edinburgh to do research in solid-state physics with Max Born at the University of Edinburgh and shared a desk with Klaus Fuchs (*q.v.*). After his internment and deportation to Canada (where conditions were so poor that he went on hunger strike), he returned to do war work at the University of Southampton, after which he moved to Manchester to work with Patrick Blackett, a future Nobel laureate in physics. He did research in astrophysics (cosmic rays), first in Southampton, then in Manchester and Leeds, and had a distinguished academic career in the Universities of Edinburgh, Southampton, Manchester and Leeds. He was the author of *Science and Technology in France and Belgium* (1988), and co-author of *British Science Policy* (1984). In 2004 he published his memoirs: *A Physicist's Labour in War and Peace. Memoirs 1933–1999*. He retired to London with his wife, Marcelle Kellermann, author of *A Packhorse called Rachel*, a novel based on her experiences in the French Resistance. He died on 15 November 2012.[8]

KUENSSBERG, DR EKKEHARD (ULRICH GUSTAV) VON – medical practitioner. Born in Heidelberg on 17 December 1913 and studied at the Universities of Innsbruck, Heidelberg and Edinburgh. A distinguished general practitioner with a practice in Edinburgh, he was a member of various committees, and president of the Royal College of General Practitioners from 1976 to 1979 and of the European General Practice Research Workshop. In 1967 he was given the Foundation Council Award, RCGP and in 1974 the Hippocrates Medal. He died in Edinburgh on 27 December 2001. The Scottish television journalist Laura Kuenssberg (b. 1976) is his granddaughter.

LEVIN, DR ERNST JULIUS – neurologist. Born in Berlin on 8 April 1887, he studied medicine in Munich, Heidelberg und Berlin, practising as a neurologist in Munich until his emigration to Britain. In 1935 he was in Osnabrück political prison. From 1943 he worked as a respected neurologist at the Royal Infirmary in Edinburgh. He died on 18 June 1975.

LIEBESCHÜTZ, DR HANS – classicist. Born in Hamburg in 1893, he taught Latin at the Lichtwark School there. From 1934 to 1939 taught at the Lehranstalt für die Wissenschaft des Judentums (Institute for the Science of Jewry) in Berlin. From 10 November until 4 December 1938 he was imprisoned in Sachsenhausen concentration camp. In February 1939 he left Germany with his wife and three

---

[8] *Cf.* also Appendix Four: A Memoir of Hans Gál, pp. 224–25, below.

children and settled in England. After his release from internment he taught Latin at various secondary schools in Lancashire and Cheshire. After the war he taught history at the University of Liverpool. He died in Liverpool in 1978.

PAUNZEN, ARTHUR – artist. Born in Vienna on 4 February 1890, he studied under Ludwig Koch and at the Académie Julian in Paris. He migrated to Britain in 1938. Among his best-known works are six prints inspired by Gustav Mahler's *Das Lied von der Erde*. Further works include among others ten large-scale nude lithographs and six illustrations of Dostoevsky's Raskolnikow, the main character in *Crime and Punishment*, as well as portraits and landscapes. His works were acquired by the British Museum, the Stockholm Engraving Collection and the Albertina in Vienna. He died in internment on the Isle of Man on 9 August 1940.

REIZENSTEIN, FRANZ THEODOR – composer and pianist. Born in Nuremberg on 7 June 1911 and studied at the Hochschule für Musik in Berlin. He emigrated to London in 1934, and studied composition with Ralph Vaughan Williams at the Royal College of Music. Between 1941 and 1945 he worked as a railway ticket-collector and gave several minor performances in support of the welfare work (with the YMCA) of Winston Churchill's wife. He taught composition at the Guildhall School of Music and worked as composer and concert pianist. From 1958 to 1964 he taught piano at the Royal Academy of Music. From 1964 to 1968 he was professor of piano at the Royal Manchester College of Music, and in 1966 professor at the Music Faculty of Boston University, USA. In 1964 he was awarded the culture prize of the city of Nuremberg, and became an honorary citizen. He composed choral works, radio operas, chamber music and piano works, among them twelve preludes and fugues (1955), and two radio operas *Men against the Sea* (1949), and *Anna Kraus* (1952). His orchestral works include concertos for violin and for cello, two overtures and a Ballet Suite (1946), *Let's Fake an Opera*, and the *Concerto popolare*, both written in 1958. He composed many piano pieces of which the best-known is a set of *Variations on 'The Lambeth Walk'*, which treats its eponymous popular song in the style of Chopin, Verdi, Beethoven, Mozart, Schubert, Wagner and Liszt. His Piano Quintet, Op. 23 (1959), is especially highly regarded. He died on 5 October 1968.

ROSENZWEIG, DR ALFRED – musicologist, critic and publicist. Born in Vienna on 21 August 1897, he obtained his doctorate in 1923 under Guido Adler at the University of Vienna, with a dissertation on the 'Developmental History of Richard Strauss' Music Dramas'. He fled to England in 1938, now writing under the name of Alfred Mathis, for *Music & Letters* in particular. In the war years, as a critic and writer on music for the *Zeitspiegel*, the magazine of the Austrian Centre, he promoted especially music which was branded 'degenerate' by the Nazis. His work on Mahler, *Gustav Mahler: Neue Erkenntnisse zu seinem Leben, seiner Zeit, seinem Werk*, remained unfinished, and for a while the manuscript was thought lost, but it was published, in a translation by Jeremy Barham, as *Gustav Mahler: New Insights into his Life, Times and Work*, ed. Jeremy Barham (Ashgate, Aldershot), in 2007. He died in London on 11 December 1948.

SCHNEIDER, DR HUGO – dentist. Born in Karvina, in the present-day Czech Republic, in 1897. He studied medicine at the University of Vienna, graduating in 1922, and became a dentist. He emigrated in 1938, staying illegally in

Czechoslovakia and Poland. He came to Great Britain in 1939 as one of only 40 Austrian dentists to receive permission from the British government to practise as dentists after completing British dental training. Since dentists were needed, he was released from internment after only four months, and from 1941 he was a dentist in Edinburgh. He died there in 1968.

SIMSON, PROFESSOR WERNER VON – jurist. Born Kiel, 21 February 1908. Studied law in Berlin and Freiburg, graduating in Freiburg in 1935. In 1938 he moved to England and worked there as a lawyer until 1955. Returned to the continent in 1955, working as a lawyer at the European Court in Luxemburg, advising in this capacity both the Federal Government and private businesses. In 1968 he was appointed to the chair of national, international and European Community law in Freiburg. He remained there until his retirement in 1976. He published many works relating to European law. He died in Freiburg on 20 September 1996.

STEIN, DR ERWIN – musician. Born Vienna, 7 November 1885. Studied musicology at the University of Vienna and worked as a conductor. Until 1938 he was artistic adviser to Universal Edition in Vienna. He emigrated to London in 1938, and worked as editor and publisher with Boosey & Hawkes. After the war he re-organised Covent Garden Opera and from 1947 was director of the English Opera Group. He was the father of Marion, Countess of Harewood, later wife of the Liberal politician Jeremy Thorpe. He died in London on 19 July 1958.

SUGAR, DR MAX – ear, nose and throat specialist. Born as Miksa Slier in Hungary in 1896. He was an Austrian citizen. He emigrated to Great Britain and lived in Edinburgh from 1939. He took British citizenship in 1947. He first worked as ear, nose and throat specialist in Edinburgh before emigrating in 1948 to Jamaica, where he worked in Kingston Public Hospital.

TOVEY, PROFESSOR SIR DONALD FRANCIS – musicologist, pianist and composer. Born Eton, 17 July 1875. A highly regarded pianist, scholar and composer whose works were performed in Berlin, London and Vienna in the early years of the twentieth century, he was Professor of Music at the University of Edinburgh from 1914 until his death and founded the Reid Orchestra there. In 1925 and 1927 he gave piano recitals in the USA. His books include *A Companion to Beethoven's Pianoforte Sonatas* (1931), *Essays in Musical Analysis*, seven volumes, 1935–37, 1939; *A Musician Talks*, 1941. He composed the opera *The Bride of Dionysus* (1907–18), a symphony (1913), concertos for piano (1906) and cello (1935) and much chamber music. He edited Bach's *Art of Fugue* and wrote an accompanying essay, *A Companion to 'The Art of Fugue'* (1931). He was music advisor for the 14th edition of the *Encyclopaedia Britannica*. He was knighted in 1935 and died in Edinburgh on 10 July 1944.

ULRICH, DR HERMANN – judge and music-critic. Born Mödling (Vienna), 15 August 1888. Studied law in Vienna and music in addition. He emigrated to Great Britain in 1939. He was author and assistant on the *Zeitspiegel* (a review produced by the Free Austria Movement during the War years) and worked at the Austrian Centre. In 1942 he became honorary member and secretary of the Austrian Musicians Group. He returned to Austria in 1946 and became Second President of the High Court and from 1958 President of the Patent Court in Vienna. He died in Vienna on 26 October 1982.

WEISS, PROFESSOR ERWIN. Pianist and composer. Born in Vienna on 6 October 1912. Studied piano with Alexander Manhart and Walter Kerschbaumer. From 1927 until 1934 he was a member of the Austrian Socialist Party, and organised concerts in support of the organisation. From 1934 until 1938 was a member of the proscribed Revolutionary Socialists, and organised concerts to raise money for that party. From 1936 pursued a career as concert pianist in Vienna, London and Paris. After an illegal stay in Switzerland (1938) he lived for seven months in France. He emigrated to Britain in 1939. Between 1941 and 1945 he worked in the armaments industry. During the war he directed the Young Austria choir. He worked at the Austrian Centre and the Austrian Labour Club. In November 1945 he returned to Austria at the invitation of the Austrian Socialist Party. He was active as a concert pianist and piano teacher at the Vienna Conservatoire. From 1950 he was known by the name of Peter Falk. In 1951 he received the promotional prize for composition of the City of Vienna. After 1960 he was Director of the Conservatoire for 20 years and organised cultural and musical programmes for the Workers' and Employees' Chamber. In 1971 he was awarded the Austrian Ehrenkreuz ('Cross of Honour') for Science and Arts. Among his works are the song-cycle *Geflüster der Liebe* ('Whispers of Love'); the cantata *Für alle die starben lange vor der Zeit* ('For all who died long before their time') for two soloists and choir, and *Das Lied der Motoren* ('The Song of the Motors'). He died in Vienna on 13 September 2004.

WEISSENBERG, PROFESSOR KARL – chemist. Born in Vienna on 11 June 1893. Studied mathematics in Vienna, Berlin and Jena. From 1929 he was a member of the Kaiser Wilhelm Society for Physical Chemistry. From 30 September 1933 had to give up this position as well as his professorship at Berlin University. After a short stay in Paris he went to Southampton in 1934, where he began to work on the spectroscopy of molecules. He became a British citizen in 1939. He made important contributions to the study of crystallography and rheology. He died in the Hague on 6 April 1976.

Appendix Two

Contents of the CD

Huyton Suite **for flute and two violins, Op. 92** (1940)   **18:26**

1	I	*Alla marcia*	2:29
2	II	*Capriccio*	5:32
3	III	*Canzonetta con variazioni*	6:11
4	IV	*Fanfaronata*	4:14

Philippa Davies (flute); Paul Barritt and Marcia Crayford (violins)

What a Life!**: Music from the Camp Revue** (1940)   **19:53**
Reconstructed from the manuscript by Michael Freyhan

5	No. 1	Entrance March	3:15
6	No. 2	Barbed-Wire Song	2:07
7	No. 3	Women's Song	1:14
8	No. 4	The Ballad of the German Refugee	2:12
9	No. 5	Entr'acte	1:16
10	No. 6	'Keep Fit'	1:23
11	No. 7	Quodlibet	1:19
12	No. 8	Broom Song	0:53
13	No. 9	Song of the Double Bed	1:26
14	No. 10	Serenade	2:15
15	No. 11	Finale	2:33

Norbert Meyn (tenor)
Thomas Guthrie (baritone)
Katalin Kertész and Charlotte Edwards (violins)
Andrew Byrt (viola)
Peter Freyhan (cello)
Raffaello Orlando (clarinet)
Edward Beckett (flute)
Michael Freyhan (piano: 1920s Blüthner)

16	**'The Ballad of Poor Jacob'**	**17:41**

Thomas Guthrie (speaker)
Michael Freyhan (piano: Hans Gál's 1911 Blüthner)

What a Life!: Piano Suite from the Camp Revue (1940)   **13:05**

Texts omitted from the recording are shown in italics.

6 **No. 2, Der Song vom Stacheldraht**

Die Möwen sehen den Stacheldraht,
Den man in Douglas errichtet hat,
Und weil kein Draht hier früher war,
Ist ihnen der Zweck des Drahtes nicht
    klar.

Sie debattieren mit viel Geschrei,
Was wohl der Sinn des Drahtes sei,
Und kommen zu keinem Resultat.
Warum lebt der Mensch hinter
    Stacheldraht?

The Barbed-Wire Song

The seagulls are in a curious mood –
Maybe they are getting too much food.
One thing they all very much deplore
Is the ugly barbed wire that grows up the
    shore.

So in the seagulls' parliament
There was a great debate on that end,
And many of them did then enquire:
'Why are human beings behind a wire?'

7 **No. 3, Frauen-Song**

Die Frauen gehen aussen vorbei,
Die Männer innen herum.
Es könnte auch sein, dass es
    umgekehrt sei,
Dann wäre es genau so dumm.

Women's Song

The women walk along outside.
The men inside must come.
The other way round also could have been
    tried,
And that would be just as dumb

8 **No. 4, Die Ballade vom deutschen Refugee**
Otto Erich Deutsch

Am Pfingstsonntag, im strahlenden
    Morgenschein,
Nach des Frühstücks bescheidenem
    Schmaus,
Fanden sich zwei sehr freundliche
    Herrn bei uns ein,
Mit dem Auto bereit vor dem Haus.
Und im Rathaus, da traf ich noch
    andere dann,
Die so freundlich geholt worden warn,
Und dort sagte uns ein viel höherer
    Mann,

The Ballad of the German Refugee
Translation by Anthony Fox

On Whitsunday the sun shone as bright as
    could be,
After breakfast's quite modest
    treat,
When two friendly gentlemen visited me,
With a car waiting out in the street.
And then in the Town Hall I met others,
    too,
Who had kindly been brought there that
    day,
And there we were met by a higher man,
    who

Dass wir bald über Land sollten fahrn.	Told us we'd soon be going away.
Hier ist die Ballad' vom deutschen Refugee,	This is the ballad of the German refugee
Wer sie nicht erlebt hat, der begreift sie nie, nein, der begreift sie nie.	If you haven't been one you never will see, no, you'll never see.
Lieber, guter, braver deutscher Refugee,	Dear, good, honest German refugee,
Leider müssen wir Dein Wochenende stören, kleiner Refugee.	Sorry but we must disturb your weekend, little refugee.

Und wir glauben, dass unsere Gastfreunde wohl	*And our hosts they had probably wanted, we thought,*
Uns nur zu einer Pfingstfahrt vereint.	*Just to give us an outing at Whit.*
Deshalb packten wir unsere Koffer nicht voll	*So we didn't pack cases as full as we ought*
Und wir haben auch garnicht geweint.	*And we didn't cry one little bit.*
Denn der Abschied von unseren Lieben war kühl,	*For the parting from all of our loved ones was cool,*
Mit dem wartenden Fremden dabei,	*With the strangers all there in the way,*
Und das Ganze schien uns nur ein Sonntags-Spiel	*And it seemed like a Sunday day-trip with the school*
Nach dem grauen Alltags-Einerlei.	*After week-days of ordinary grey.*
(Refrain)	*(Refrain)*
Auf der Fahrt zu dem nächsten Bestimmungsziel	*As we travelled along to our next journey's end*
Wurde uns allmählich erst klar,	*To us all it began to be clear*
Dass wohl keiner von uns, die erduldet so viel,	*That none of us sufferers yet could pretend*
Schon am Ziel seines Leidenswegs war.	*That our misery's end was now near.*
Nach den grossen Männern des Dritten Reichs,	*There was first the Third Reich with all its great men,*
Die uns raubten die Heimat, die Ruh',	*They who stole from us homes and peace, too,*
Kamen nun unsre Freunde diesseits des Teichs	*But our friends on this side of the pond came just then*
Mit dem Trost 'I am sorry for you!'	*And explained: 'I am sorry for you!'*
(Refrain)	*(Refrain)*
Grosse Männer, die gab es wohl immer schon,	*Though great men there have certainly been not a few,*
Seit King Pharao Übles getan:	*Since King Pharoah and his evil plan:*
Kaiser Nero und Kaiser Napoleon,	*There was emperor Nero, Napoleon, too,*
König Attila, Herr Dschingiskhan.	*King Attila and Lord Ghenghis Khan.*
Aber Männer von so einem Hochformat	*But the men who on such a grand scale are so great*
Und von solch einer Heldennatur,	*And with such a heroic mind,*
Dieses auserlesene Triumvirat,	*This so highly selected triumvirate,*
Das gibt es in Deutschland nur. (Refrain)	*In Germany only you'll find. (Refrain)*
Ganz allmählich setzte vom Mainland her	*From the mainland our people continued to flee*

Unser Volk seine Wanderung fort,	*And now reached the Atlantic coast,*
Hin nach Liverpool, an das atlantische Meer,	*They first came here to Liverpool, next to the sea*
Bis wir fanden uns in diesem Port.	*Until this port became then our host.*
Hier nun gab es, auf engem Raum gebaut,	*So here now packed tightly alongside the shore,*
Ein Geviert von Hotels feiner Art,	*Was a fine hotel quarter, quite smart,*
In die keiner von uns sich je hätte getraut,	*One that none of us would have dared enter before,*
Weder table d'hôte noch à la carte.	*Neither table d'hôte nor à la carte. (Refrain)*
(Refrain)	

In den leeren Gasthöfen fanden wir	*In the empty hotels we could now have a dish*
Die Früchte der Isle of Man,	*Of the fruits of the Isle of Man*
Darunter das lederne Stockfisch-Tier,	*Not excluding the leathery dried-up cod fish*
Dessen Duft nimmer wollte verwehn.	*Whose aroma we never could ban.*
Ohne jegliche Vorbereitung kam	*And without any preparation there came*
Je ein Gentleman-Koch ins Haus,	*Then a gentleman-cook to each place,*
Der ergreift dort den Kochlöffel ohne Scham	*And he took up the cook's spoon without any shame*
Und machte das Beste daraus.	*And did what he could with good grace.*
(Refrain)	*(Refrain)*

Jede Küche im ganzen Lager kann	*So now every kitchen throughout the camp can*
Nun kochen die Speisen, als ob – ,	*Cook its meals – and each in its own ways,*
Was hinaufschickt freilich der gute Mann,	*Although what is sent up to us by the good man*
Findet selten ein einiges Lob.	*Rarely meets with unanimous praise.*
Doch die Küche, sie tröstet sich damit –	*But the kitchen is always completely consoled*
Essen müssen's die Kerle ja doch.	*By the fact that we all have to eat.*
Und verzweifeln wird sie wohl niemals nit;	*And despair will now probably never take hold;*
Das Beste bleibt immer beim Koch.	*As the cook gets the best of the meat.*
(Refrain)	*(Refrain)*

Wenn wir manchmal in diesen Wochen auch	*If in all of these weeks we have not often heard*
Das Geschehen der grossen Welt	*Of the wide outside world's great events,*
Übersehen über den eigenen Bauch,	*Though beyond our own navels we've not often stirred*
So war damit kein Urteil gefällt.	*It was not through our own real intents.*
Was gekränkt uns und unseren Stolz verhöhnt,	*What has hurt us and what to our pride has been done*
Wird gewiss bald vergessen sein,	*We will soon quite forget, it is true,*
Wenn der Sieg nur am Ende die Sache krönt,	*When the victory comes and the crown is then won*
Die wir haben mit England gemein.	*That we'll share then with England, too.*
(Refrain)	*(Refrain)*

Hatte einst das gemeinsame Vaterland	*And although once by our common fatherland*
Uns zu Paaren hinausgejagt,	*We were one by one thrown right out,*

So hat wieder vereint uns hier ein Band,
Das vielleicht nicht jedem behagt.
Doch das Gastland hat uns geladen zart
Auf der Insel zum Rendezvous,
Und trotz unserer sehr verschiedenen
    Art
Gibt es Freunde auf Du und Du.
(Refrain)

We are now reunited here by a band
That not all of us like much, no doubt.
But we've all been invited by our gentle host
To this island rendez-vous here,
And despite all the ways that we differ the
    most
We've made friends here to whom we are
    dear. (Refrain)

Alle Manxer, sie sehen uns dieses Mal
Mit gemischten Gefühlen getrennt:
Auf Port Erin fiel nur die Damenwahl,
Sieben Plätze sind uns gegönnt.
Frau'n und Mädchen gibt es dreitausend
    bloss,
Männer aber doch dreimal so viel;
Liesse man die verschiedenen
    Lager los,
Ja, das gibt eine tolle Quadrill'!
    (Refrain)

All the Manxers can see us this time around
Kept apart, and our feelings are mixed:
While Port Erin was chosen as ladies' ground
Seven places for us have been fixed.
Though of women and girls there are three
    thousand here
There are three times as many men
If the different camps were let loose, then I
    fear
There would be a few goings-on then!
    (Refrain)

Und in jeden der vielen Lager hat
Sich entwickelt nach kurzer Frist
Ganz von selber so eine Art von Staat,
Dessen Kleinbürger man nun ist.
Wenn wir leben auch in den Tag
    hinein,
Wissen wir ganz verlässlich doch dies,
Dass beendet wird dieses Scheindasein
Eines Tages ja durch Release.
    (Refrain)

And in each of the camps, inside the gate,
After quite a short time came to be
As if all by itself a kind of state
Of which we are the bourgeoisie.
As from day to day now our lives we must
    spend
There is one thought that gives us some peace,
That this pseudo-existence will finally end
When one day we all get our release.
    (Refrain)

Nicht als Kriegsgefangene angesehn,
Nur gefangen für diesen Krieg,
Mit gebundenen Händen,
    wir erflehn
Unsrer Wärter baldigen Sieg.
Da sich Englands alte Grösse
    bewährt
In dem Kampf um die Freiheit der Welt,
Ist bald unsere Schicksalsfrage
    geklärt,
Und die Schranke des Stacheldrahts fällt.

It is not now as pris'ners of war, no indeed,
But as prisoners just for this war,
With our hands tightly bound for our guards
    we must plead
That the victory soon they may score.
Since the ancient greatness of England is
    shown
In the fight for the freedom of all,
Then our own fate it will clearly soon be
    known
And at last then the barbed wire will fall.

Das war die Ballad' vom deutschen
    Refugee,
Wer sie nicht erlebt hat, der begreift sie nie.

This was the ballad of the German
    refugee,
If you haven't been one you will never see.

9 **No. 5 Entr'acte** (instrumental)

10 **No. 6, Keep Fit**
Every morning in the street,
You can hear the pit-a-pat of feet,
There are rows of people doing gym,
To keep them beautiful and slim.

Each one tries his best,
They're throwing out their chest,
It's beauty culture, don't forget,
And brings down weight and fat!

Trying hard to keep in shape
For times to come outside the gate,
Also for the time which is quite near,
To join the British pioneer!

11 **No. 7, Quodlibet**

	Quodlibet
Auch ich war ein Jüngling mit lockigem Haar,	I, too, was a young man with long curly hair,
An Mut und an Hoffnungen reich,	With courage and hope was replete,
Am Amboss seit jeher ein Meister fürwahr,	With me on the anvil no-one could compare,
Am Fleisse kam keiner mir gleich.	In labour no-one could compete.
Ich liebte den Frohsinn, den Tanz, den Gesang,	To dance and to sing I just could not resist,
Ich küsste manch Dirnlein mit rosiger Wang,	And many a rosy-cheeked maiden I've kissed,
Ihr Herz hat mir manche geweiht.	And me many girls would have wed.
Köstliche Zeit, das war eine köstliche Zeit.	Oh then what a great life I led.
etc.	etc.

12 **No. 8, Besen-Song**

	Broom Song
Der Besen kehrt die Stube rein,	The broom sweeps clean, as is well known,
Doch tut er das nicht von sich selber allein,	But it doesn't sweep by itself all alone,
Er hat keinen Sinn für Wohnungskultur,	With elegant style it has no success,
Ist hölzern und faul und gleichgültig nur.	It's wooden and slow and couldn't care less.
Es muss einer sein, der sich da regt,	There must be a person behind the scenes,
Es muss einer sein, der ihn bewegt,	There must be a person who intervenes,
Es ist der Mensch, nicht der Besen, der fegt!	It's not the broom but the human that cleans!

13 **No. 9, Der Song vom Doppelbett**
Das Doppelbett hat ein Tischler gemacht,
Der hat sich dabei was ganz and'res
    gedacht,
Denn dass zwei Männer hier drinnen
    liegen,
I'm sorry, davon hat keiner Vergnügen!

The Song of the Double Bed
The most delightful gift of all
Is a wife not too tall and a bed not too
    small
But put two men in a bed
    together?
I'm sorry: it is for neither a pleasure!

14 **No. 10, Serenade**
Jeden Abend, wenn es dunkelt,
Und das Meer schon nächtlich funkelt,
Klagen laut im Mondestrahl
Tolle Kater ihre Qual.

Serenade
Ev'ry ev'ning, when it's dark'ning,
And by night the sea is sparkling,
In the moonlight's glowing beams
Crazy tomcats voice their screams.

Wenn in unsrem stillen Campe
Leser sitzen bei der Lampe,
Da ertönt im süssen Klang
Serenading ein Gesang:

When in this our silent camp-site
Readers sit beneath the lamp-light,
Then rings out with sweetest strain,
Serenading, this refrain:

'Put that light out! Put that light out!
Hurry up, hurry up, put it right out!
In the window on the right I still see a
    little light!
What a nuisance, what a nuisance every
    night!'

15 **No. 11 Finale** (instrumental)

16 **Die Ballade vom armen Jakob**
Norbert Elias

The Ballad of Poor Jacob
Translation by Anthony Fox

Bild: Zwei Chöre in
    Kampfstellung

Scene: Two choruses in a confrontational
    posture.

Chorführer (treten zwischen die
    Kämpfenden und sagen):
Warum könnt ihr euch denn nicht
    vertragen?
Warum wollt ihr denn euch selber schlagen?
Das tut schliesslich nur euch selber weh!
Statt euch miteinander zu verkrachen
sucht euch lieber einen Schwachen
und verdrescht ihn und verhaut ihn
und verprügelt ihn gemeinsam
mit Juchheiserassa und Juchhe!

Chorus leaders (step between the
    combatants and say):
Why can't you be like a sister or
    brother?
Why do you both try to thrash one another?
You'll just hurt yourselves that way!
Instead of fighting why not seek
someone who is poor and weak
and then thrash him and then beat him
and then punch him both together
with hoorah and with hooray!

Chor:
mit Juchheiserassa und Juchhe!

Chorus:
with hoorah and with hooray!

I

<table>
<tr><td>

Sprecher:
Hört! Hört! Die wahre Geschichte von
   dem armen Jakob!
Der war schon als Kind etwas
   schwächlich.
Seine Stirn war blass, seine Augen
   auffallend gross
und er hatte die eigentümliche
   Gewohnheit
den Finger an die Nase zu legen und
   nachdenklich ins Blaue zu sehn.
Das war natürlich etwas aufreizend.
Es kam wohl daher dass er bei Fremden
   aufwuchs.
Und jedesmal wenn seine Pflegemutter
und sein Pflegevater sich zankten
wenn der Mann sagte: Verdammte Kröte!
und die Frau: Dieb, Zuhälter und so weiter
wie das in jeder Ehe gelegentlich einmal
   vorkommt
wenn das Geschirr flog und es gerade so
   aussah
als wollten sie sich gegenseitig verprügeln
die Frau mit dem Besen und der Mann
   mit der Faust
oder was ihm gerade in die Hand kam
   dann
sahen sie sich plötzlich ganz vertraulich an
gaben sich die Hand: So!
und ohne ein weiteres Wort zu sagen
schlugen sie alle beide im Verein
auf den armen kleinen Jakob ein

Chor:
schlugen alle beide im Verein
auf den armen kleinen Jakob ein

Sprecher:
bis ihnen die Puste ausging
und bis da schliesslich auch nicht mehr
   viel zu schlagen war
und am Ende machte ihnen die ganze
   Geschichte keinen Spass mehr... da
schickten sie den Jakob ohne Geld
in die weite, weite Welt

Chor:
in die weite, weite Welt.

</td><td>

Speaker:
Listen, listen! To the true story of
   poor Jacob!
Even as a child he was a weakling.
His brow was pale, his eyes
   strangely large
and he had the unusual habit
of putting his finger on his nose and gazing
   pensively into the distance.
That was of course rather provocative.
That may have been because he was brought
   up by strangers
and whenever his foster-mother
and his foster-father were arguing
when the husband said 'Damned cheek!'
and the wife: 'Thief, pimp', and so on
which happens from time to time in every
   marriage
when the crockery was flying and it
   looked
as if they were going to thrash each other
   the wife with the broom and the man
   with his fist
or whatever he could lay his hands on,
   then
suddenly they looked at each other in a
   friendly sort of way,
shook hands: like this!
and without another word
they both knew what they should do:
they beat poor Jacob black and blue.

Chorus:
they both knew what they should do:
they beat poor Jacob black and blue.

Speaker:
until they ran out of breath
until there was nothing much more
   to beat
and the whole business was not much fun
   any more... then
they sent him off, without delay,
penniless upon his way.

Chorus:
penniless upon his way

</td></tr>
</table>

II

Sprecher:
Auf diese Weise kam er nach München.
Da waren alle sehr freundlich zu ihm
und halfen ihm und pflegten ihn und
    sagten: Armer, kleiner Jakob!
Und er begann auch bereits ganz hübsch
    Geld zu verdienen
mit Reklamezeichnen und kurzen
    Artikeln und so
denn er hatte eine recht
kluge und geschickte Feder.
Dann war da auch ein kleines Mädchen
Else
mit Grübchen in den Backen
und auch sonst noch diesem und jenem
    was gut
und freundlich anzusehen war. Die hatte
    er gern.
Und er fing auch schon an sich ganz wohl
    zu fühlen in dieser Welt
und zu träumen wie man eben
    so träumt:
Heirat, Kinder, eine kleine Wohnung
    draussen im Grünen...
Aber es waren damals stürmische Zeiten
    in München.
Es gab da graue Soldaten, die
    marschierten drohend durch die
    Strassen.
Und braune mit prallen Hosen und
    niedrigen Stirnen
die rempelten alle Leute an und schlugen
    Schaufenster ein
und hielten grosse Reden mit Geraufe
    und Messerstecherein.
Und eines Abends als der kleine Jakob
irgendwo in einem Lokal mit seinem
    Mädchen beim Bier sass
da kamen ein paar von den Braunen
    herein
richtige Bullen mit Stiernacken und
    groben Gesichtern
und fingen an Skandal zu machen, und
    die Grauen
die da an den Tischen sassen, standen auf
und sagten sie sollten ruhig sein.
Da beschimpften sie sich gegenseitig und
    nannten sich Spitzel,

Speaker:
In this way he came to Munich.
There everyone was very kind to him
and helped him and looked after him and
    said: Poor little Jacob!
And he began to earn lots of money with
    advertising drawings
and short articles and
    suchlike
for he had a really
clever and skilful pen.
And then there was a little girl
Elsie
with dimples in her cheeks
and all sorts of things that
    were good
and nice to look at.
    He liked her.
And he really began to feel rather happy in
    this world
and to dream the sort of things that people
    dream:
marriage, children, a little house in the
    country...
But those were stormy times
    in Munich.
There were grey soldiers marching
    threateningly through
    the streets.
And brown ones with bulging trousers and
    low brows
who jostled everyone and smashed shop
    windows
and made big speeches with violence and
    stabbings.
And one night when little Jacob
was sitting somewhere drinking beer with
    his girl in a pub
a couple of brown ones came in
real oxen with necks like bulls and coarse
    faces
and began to make a scene, and the grey ones
sitting there at the tables stood up
and told them to shut up.
Then they swore at each other and called
    one another informers,
murderers, Jews' lackeys and God knows
    what.

Mörder, Judenknechte und Gott weiss was.
Und es sah schon so aus, als ob sie
    übereinander herfallen wollten
und als ob es Mord und Totschlag geben
    würde
da sahen sich die Grauen
und die Braunen
plötzlich ganz vertraulich an
gaben sich die Hand: So!
und sagten:
Warum können wir uns nicht vertragen?
Warum sollen wir uns selber schlagen?
Das tut schliesslich nur uns selber weh!
Statt uns miteinander zu verkrachen
suchen wir uns lieber einen Schwachen
und verprügeln ihn gemeinsam
mit Juchheiserassa und Juchhe!

Chor:
mit Juchheiserassa und Juchhe!

Sprecher:
Und dann schlugen alle im Verein
auf den armen kleinen Jakob ein
bis sie die Puste verloren
und das Licht ausging.
Da kroch der kleine Jakob auf allen
    Vieren ins Freie
und versteckte sich irgendwo und heilte
    seine Wunden so gut es ging.

Und dann zog er wieder ohne Geld
ein Stück weiter in die weite Welt.

Und die Else hat er nie mehr wiedergesehn.

And it looked as if they were going to attack
    one another
and there would be murder and killing
and then
the greys and the browns suddenly looked
at one another in a friendly sort of way
shook hands: like this!
and said:
Why can't we get along
    like a sister or brother?
Why is each of us trying
    to thrash the other?
We'll just hurt ourselves that way!
Instead of fighting why not seek
someone who is nice and weak
and we'll punch him both together
with hoorah and with hooray!

Chorus:
with hoorah and with hooray!

Speaker:
they all knew what they should do:
they beat poor Jacob black and blue.
until they ran out of breath
and the light went out.
Then little Jacob crept outside on all fours
and hid somewhere and healed
    his wounds
as well as he could.

Again he went, without delay,
penniless a little further on his way.

And he never saw Elsie again.

III

Sprecher:
So kam er schliesslich an die holländische
    Grenze.
Da stand ein grosser Mann in Uniform
und fragte wo er hin wollte.
Und der kleine Jakob sagte: Wo anders hin.
Der Mann aber sah ihn von oben bis
    unten an
fragte ihn nach Papieren und Geld
und als der kleine Jakob gar nichts
    vorzeigen konnte
da sagte er: Hier kannst du nicht herein.

Speaker:
So at last he came to the Dutch
    border.
There stood a big man in uniform
who asked where he was going.
And little Jacob said: Somewhere else.
But the man looked him up and down
asked him for his papers and money
and when little Jacob couldn't show
    anything at all
he said: You can't come in here.
And when little Jacob begged and said:

Und als der kleine Jakob bettelte und sagte:
Wenn ich wieder zurückmuss, da
    schlagen sie mich tot
da sagte er: Armer kleiner Jakob
so leid es mir tut, hier kannst du nun mal
    nicht herein!
Das ist gegen die Regulationen. Und
    deinesgleichen
wollen wir hier überhaupt nicht, so leid es
    mir tut.
Aber wenn du willst
könn' wir dich über die Grenze nach
    Belgien schaffen
vielleicht behalten die dich.
Da sagte der kleine Jakob: Ja.

Chor:
Und so wurde er also heimlich bei Nacht
über die Grenze nach Belgien gebracht.

Sprecher:
Da stand er nun in einem grossen
    dunklen Walde und fürchtete sich ein
    bisschen.
Denn er wusste ja gar nicht wohin er
    gehen sollte
und es regnete und Hunger hatte er auch.
Aber als er ein paar Schritte gegangen war
da stand schon wieder ein Mann in
    Uniform
klein, mit schwarzem Schnurrbart, der
    schrie: Halt, wer da?
Und als er den kleinen Jakob erkannte, da
    sagte er:
Du bist heute schon der dreiundzwanzigste!
Wenn ich nur diesen Holländer mal
    erwischen könnte
der euch herüberschmuggelt.
Aber als er sah dass der kleine Jakob
    hungrig war
da gab er ihm ein Stück Brot
und als er sah dass ihm kalt war
da gab er ihm seinen Mantel
denn er hatte im Grunde ein mitleidiges
    Herz.
Und dann warf er ihn in das Gefängnis zu
    den anderen zweiundzwanzig.
Da lag nun der kleine Jakob
und fühlte sich ganz wohl
denn es war wenigstens nicht so nass
und zu essen bekam er auch.
Aber er konnte da nicht lange bleiben

If I have to go back they'll beat me
    to death
then he said: Poor little Jacob
I'm sorry, but you just can't
    come in!
It's against the regulations. And we don't
    want
people like you at all, I'm sorry.
But if you like
we can put you over the border into
    Belgium
perhaps they'll have you.
Then little Jacob said: Yes.

Chorus:
And so to Belgium he was brought at night
over the border out of sight

Speaker:
There he now stood in a big dark
    wood and was a
    little afraid.
For he didn't know where
    to go
and it was raining and he was hungry too.
But when he had gone a few steps
there stood a man in uniform
    again
small, with a black moustache, who
    shouted: Halt, who goes there?
And when he recognised little Jacob
    he said
You're already the twenty-third today!
If only I could catch this Dutchman
Who's smuggling you over.
But when he saw that little Jacob
    was hungry
he gave him a piece
    of bread
and when he saw that he was cold
he gave him his coat
for he really had a sympathetic
    heart
And then he threw him into prison along
    with the other twenty-two.
There lay little Jacob now
and felt quite happy
for at least it wasn't so wet
and he got something to eat too.
But he couldn't stay there long.

Chor:
denn er wurde schon in der folgenden
    Nacht
über die Grenze nach Holland
    zurückgebracht.

Sprecher:
Als er da ein paar Schritte gegangen war
da stand schon wieder der Holländer und
    sagte:
So leid es mir tut, hier kannst du nun mal
    nicht bleiben.

Chor:
Und dann wurde er in der folgenden
    Nacht
wieder nach Belgien zurückgebracht.

Sprecher:
So flog er wie ein Spielball immer hin und
    her
und der kleine Jakob fürchtete sich ein
    bisschen und dachte:
Wenn ich es nur aushalte! Wenn ich es
    nur aushalte!
Aber eines Nachts
kam der Belgier grade dazu
wie der Holländer ihn in den dunklen
    Wald brachte.
Da zankten sich die beiden
und schrien auf einander ein.
Und der Holländer sagte: Du hast
    angefangen!
Und der Belgier sagte: Du hast angefangen!
Und sie schrien und schimpften und
    tobten so laut
dass der Mond sich hinter den Wolken
    versteckte.
Aber als es gerade so aussah, als ob es
    Mord und Totschlag geben würde
und als der kleine Jakob schon zu
    fürchten begann
sie würden sich etwas zu leide tun
da sahen sich die beiden plötzlich ganz
    vertraulich an
gaben sich die Hände: So!
und sagten:
Warum können wir uns nicht vertragen?
Warum sollen wir uns selber
    schlagen?
Das tut schliesslich nur uns selber weh!
Statt uns miteinander zu verkrachen

Chorus:
And back into Holland he was brought that
    night
over the border out of sight.

Speaker:
When he had gone a few steps
the Dutchman was there again
    and said:
I'm sorry, but you can't
    stay here.

Chorus:
Then back into Belgium he was brought
    that night
over the border out of sight

Speaker:
So he flew back and forth like a
    ball
and little Jacob was a little afraid and
    thought:
If I can just hold out! If I can just
    hold out!
But one night
the Belgian came along
just when the Dutchman was taking him
    into the dark wood
The two of them quarrelled
and shouted at each other.
And the Dutchman said: You
    started it!
And the Belgian said: You started it!
And they shouted and cursed and
    quarrelled so loudly
that the moon hid behind
    the clouds.
But when it looked as if there would be
    murder and killing
and when little Jacob
    began to fear
that they would hurt each other then
they suddenly looked at each other in a
    friendly sort of way
shook hands: like this!
and said:
Why can't we get along with one another?
Why is each of us trying to thrash the
    other?
We'll just hurt ourselves that way!
Instead of fighting why not seek

suchen wir uns lieber einen Schwachen
und verhauen und verdreschen und
    verprügeln ihn gemeinsam
mit Juchheiserassa und Juchhe!

Chor:
mit Juchheiserassa und Juchhe!

Sprecher:
Und dann schlugen beide im Verein
auf den armen kleinen Jakob ein

Chor:
und dann schlugen beide im Verein
auf den armen kleinen Jakob ein

Sprecher:
bis ihnen die Puste ausging
und bis da schliesslich auch nicht mehr
    viel zu schlagen war.
Dann wurde der kleine Jakob von dem
    Belgier
an die französische Grenze gebracht.
Und so zog er wieder ohne Geld
ein Stück weiter in die weite Welt

Chor:
und so zog er wieder ohne Geld
ein Stück weiter in die weite Welt.

someone who is nice and weak
then we thrash him and we beat him and we
    punch him both together
with hoorah and with hooray!

Chorus:
with hoorah and with hooray!

Speaker:
they both knew what they should do:
they beat poor Jacob black and blue.

Chorus:
they both knew what they should do:
they beat poor Jacob black and blue.

Speaker:
until they ran out of breath
until there was nothing much
    more to beat.
Then little Jacob was taken by the
    Belgian
to the French border.
Again he went, without delay,
penniless further on his way.

Chorus:
Again he went, without delay,
penniless further on his way.

IV

Sprecher:
So kam er schliesslich nach der grossen
    Stadt Paris.
Da ging er in den Strassen umher und
    staunte
über die vielen fröhlichen Menschen
die vor den Cafés bei den Koksöfen sassen
und fühlte sich sehr allein
denn er konnte gar nicht froh sein
und er fror und hungerte.
Nur in den Asylen wo er schlief
da fand er viele die waren wie er
blass mit schäbigen Kleidern und
    unrasiert.
Sie spielten Karten und erzählten sich
wie es ihnen ergangen war
bis der Wärter das Licht auslöschte.

Speaker:
So at last he came to the great city of
    Paris.
He walked around in the streets
    amazed
at all the happy people
sitting outside the cafés by the coke stoves
and felt very alone
for he couldn't be happy at all
and he was frozen and hungry.
But in the hostels where he slept
he found many people like him
pale with shabby clothes and unshaven.
They played cards and told one another
what had happened to them
until the warden put out the light.

Aber dann wurde es Frühling. Im Luxemburg-Garten kamen die gelben Narzissen ans Licht. Die Luft duftete nach Sonne, jungen Blättern und Aperitifs und eines Mittags als er auf einer Bank mit einem jungen Mädchen zusammensass, da sprach er sie an. Sie plauderten vom Wetter und sahen dass sie sich gern hatten. Sie blieben beieinander bis zum Abend und tanzten zusammen in einem kleinen rauchigen Lokal und sagten Du zueinander.	But then it was spring. In the Luxembourg Gardens the yellow daffodils came out. The air had the scent of sunshine, new leaves and aperitifs and one day when he was sitting on a bench with a young girl, he spoke to her. They chatted about the weather and saw that they liked each other. They stayed together till the evening and danced together in a smoky little café and were on first-name terms.
Da begann er sich wohl zu fühlen in den schmalen Hotelzimmern unter den Dächern von Paris und lernte viele Menschen kennen, die waren sehr freundlich zu ihm und halfen ihm und machten ihm Komplimente und grosse Firmen gaben ihm Aufträge für Plakate und Modeentwürfe und er fing bereits an sich einen Namen zu machen	Then he began to feel happy in the narrow hotel rooms under the roofs of Paris and got to know a lot of people who were very kind to him and helped him and complimented him and big companies signed him on for posters and fashion designs and he started to make a name for himself.
Da holte ihn die Polizei weil er keine Arbeitserlaubnis hatte und sperrte ihn ins Gefängnis. Und als kurz darauf der grosse Krieg ausbrach zwischen Deutschland und Frankreich und England wurde er mit vielen seinesgleichen in ein Lager geschafft.	The police arrested him because he didn't have a work permit and shut him up in prison. And when soon afterwards the great war broke out between Germany and England and France he was put into a camp with many others.
Da hungerte er sehr, denn es gab gewöhnlich nur Kartoffelsuppe, Kaffee und Brot. Sie machten sich Spielkarten aus alten Kartons und kneteten sich Schachfiguren aus altem Brot und wenn es regnete dann rann der Schmutz in ihre Hütten. Die grauen Ratten kamen aus ihren Löchern und frassen was sie konnten.	He was very hungry there, as there was usually only potato soup, coffee and bread. They made packs of cards out of old cartons and kneaded chess pieces from old bread and when it rained the dirt ran down into their huts. The grey rats came out of their holes and ate everything they could find.
Und dann eines Tages hörte man das Trommelfeuer der grossen Kanonen in der Ferne.	And then one day they heard the drumming noise of large guns in the distance.

Die Offiziere wurden böse und aufgeregt
und drohten mit Revolvern, wenn
einer zu nahe ans Gitter kam.
Dann ratterten ganz in der Nähe
    Maschinengewehre
Flugzeuge kreisten niedrig über dem Lager.
Zweihundert Schritte von seinem
    Eingang erschien
auf Motorrädern eine Handvoll Deutscher
und forderte
dass man ihnen die Insassen übergab…

Da weigerten sich die Franzosen.
Sie sammelten sich um ihre
    Maschinengewehre
und einige rückten gegen die Deutschen
    vor.
Aber als es gerade so aussah
als wollten die Franzosen sich zur Wehr
    setzen
und als würde es ein blutiges Gefecht
    geben
da traten auf beiden Seiten die Offiziere
    hervor
winkten beruhigend ihren Soldaten,
    gingen
ernst in gemessenem Schritt auf einander
    zu
grüssten
schlugen die Hacken
und dann
sahen sie sich plötzlich ganz vertraulich an
gaben sich die Hände: So!
und sagten:

Warum sollen wir uns nicht vertragen?
Warum wollen wir einander schlagen?
Das tut schliesslich nur uns selber weh!
Statt uns miteinander zu verkrachen
suchen wir uns lieber einen Schwachen
und verhauen und verdreschen
und verprügeln ihn gemeinsam
mit Juchheiserassa und Juchhe!

Chor:
mit Juchheiserassa und Juchhe!

Sprecher:
Und dann schlugen beide im Verein
auf die Leute in dem Lager ein

The officers became angry and nervous
and threatened anyone with revolvers
who came too near the fence.
And then machine guns chattered nearby
planes circled low over the camp
two hundred paces before the entrance
there appeared a handful of Germans on
    motor cycles
and demanded
that the inmates should be handed over to
    them…

The French refused.
They gathered round their
    machine guns
and some advanced on the
    Germans.
But when it looked as if
the French were going to defend
    themselves
and there would be a bloody conflict
the officers on both sides stepped
    forwards
waved soothingly to their soldiers,
    moved
towards one another at a moderate
    pace
greeted one another
clicked their heels
and then
looked at one another in a friendly sort of
    way
shook hands: like this!
and said:

Why can't we get along with one another?
Why is each of us trying to thrash the other?
We'll just hurt ourselves that way!
Instead of fighting why not seek
someone who is nice and weak
then we thrash him and we beat him
and we punch him both together
with hoorah and with hooray!

Chorus:
with hoorah and with hooray!

Speaker:
they both knew what they should do:
they beat the people black and blue.

Chor:
und dann schlugen beide im Verein
auf die Leute in dem Lager ein

Sprecher:
bis ihnen die Puste ausging
und bis da schliesslich auch nicht mehr
        viel zu schlagen war.
Französische Wachen versteckten am
        Abend
den Jakob und einige andre im Ufergebüsch
sie brachten sich nachts mit ihnen
        zusammen in Sicherheit.
Und dann zog der Jakob ohne Geld
wieder ein Stück weiter in die Welt

Chor:
und dann zog der Jakob ohne Geld
wieder ein Stück weiter in die Welt.

Chorus:
they both knew what they should do:
they beat the people black and blue.

Speaker:
until they ran out of breath
until there was nothing much
        more to beat.
In the evening French guards hid
Jacob and some others in the
        undergrowth
at night they got to safety
        with them.
Again went Jacob, without delay,
penniless further on his way.

Chorus:
Again went Jacob, without delay,
penniless further on his way.

V

Sprecher:
Ja, liebe Leute, dieses ist
die wahre Geschichte von dem armen
        Jakob.
Er wanderte von Land zu Land
über die weite Erde hin
ruhte hier ein wenig, rastete dort eine Weile
aber er konnte nirgends lange bleiben.
Denn immer wenn die Unruhe unter den
        Völkern wuchs
wenn sie sich lauter und lauter bedrohten
        mit Tod und Zerstörung
gefangen im Dickicht ihres gegenseitigen
        Hasses
wie Fische im Netz
dann war er unter den ersten den sie
        schlugen.
Und er musste weiterwandern
vorbei an den anderen die noch ruhig vor
        ihren Häusern sassen
und er sagte ihnen, sich bereit zu halten für
        das Ungewitter das im Kommen war.
Aber die Menschen hörten ihn nicht.
        Denn er war ja machtlos
und ein Geschlagener.

Speaker:
Yes, dear people, this is
the true story of poor
        Jacob.
He wandered from country to country
over the wide earth
rested a little here, stopped for a while there
but he could stay nowhere for long.
For always when disorder grew among
        peoples
when they threatened louder and louder
        with death and destruction
trapped in the thicket of their mutual
        hatred
like fish in a net
then he was one of the first they
        struck.
And he had to move on
past the others who were still sitting
        peacefully in front of their houses
and he told them to be ready for the
        approaching storm.
But the people didn't listen to him. For he
        was powerless
and a beaten man.

Furchen zogen über sein Gesicht und
        Narben über seinen Leib
und sein Haar wurde grau.
Aber die Augen blieben klar

Furrows cut across his face and scars across
        his body
and his hair became grey.
But his eyes stayed clear

und stark auf ihre Weise
denn er hatte Vieles gesehen:
die Menschen von innen, Schläger und
    Geschlagene
ohne ihre Verhüllungen.
Und es gab nur noch wenig vor dem ihm
    schauderte.

Da redete er nicht mehr viel. Die kleinen
    Falten
zogen sich fester um seinen Mund.
Nur manchmal
wenn er für Monate gefangen sass mit
    anderen Geschlagenen
oder an Deck eines Schiffes
auf der Reise nach einem unbekannten
    Land
oder auch
in einer der kleinen Tavernen am Rande
    der südlichen Städte
wo man die warmen Nächte hindurch
billigen Wein trank und Geschichten
    erzählte und Lieder sang
da begann er manchmal zu erzählen:
von den Erschlagenen und von denen die
    sich gerettet hatten
von den Liebesleuten, die
    auseinandergerissen wurden und sich
    nie mehr fanden
und von denen die verschickt wurden
ohne zu wissen wohin.

Er erzählte von Feinden und wie sie zu
    bekämpfen, denn so ist unsere Erde
aber ohne Bitterkeit
und dass auch sie Getriebene sind wie wir
    alle
und im Grunde ohne Schuld.
Er erzählte von den Menschen und wie er
    Gefallen an ihnen fand
auch ohne ihre Masken
kunstfertig wie sie waren und verspielt
    und arbeitsam
faul und verträumt und grausam, grosse
    Kinder
wenn man sie spielen liess
und wilde Tiere wenn die Furcht sie
    packte
und die Wut über sie kam
und am nächsten noch den andern
    Menschen auf die er wartete
wenn sie ganz machtlos waren
oder teilten die Macht.

and in their own way strong
for he had seen much:
people from within, the beaters and the
    beaten
without their disguises.
And there was little left that made him
    shudder.

He no longer talked much. The little
    creases
became firmer around his mouth.
But sometimes
when he was imprisoned for months with
    others who were beaten
or on the deck of a ship
sailing to an unknown land
or else
in one of the little taverns on the edge of the
    southern cities
where through the warm nights
one drank cheap wine and told stories and
    sang songs
then he sometimes began to tell:
of those beaten down and those who had
    escaped
of lovers who were torn apart and lost each
    other for ever
and those who were sent away
not knowing where to.

He told of enemies and how to fight them,
    for such is our earth
but without bitterness
and they, too, are hounded like all
    of us
and basically guiltless.
He told of people and how he had taken
    pleasure in them
even without their masks
skilful as they were and playful and
    industrious
lazy and dreamy and cruel, big
    children
when one let them play
and wild animals when fear gripped
    them
and rage came over them
and most of all the other people he was
    waiting for
when they were quite powerless
or shared power.

So erzählte er bis zum Morgengrauen.
Und sang ihnen Lieder und trank den
    Wein
und wenn sie unruhig wurden und in
    Unmut
zu raufen begannen: über Äpfel oder ein
    Fässchen Wein
dann redete er ihnen zu sich zu
    vertragen
und sich die Hände zu geben:
So!
und er sprach zu ihnen und sagte:

Warum können wir uns nicht vertragen?
Wir haben nichts als uns.
Warum sollen wir uns selber schlagen
und wehtun?
Diese Erde hat genug des Guten
Früchte, Wein und Korn
warum solln die Schwächeren im Zorn
der Stärkeren verbluten?

Raufen wir uns um ein Fass voll Wein
bricht das Fass in Trümmer, hat am Ende
    keiner was
schenket friedlich ein
jeder kriegt ein Glas.

Da sangen sie alle und tranken
und der alte Jakob freute sich der
    Menschen so wie sie waren
bald gut, bald schlecht, wie es die
    Zeitläufe brachten.

Aber am Morgen machte er sich wieder
    auf seinen Weg
und wenn sie ihn nicht totgeschlagen
    haben.

Sprecher und Chor:
wandert er noch immer ohne Geld
ein Stück weiter um die weite Welt.

So he spoke until dawn.
And he sang them songs and drank the
    wine
and when they became restless and in ill-
    humour
began to squabble: about apples or a cask
    of wine
then he told them to get along with each
    other
and to shake hands:
like this!
and he spoke to them and said:

Why can't we be like a sister or brother?
We only have us.
Why do we both try to thrash one another?
and are both hurt?
On this earth enough goodness grows
Fruit and wine and grain
why should the weaker suffer pain
from the stronger's angry blows?

If we fight over a barrel of wine
when the barrel breaks, there's wine for
    none
if we pour out the wine in peace
there's enough for everyone.

Then they all sang and drank
and old Jacob enjoyed people as
    they were
sometimes good, sometimes bad, according
    to the times.

But in the morning he set off
    again
if they haven't beaten him to
    death.

Speaker and Chorus:
and still he goes, without delay,
penniless a little further on his way.

Appendix Three
Hans Gál in Conversation
MARTIN ANDERSON

This conversation, first published in the *Journal of the British Music Society* (Vol. 9, 1987, pp. 33–44), was recorded at Dr Gál's Edinburgh home in December 1986, less than a year before his death on 3 October 1987, and shows his wit and wisdom undiminished by age. As a performing musician, too, he was in full command of his faculties: at the end of the interview he sat at the piano and played me some extracts from Bach's *Well-Tempered Clavier* with extraordinary sensitivity of touch.

The gentle humour evident in his conversation had already surfaced in an exchange before I began recording. I asked him: 'There's a rumour that you played the piano to Brahms – is that true?' His answer stopped me in my tracks: 'What do you think? I was only six when he died'.[1]

Although you are Austrian by birth, Gál isn't an Austrian name, is it?

Gál is an Hungarian name. My father was Hungarian.

Had he settled in Austria by the time you were born?

He came to Vienna as a student, and became a doctor of medicine. It was a middle-class family. Both my grandfathers were doctors, too – it was a family of doctors.

Were you then, like Berlioz, destined to become a doctor, and not a musician?

No, no. I never intended to become anything else. In this respect my feelings were perfectly in balance when I left school at eighteen.

Did your parents help you?

My parents couldn't help me much. Right from my student time I had to make my own existence as a teacher. I had pupils in Vienna from the age of eighteen or nineteen.

Were you composing already?

Oh yes. I started composing at eleven or twelve, and during my years at secondary school I wrote an awful lot of music.

All of which, I believe, you have since disowned.

---

[1] In the summer months in Gál's childhood his family rented a house in Heiligenstadt, diagonally across the street from the house Beethoven used to occupy. An old lady who lived locally told the young Gál that, as a member of a gang of children, she used to tease the deaf Beethoven in the street and throw snowballs at him in the winter (e-mail from Eva Fox-Gál to Martin Anderson, 29 April 2014).

I disowned them very soon, all these early works. I must have written towards a hundred songs around then.

So how old were you when you composed your first acknowledged composition?

Only after having had my sound training – not at the University: one didn't get a musical training at the University. One could go to the Conservatoire, which I did not, or one could have private tuition, which I had. My teacher was Mandyczewski.[2]

You collaborated with Mandyczewski on the Brahms edition, didn't you?

Later, yes; but I became his pupil when I was nineteen.

Which made you a 'grand-pupil' of Nottebohm.[3] Did you know Robert Fuchs[4] at the Hochschule?

Yes, Fuchs I knew personally. He taught at the Conservatoire. My only teacher was Mandyczewski. I became a musician in every respect during my early twenties, but by the time I had become 'mature' the First World War started, and after a year I was in the army.

What were you doing in the army?

I had different occupations, but after the first few months was not in the front line any more. I had to do with administration and things like that, with war prisoners. I got round all the different parts of the War in the Austrian army: I was in Serbia, in Hungary, in Poland, in Italy.

Was your suite of Serbian dances based on what you heard there?

Yes, the *Serbian Dances*[5] came from that time in Serbia, when I was travelling round the country. At the end of the War I was in the Austrian part of Italy. It was not a joke, you know: it was a very convulsive time, the end of the Austrian monarchy in 1918, when it fell into pieces. One has forgotten this part of history, you know. Austria was the only country in Europe at the time of the First World War without a parliament. Parliament had become a problem of different parties working against one another. It was not workable, and so it was dissolved in 1912. Austria was then ruled by a Prime Minister, who was never elected: he was nominated by the Emperor. Then the old Emperor died towards the end of 1916, and in the spring of 1917 the young Emperor, Karl, convoked the parliament – and the first thing the parliament did was to dissolve the monarchy. This was the situation in 1918. Of course, there was still the army who kept the country somehow together, and then

---

[2] *Cf.* note 3 on p. 13, above.

[3] Gustav Nottebohm (1812–82) is chiefly remembered as a pioneering Beethoven scholar, being the first to make a systematic study of Beethoven's manuscripts, the sketches and exercises in particular. His own compositions consist chiefly of chamber works and piano music.

[4] Fuchs (1847–1927) was the composer of three symphonies, five orchestral serenades (which became so popular that he was nicknamed 'Serenaden-Fuchs'), two operas and a substantial body of chamber music. Although Fuchs counted Brahms among the many admirers of his music, it was as a teacher that he is best remembered, his students including Enescu, Korngold, Mahler, Schmidt, Schreker, Sibelius, Wolf and Zemlinsky.

[5] *Serbische Weisen* ('Serbian Tunes'), Op. 3, for piano duet or small orchestra, composed in 1916.

this was dissolved in the autumn of 1918. At that time I went home to Vienna on the day when the Austrian republic was constituted: 12 December 1918.

What kind of state was musical life in Vienna in after the War?

It took two or three years before everything became workable again. But for an Austrian composer the chief part of his activity was in Germany. Germany had consisted of forty or fifty principalities. Every principality had a duke or king at its head, and as it was the custom at that time he had to have a court theatre, which did opera. So there were fifty permanent operatic theatres in Germany at that time – a tremendous musical activity. Every opera had its orchestra. So there was a kind of musical life which is difficult to imagine knowing the musical life of this country, where nothing similar ever existed.

So the system of court theatres survived the War?

Yes, when the kings and dukes had to go at the end of the World War, the cities or the states took over, because the theatres existed and one couldn't let them disappear. I became known as an operatic composer just after the First World War – I had my first operatic performance in Breslau in 1919.

Which opera was that?

Der Arzt der Sobeide.[6] It was published at the same time. When an opera was performed, there was no difficulty with the publisher: one knew there would be some response. And this was the case at that time. Two years later came my main operatic success, *Die heilige Ente*, which had its first performance in Dusseldorf, conducted by George Szell.[7] So my first big steps in publicity came through opera, although, of course, I had written a lot of chamber music at the time, and orchestral music also.

You were also active as a pianist, weren't you?

Oh yes. I had a good pianistic training. My teacher, Richard Robert,[8] was the teacher of Rudolf Serkin, of Clara Haskil; he was practically the best piano teacher in Vienna at that time. I came to him when I was about fifteen, and I had a very sound pianistic training, and started teaching, piano first and later composition, because I had to maintain myself.

---

[6] 'Sobeide's Doctor', comic opera in a prologue and two acts, Op. 4 (1917–18), to a libretto by Fritz Zoref. The premiere was conducted in Breslau (today Wrocław in Poland) on 2 November 1919 by Julius Prüwer.

[7] 'The Sacred Duck', 'A Play with Gods and Men' in a prelude and three acts, Op. 15 (1920–21), premiered on 29 April 1923. *Cf.* pp. 15 and 16, above.

[8] The Vienna-born Robert (*né* Spitzer; 1861–1924) was hugely esteemed as a piano pedagogue, although he was also a composer (writing songs, chamber music and an opera, *Rhampsinit*), the editor (1885–91) of the journal *Neue Musikalische Rundschau* and a critic for a number of Viennese newspapers. His own teachers included Julius Epstein and Anton Bruckner; among his other distinguished students were the conductor Kurt Adler, composer and pianist Julius Chajes, composer Wilhelm Grosz, pianist Marjan Rawicz (who, with Walter Landauer, formed the popular piano duo Rawicz and Landauer, themselves interned on the Isle of Man in 1940), composer-conductor Alfred Rosé, composer Marcel Rubin, conductor Rudolf Schwarz (later a champion of Gál's music), composer and music-therapist Vally Weigl and musicologist Viktor Zuckerkandl.

Were you teaching privately?

Yes. And when in 1909 my teacher Robert became the Director of the New Conservatoire in Vienna, there I taught piano and harmony and counterpoint. I had a full occupation. I don't think I ever had a time without a full ten hours' daily work, besides composition.

Did you ever resent teaching for taking time away from composition?

No, I couldn't say that. I accepted things as they came, without asking questions. You mustn't forget that it was a situation when, with respect to the regular proceedings of the day, one didn't ask any questions. One accepted things as they were. There were rich and poor, and the poor had to work. I was more or less poor. I had three sisters who too had to work. My sister Erna became a pianist. My other two sisters worked at the office of a bank.[9]

You were composing a lot by this time. Were these commissions, or were you just writing in the hope that someone would come along and perform them?

I couldn't call them commissions, because 'commission' means one pays for something; but if somebody asked me for a composition I did write it. My first work that was published, *Von ewiger Freude*, a work for female chorus, organ and harp, was written for an occasion.[10] My teacher Mandyczewski had a female chorus, and there was a performance in the biggest hall in Vienna, the Musikvereinsaal. It was on a poem from the seventeenth century. At that time nobody spoke of Baroque poetry, but I found it somewhere in a collection; it appealed to me, and so I wrote music to it. Much later, at least ten years later, there came the fashion for Baroque poetry in Germany, poetry written at the time of the Thirty Years' War. Any instigation, any claim, was sufficient to make me write music.

You were writing in the Vienna of the 'Second Viennese School'. How was your music regarded by your contemporaries?

I don't think I was ever conscious of conforming with anything. I wrote the music that came to me spontaneously. I had made music from my childhood. At that time the chance of listening to music was restricted to public occasions – there was no wireless – so that in a centre of music such as Vienna there were no more than two dozen orchestral concerts throughout the year.

Is that all? We are conventionally told of Vienna in the first thirty years of the twentieth century as being alive with music.

It *was* alive with music. Yet everything was restricted to the comparatively rare chance of public performance. The Philharmonic Orchestra in Vienna gave eight concerts a year. There were two more orchestras, and everyone had, I think, a dozen concerts a year. This was the supply of orchestral music. Chamber music was a rare occasion in public. There was the Rosé Quartet, the members of which were members of the Philharmonic Orchestra;

---

[9] *Cf.* Appendix One, pp. 183 and 185, above.

[10] Gál's Op. 1 (though his fourth acknowledged composition), *Von ewiger Freude* was first performed in the Gesellschaft der Musikfreunde on 16 February 1913, with the Albine Mandyczewski Chorus conducted by Eusebius Mandyczewski; the organist was Alois Kofler.

Rosé was its leader.[11] They gave six string-quartet recitals throughout the season – not more.

The positive side of this situation was that one studied a score soundly before first hearing it. The only primary possibility of getting acquainted with great music was the piano duet. I had two piano-playing sisters, and we played everything, up to Brahms and Bruckner and Mahler. Every work that was published was first published as a piano duet; it was the way of selling music at the time. One knew music from the inside. Before I went to an orchestral concert I studied all the scores. I don't think that a young musician nowadays makes such a sound acquaintance with the score as we did then. Things changed enormously with the advent of radio – it changed the world of music. I had an engagement with the Vienna Radio – it must have been in 1927 or '28. It was the first time for Vienna Radio that contemporary music was actually performed for a broadcast, and with me on the same occasion was Richard Strauss, who accompanied the singer Steiner[12] in his songs. I played my 'Heurigen Variations'[13] on that occasion.

Was there no sense of conflict with more radical composers?

No. These things came later. When broadcasting became such a widely spread activity, there was room for everything in it. Then, in 1929, I became director of the College of Music in Mainz, in West Germany. I was there for three years, until the advent of Hitler, and then I was thrown out. I came back to Vienna in 1933.

You were conducting quite a bit by then, weren't you?

In Vienna, yes. And then in 1938, when the Nazis came to Vienna, we left instantly and came to this country.

Why Britain?

We intended to go to America. We came to Britain as a first step, because we had friends here. I had invitations to America, several very serious invitations. Now I became acquainted with Tovey,[14] and Tovey invited me to Edinburgh.

How did you meet him?

I knew of him, and he knew of me. We met in London. He invited me to Edinburgh because he wanted to bring me to the University. But then the War started, and I was interned as an enemy alien. I spent half a year on the Isle of Man, and then it was too late to go to America during the War.

What were conditions like in the internment camp? I know you wrote music there.

---

[11] Arnold Rosé (1863–1946) formed the Rosé Quartet in 1886 and led it for the 55 years of its existence; it was disbanded in 1938. He and his cellist brother Eduard both married sisters of Gustav Mahler.

[12] The baritone Franz Steiner (1876–1954), a student of Johannes Ress in Vienna and Johannes Messchaert in Frankfurt and, from 1905, a singer of international repute. Also a Jew, he had to flee Austria in 1938 and became an important teacher in Mexico City.

[13] *Variationen über eine Wiener Heurigenmelodie* ('Variations on a Viennese "Heurigen" Melody'), Op. 9, for piano trio (1914).

[14] *Cf.* Appendix One, p. 194, above.

First at Huyton, near Liverpool, and then on the Isle of Man, we organised ourselves as well as possible, and there was music. There was a lot of music. We performed a play to which I wrote the music. One of my compositions there was my *Huyton Suite* for flute and two violins, for the only musicians who had their instruments with them. It was performed everywhere – in the different tents and houses. It was a curious life. I was interned for five months from May to the end of September. And then I was released because of a skin disease which was very, very torturing and which I kept for many years. Others remained there until the spring of '41; they were all interned in May 1940. It was a very curious policy, to intern Hitler's best enemies!

I first came to Edinburgh in April 1938. Tovey invited me to organise the Reid Library, which at that time consisted of cases and boxes full of music and books. I spent the summer of 1938 and the following winter at the Reid Library here, and in the end produced a catalogue of valuable music and books, both manuscript and printed.[15] I had my own system, with the place of the music and a number: the only reasonable way is to place the music according to its size because you cannot do it any differently. I brought things into order. It's a very valuable library brought together by chance and luck over a long period. There were Reid Professors all through the nineteenth century – good and bad musicians, and no musicians at all; it was a very curious institution. Tovey, of course, was an eminent musician and a splendid spirit. Unfortunately, he fell ill already during that first year of our acquaintance, towards the end of 1938.

He was quite severely rheumatised by then, wasn't he?

Well, he was catastrophically hit by a sort of deterioration of the whole body. He died during the time when I was on the Isle of Man, in the summer of 1940. But without him we probably would have gone to America before the War. And then it became impossible, and so we remained here after the War, when I became a lecturer at the University. I had been teaching in Edinburgh already during the War. And I was teaching at the University long over my proper age: I was 70 when I retired. Chance decides so many things in life. Chance decided that we remained in Edinburgh.

Were you composing all the time?

I have always written music. I have also written several books, but in practice I never wrote a book without a publisher asking for it. It was not my proper vocation, but when I did it, I did it with my fullest interest, and so things came out that have made their way. I wrote in German to begin with. One of my books I translated myself into English, on Schubert, but the others were translated by others. I wrote four monographs – Brahms, Wagner, Schubert and Verdi – and this one here, of *Letters of Great Musicians*, was republished in German, and more recently also in Spanish, called *The Musician's World*.[16] This, too, was based on my experience at the Library. I would never have written it without having a thorough knowledge of the literature. I spent the summer of 1940 at the Reid Library, organising it, but

---

[15] *Catalogue of Manuscripts, Printed Music and Books of Music up to 1850 in the Library of the Music Department of the University of Edinburgh*, Oliver and Boyd, London, 1941.

[16] *Cf.* note 5 on p. 181, above.

my main activity was reading. All the important sources of music were available there. General Reid was a lover of music, and he founded this library in the early nineteenth century.

You had been widely performed in Germany and Austria before the War.

Oh yes. At the time, before 1933, my operas were performed everywhere. There were so many operatic theatres, as I told you. Three operas of mine came out in the 1920s.[17]

Did you find you had virtually to begin again when you came to Britain?

Yes, it was practically a new start. Again, my chief stimulus was the urge to create. I always wrote music, until at the age of 86 or 88 I closed my workshop and decided: 'Now it's enough'. One mustn't go on beyond a certain age.

Why not?

When one is too old, there are limits. My last work that was published was a set of 24 fugues for piano.[18]

You seem to have been luckier with publishers than with performances.

I was never very active in promoting my own cause, and when came to this country, not far off 50, I was practically unable to do it, so what happened on my behalf happened through friends, through musicians who were interested in my work – through others. I was much too passive to do anything. I always cultivated my piano-playing. I played much in public here too, especially at a time when the Edinburgh lunch-hour concerts were started during the War. It must have been in 1942 or '43. Tertia Liebenthal,[19] long forgotten now, was the foundress of these lunch-hour concerts, every Wednesday, and there I played frequently, both as a solo pianist and as a song accompanist or in chamber music. I still play, after four operations each, my hands are still able to play. The operations were for hardening tendons: first the left hand then the right hand. You can see that the surgeon had made much progress between the operations – he learned his job on my hands!

---

[17] Gál's third opera from the 1920s was *Das Lied der Nacht*, Op. 23, a 'Dramatic Ballad in Three Scenes' to a libretto by K. M. von Levetzow, first performed in Breslau on 24 April 1926 conducted by Fritz Cortolezis (1878–1934), who was chief conductor there from 1925 to 1929. Gál's fourth and last opera was *Die beiden Klaas*, Op. 42 (1932–33), a three-act comic opera, again to a libretto by von Levetzow, which awaits a professional production.

[18] Gál understates his own longevity as a composer: after the 24 Fugues, Op. 108 (1979–80), he composed a Sonata and Suite for solo cello, Op. 109a and b (1982), a set of *Four Bagatelles* and a Sonatina for solo treble recorder, Op. 110a and b (1983); his last work, without opus number, was a *Moment Musical*, also for solo treble recorder (1986).

[19] An Edinburgh native (with a Russo-German father from Königsberg), Tertia Liebenthal was born in 1889 and lived all her life in the house where she was born, 34 Regent Terrace (Sir Herbert Grierson, patron of the Gáls during their early days in Edinburgh, lived at No. 12). An amateur violinist, she played in Tovey's Reid Orchestra for some years. She founded the lunch-hour concerts at the Edinburgh Society of Musicians in 1941 and on 4 March 1970 collapsed as she made an announcement during the 699th concert, dying later that day. (The 700th concert, where the performers were Peter Pears and Benajmin Britten, was therefore dedicated to her memory.) The cellist Moray Welsh provides a pen-portrait of her at www.moraywelsh.com/tertia.html.

I still play as far as I can; as an old man one has one's limits. But the ear is fine. Fortunately the ear has hardly deteriorated. It lost a little bit of sharpness of hearing, but no trouble with pitch at all.

I believe you heard Mahler conduct in Vienna.

Yes, it was always an extraordinary experience. I attended one of his earliest performances at the Wiener Hofoper. It was Auber's *Fra Diavolo*, curiously.

But that was in 1897!

Yes, that is correct. I was only a small boy, but in those days it was the custom for children to go to the opera with their parents, and so we went to see *Fra Diavolo*. We heard Mahler conduct quite often at the opera house, where he remained until 1907. It is extraordinary how these things stick in the memory. But it was the most marvellous conducting – in all these years I've never heard anything to equal it.

You were also acquainted with Franz Schmidt, I believe.

Oh yes. Schmidt was one of the most completely natural musicians I have ever met, an extremely gifted man and very capable indeed. Unfortunately, he had no sense of literary taste and so he chose these atrocious libretti, to which he wrote marvellous music. But he was a profound musician.

And you were a student together with Georg Szell, I believe.

'Student' only as far as we both had the same teacher, Robert, in Vienna. I was seven years older than he, and he was practically a child when I first met him. He was an enormously mature child. He had started very early; he was splendid at the piano; and he was immensely gifted as a composer. There are two elements the combination of which results in the perfect musician: a perfect ear and a perfect sense of rhythm. Szell had both: physically he was the most perfect musician I have ever met. At the age of sixteen Szell wrote a set of orchestral variations on a theme of his own, which at that time was performed everywhere in Germany. It was a tremendous success. And three years later he wrote his last work.[20] He was never able to work any more. When his sense of self-criticism became awake, composing was something he put aside because it was too much bother. He had never learned to work. His sharpness of musical mind was so enormous that a look into a score was sufficient for him to know everything. So, as a conductor, he hardly had to work: it came to him, so to speak, by itself. And when with this sharpening self-criticism composing became something difficult, he just put it aside; he didn't do it any more.

Have you found composing difficult at any point in your career, patches when nothing seems to come?

For me the process of composition was always concentration to the utmost, and to every detail. I never put something on paper without being sure of its necessity.

---

[20] The young Szell had a contract with Universal Edition, which brought out his Quintet for Piano and Strings in E major, Op. 2 (1911), the *Drei Kleine Klavierstücke*, Op. 6 (undated; published in 1922), and two orchestra works, *Orchestervariationen über ein eigenes Thema*, Op. 4 (1918), and a *Lyrische Ouvertüre*, Op. 5 (1921).

During many, many years in this country during the latest twenty or 25 years of my life as a composer, I mainly wrote chamber music. It was because of the intimacy and the feeling of being perfectly in balance with myself. I can't express it in any different way. So, besides the *Huyton Suite* for flute and two violins, I wrote a Trio for oboe, violin and viola[21] – the most transparent sound, where every note is so essential that one couldn't do without it. Anyway, I had the chance of having so much music published – more than a hundred works. The earlier ones, many of them, are out of print, and many not republished so far. Publishers, too, have their interests to think of, and so music goes out of commission. But I have had works published by more than a dozen publishers. My operas, of course, were published: they couldn't have been performed without that.

Do you ever feel resentful that so little of it gets heard nowadays?

This is regrettable. But I am confident of not having published anything about which I could say that I was sorry to have done it. So far I have a good conscience.

Do you ever look back and say of your music: 'Ah, I must have been listening to Reger, say, or Brahms'?

No, as to the identity of my music, I have always remained self-confident![22]

---

[21] Gál's Op. 94, composed in 1941.
[22] *Cf.* also Martin Anderson, 'Hans Gál and Egon Wellesz: Parallel Lives, Divergent Aesthetics', in Michael Haas and Marcus G. Patka (eds.), *Musik des Aufbruchs: Hans Gál und Egon Wellesz, Continental Britons*, Mandelbaum Verlag, Vienna, 2004, pp. 15–32.

Appendix Four
A Memoir of Hans Gál

WALTER KELLERMANN

In this memoir Walter Kellermann, who was both a fellow-internee and personal friend (*cf.* also Appendix One: Personalia, p. 193, above), expanded upon material written as part of his autobiography, *A Physicist's Labour in War and Peace, Memoirs 1933–1999*, published in 2004 by Stamford House, Peterborough.

I met Dr Gál before the war at a house in Edinburgh where the sisters Turk had created a welcoming atmosphere for any refugee who wanted to visit. Bertha and Martha Turk had settled in a comfortable house in the South of Edinburgh. Martha had been a doctor in Germany and had re-qualified at the Edinburgh medical school, but decided not to practise medicine again and to retire. Many of the friends she had made at medical school kept dropping in at the weekend. Gradually other refugee academics, too, who had found a temporary home in Edinburgh, found their way to the house. I learned that Dr Gál, a brilliant musicologist and composer, originally from Vienna, had been the youngest director appointed at the Mainz Conservatorium. Professor Tovey, the authority on Beethoven, Professor of Music at the University, was aware of Dr Gál's reputation and had welcomed him, at first on a temporary basis, in his Department. Hans was older than I, but we soon developed a mutual understanding growing into mutual empathy and friendship. He had a very sharp mind and would speak his mind with utter sincerity and yet with his great tact would not offend. On some evenings he would without prompting go to the piano and provide us with a touching rendering of a Chopin prelude or a Brahms caprice. I was close enough to be deeply affected by the tragic death of his younger, very brilliant, son[1] and could rejoice with him when his charming wife was pregnant with his daughter Eva. Our discussions ranged widely. We discussed the importance and impact of, and the Soviet reaction to, Shostakovich's latest symphony.[2] We argued about the political situation, about Chamberlain's policies and the question of whether these were going to make war more or less likely. His clear mind impressed me deeply, as did his faculty of arriving at a balanced judgment without losing his sense of humour. I was a member of an amateur

---

[1] Peter Gál (1924–42); *cf.* Appendix One: Personalia, p. 185, above.

[2] Shostakovich's Fifth Symphony was premiered on 21 November 1937, at the height of Stalin's purges. The previous year, after a series of editorial attacks in *Pravda* (approved, if not in fact written, by Stalin), Shostakovich had withdrawn his Fourth Symphony. The Fifth was rapturously received by its first audience, but the Party response was at first muted. Two months later, on 25 January 1938, an article by a Soviet journalist in *Vechernaya Moskva* described the work as 'A Soviet Artist's Creative Reply to a Just Criticism', probably the quasi-official sanction to which Kellermann refers.

224

orchestra that he conducted. On one occasion we rehearsed for a charity concert, and the soloist was the singer Sabine Kalter.[3] Both the orchestra and the singer understood each other well, but once Miss Kalter held a high note for a very long time. Yet we, the orchestra, without waiting for a sign from Dr Gál thought she was overdoing it. So almost automatically we played the final chord while she was still holding her high note. Miss Kalter was furious. Hans Gál tapped the podium with his baton and addressed us: 'Meine Damen und Herren! So lange wie der Soloist ihre Fermate zu singen wünscht, können Sie spielen, was Sie wollen, aber nur nicht die nächste Note!'[4]

Hans Gál and I as well as many of our friends were interned together in May 1940. In the camps we were in daily contact, until the British War Office decided to transport me and many other young academics to Canada.[5] When first interned Hans had no news about his wife and young family, but he was never depressed. With his sharp mind he analysed our situation which he found at the same time deplorable and ridiculous. He was struck by what he regarded as the stupidity of the military authorities who seemed unable to differentiate between Nazis and us, their convinced opponents. He, like all of us, was shocked by the way we had been treated. Yet he was hopeful also that the same British people who had offered us a helping hand and given us asylum and their friendship would triumph in the end. He was sure they would convince officialdom of our value to society and our willingness to oppose Hitler actively.

I was released from internment fairly soon and, I think, some time before him. During most of the remainder of the war my work was in the South of England and I did not see him. It was a great pleasure, I think for both of us, when we met again after the war when Hans, his wife and his daughter Eva had settled in Edinburgh. Hans then occupied a lecturing position in the Music Department of Edinburgh University. He had begun to re-establish his international contacts, was able to travel and enjoy the honours that were bestowed on him. Later still I visited him again, and I remember a long walk with him and Eva and my eldest daughter Barbara[6] across the Pentland hills which both of us loved. We kept in touch for a long time thereafter, mainly through his wife's letters. Hans never seemed to age. Even well after his retirement he stayed amazingly active, both spiritually and physically. I shall always remember him for his kindness, his optimism, his sincerity and his spirituality from all of which I benefited immensely.

---

[3] The status of the soloist suggests that Gál's amateur orchestra was held in high regard. Sabine Kalter was born in Jaroslaw, in south-eastern Poland, in 1890, was a prominent mezzo soprano whose professional debut was made at the Vienna Volksoper in 1911; she was a soloist at the Hamburg State Opera from 1915 to 1935 and at the Royal Opera House, Covent Garden, in 1935–39, when she retired from the operatic stage, although she continued to make concert appearances in London. Thereafter she taught singing in London, where she died in 1957.

[4] 'Ladies and gentlemen, as long as the soloist wants to hold her pause, you may play what you want, but just not the next note!'

[5] *Cf.* p. 94, above.

[6] Barbara Kellerman (b. 1949) is an actress, with a number of television and film appearances to her credit, perhaps the best-known being in *The Chronicles of Narnia* for the BBC in 1988–90.

Appendix Five
The Hans Gál Society

Every note Gál wrote or played had real meaning. As a composer, he never bothered to follow fashion – nor to react against it. He created in a way that was true to himself – and that is surely the only way that music can have real value.

Steven Isserlis, President of the Hans Gál Society

The Hans Gál Society is a registered charity the aim of which is to extend international awareness of Gál's life and work by supporting performances, recordings, publications, exhibitions and research, and initiating projects to help preserve Gál's legacy for future generations.

As part of its work, the Society part-manages the website www.hansgal.org which provides full information on Gál's music and how to acquire it, on available recordings, news and events, articles, books and biographical information.

The Hans Gál Society relies entirely on donations and the support of its members. New members (from all countries of the world) are always welcome and are the life-blood of the Society. For more information on the Society and how to donate, to join as a member or support the Society in any other way, please visit www.hansgalsociety.org or contact:

The Hans Gál Society
16 Blacket Place
Edinburgh
EH9 1RL
Scotland
+44/0 131 667 8819
enquiries@hansgalsociety.org
www.hansgalsociety.org

The Contributors

Martin Anderson writes for a variety of publications, including *Tempo, The Independent, International Record Review, International Piano, Fanfare* in the USA, *Klassisk Musikkmagasin* in Norway and *Finnish Music Quarterly*. He runs Toccata Press and its sister company, the recording label Toccata Classics (which has released a CD of Hans Gál's cello music), and is a committee member of the International Centre for Suppressed Music in London. The most recent books he edited for Toccata Press both involve musicians exiled by the Nazis: *Stravinsky the Music-Maker* (2011), the complete writings on Stravinsky by Hans Keller, a fellow internee of Hans Gál on the Isle of Man; and, with Aleš Březina, *Martinů's Letters Home: Five Decades of Correspondence with Family and Friends* (2013).

Richard Dove is Emeritus Professor of German at the University of Greenwich and a founder member of the Research Centre for German and Austrian Exile Studies, University of London. He has published widely on the subject of German-speaking exile in Britain, particularly on cultural and political topics. His main publications include *He was a German. A Biography of Ernst Toller* (Libris, London, 1990; German translation: *Ein Leben in Deutschland*, Steidl, Göttingen,1993); *Journey of No Return: Five German-Speaking Literary Exiles in London 1933–45* (Libris, London, 2005; German translation: *Fremd ist die Stadt und leer...*, Parthas Verlag, Berlin, 2004); *Wien-London, Hin und Retour: Das Austrian Centre in London 1939 bis 1947*, with Marietta Bearman *et al.*, Czernin, Vienna, 2004); editor, *Totally un-English? Britain's Internment of Enemy Aliens in Two World Wars*, Yearbook of the Research Centre for German and Austrian Exile Studies, Vol. 7, 2005; *Politics by Other Means. The Free German League of Culture in London 1939–1946*, with Charmian Brinson (Vallentine Mitchell, London, 2010).

Anthony Fox is the son-in-law of Hans Gál. He has a degree in Modern Languages and a PhD in Linguistics from the University of Edinburgh, and was for many years Head of the Department of Linguistics and Phonetics at the University of Leeds, publishing four books as well as linguistics articles. Since his retirement in 2003 he has continued his work in linguistics as well as looking after the archive of his father-in-law and helping to promote his works. He has also produced translations of various works, including the libretto of Gál's last opera, *Die beiden Klaas*.

Eva Fox-Gál was a lecturer in German literature in the Department of English and Related Literature, University of York (UK), from 1971 to 2001. She was a founder member of the British Comparative Literature Association, with a particular interest in the interface between literature and music. Since 1995 she has maintained a busy practice as a homeopath – both her paternal grandfather and great-grandfather were homeopathic doctors in Vienna.

As the daughter of Hans and Hanna Gál. she grew up bilingually and imbibed much of the central European culture which her parents brought with them. She is an active musician, both as pianist and as violinist, and is a committed chamber-music player. She is married, with two grown-up children and two grandsons. She is Honorary Vice-President of the Hans Gál Society.

Sir Alan Peacock was one of the most distinguished British economists of the twentieth century. Born in Ryton-on-Tyne in 1922, he was schooled in Dundee and at the University of St Andrews, where in 1942 his studies were interrupted by call-up to the Royal Navy. Graduating in 1947, he lectured first at St Andrews and then at the London School of Economics (where he conducted the LSE Orchestra), before taking up a chair in economics first at the University of Edinburgh (1956) and then at the newly founded University of York (1962). His final formal appointments were at the University of Buckingham, as Professor (1978), Principal (1980) and Vice-Chancellor (1983). In 1985 he was a co-founder and, until 1991, director of the David Hume Institute in Edinburgh. With Professor Jack Wiseman, a colleague in the Economics Department at York, he was instrumental in introducing into British intellectual life the body of thought known in the USA as Public Choice and in the UK as the Economics of Politics. But it is chiefly for his engagement with cultural economics that he will be remembered, as the author of some thirty books on various aspects of public policy, the arts especially. He was knighted in 1987. He died on 2 August 2014, as this book was going to press.

Bibliography

1. LITERATURE ON HANS GÁL

ANDERSON, MARTIN, 'Hans Gál in Coversation', *Journal of the British Music Society*, Vol. 9, 1987, pp. 33–44

FOX-GÁL, EVA, and FOX, ANTHONY, *Hans Gál: Ein Jahrhundert Musik*, Centrum Judaicum/Hentrich & Hentrich, Berlin, 2012

HAAS, MICHAEL, and PATKA, MARCUS G. (eds.), *Hans Gál und Egon Wellesz: Continental Britons*, Jewish Museum/Mandelbaum, Vienna, 2004

KONTER, ASTRID, 'Hans Gál (1890–1987) als Direktor der Musikhochschule Mainz von 1929 bis 1933', *Mitteilungen der Arbeitsgemeinschaft für mittelrheinische Musikgeschichte*, No. 81 (2007)

MONCRIEFF, MARGARET, 'Hans Gal (1890–1987): A Personal Tribute and Memoir', *The British Music Society News*, No. 97, March 2003, pp. 369–74; online at http://www.musicweb-international.com/classrev/2003/mar03/gal.htm

OLIVER, ROGER, 'Hans Gál at 95', *Tempo*, No. 155, December 1985, pp. 2–7

PURSER, JOHN, 'Hans Gál – A Personal Appreciation', *Stretto*, Vol. 7, No. 4, Winter 1988, pp. 24–27

SNIZEK, SUSANNE, *German and Austrian Émigré Musical Culture in the British Internment Camps of World War II: Composer Hans Gál, Huyton Suite and the Camp Revue* What a Life!, doctoral thesis, Faculty of Graduate Studies, University of British Columbia, April 2011, online at http://circle.ubc.ca/bitstream/handle/2429/33917/ubc_2011_spring_snizek_suzanne.pdf

WALDSTEIN, WILHELM, *Hans Gál. Eine Studie*, Elisabeth Lafite (Österreichischer Bundesverlag), Vienna, 1965

A complete bibliography of writings on Gál can be found at http://www.hansgal.com/bibliography/15.

2. LITERATURE ON INTERNMENT
Autobiographical Writing

FRIEDENTHAL, RICHARD, *Die Welt in der Nussschale*, Piper, Munich, 1956

LAURENT, LIVIA, *A Tale of Internment*, George Allen & Unwin, London, 1942

LOMNITZ, ALFRED, *'Never Mind Mr. Lom!' or, The Uses of Adversity*, Macmillan, London, 1941

NEUMANN, ROBERT, internment diary (untitled), unpublished manuscript, 123pp., Dokumentationsarchiv des österreichischen Widerstands, Vienna

SPIER, EUGEN, *The Protecting Power*, Skeffington and Son, London, 1951

TAYLOR, JENNIFER (ed.), *Civilian Interment in Britain during WW2: Huyton Camp – Eye-Witness Accounts*, Anglo-German Family History Society, London, 2012

History

CARR, GILLY, and MYTUM, HAROLD (eds.), *Cultural Heritage and Prisoners of War: Creativity behind Barbed Wire*, Routledge, New York/Abingdon, 2012

CESARANI, DAVID, and KUSHNER, TONY (eds.), *The Internment of Aliens in Twentieth Century Britain*, Routledge, London, 1993

CHAPPELL, CONNERY, *Island of Barbed Wire*, Robert Hale, London, 2005

DOVE, RICHARD (ed.), *'Totally Un-English'? Britain's Internment of Enemy Aliens in Two World Wars*, Yearbook of the Research Centre for German and Austrian Exile Studies, Vol. 7, Institute of Germanic and Romance Studies, University of London/Rodopi, Amsterdam, 2005

FEATHER, JESSICA, *Art behind Barbed Wire*, National Museums and Galleries on Merseyside, Liverpool, 2004

GARNHAM, A. M., *Hans Keller and Internment: The Development of an Emigré Musician 1938–48*, Plumbago Press, London, 2011

GILLMAN, PETER and LENI, *Collar the Lot! How Britain Interned & Expelled its Wartime Refugees*, Quartet Books, London, 1980

LAFITTE, FRANÇOIS, *The Internment of Aliens*, Penguin, Harmondsworth, 1940; new edn. Libris, London 1988

'JUDEX' (H. D. HUGHES), *Anderson's Prisoners: Refugee Case-Book*, Victory Books No. 7, Victor Gollancz, London, 1940

KAPP, YVONNE, and MYNATT, MARGARET, *British Policy and the Refugees 1933–1941*, Frank Cass, London 1997; new edn. 2013, Routledge, Abingdon and New York, 2013

LONDON, LOUISE, *Whitehall and the Jews, 1933–1948: British Immigration Policy and the Holocaust*, Cambridge University Press, Cambridge, 2003

SEYFERT, MICHAEL, *Im Niemandsland. Deutsche Exilliteratur in britischer Internierung. Ein unbekanntes Kapitel der Kulturgeschichte des zweiten Weltkriegs*, Das Arsenal, Berlin, 1984

STENT, RONALD, *A Bespattered Page? The Internment of 'His Majesty's most loyal Enemy Aliens'*, André Deutsch, London 1980

Documentary Sources

Hansard (House of Commons Debates), Vols. 362–64, 1939–40

National Archives, Kew, Foreign Office und Home Office documents

The Manx National Heritage Library maintains a comprehensive bibliography, covering histories, academic writing, camp publications prepared by the prisoners, etc., which can be consulted at http://www.gov.im/mnh/heritage/library/bibliographies/internment.xml.

Index
of Hans Gál's Compositions

General Index